D1624923

KING TOWNSHIP PUBLIC LIBRARY
NOBLETON BRANCH

Praise for
the queer advantage

"As a queer reader, you see yourself reflected on the page while also learning of the diversity within this community. The comfort of seeing that your pain was shared, and the excitement of a future where the closet need not exist. A must read for ALL people. Honey, Andrew did THAT!"

   —Benito Skinner, comedian

"I felt understood and seen within seconds of reading *The Queer Advantage*. Our biggest weaknesses in life can ultimately propel us to our highest potential. This book creates space for queer people to find their community and fosters self-healing, helping to silence the damaging voices we project on ourselves."

   —Hayley Kiyoko, singer, actor, director

"An inspirational book of positive queer histories and quotes. Loved it, and it's true there is definitely an advantage."

   —Gus Van Sant, award-winning filmmaker of *Milk* and
      Good Will Hunting

"Yes to all of this! Yes, yes to Andrew's inspiring and beautiful interviews about how otherness brings with it strength, wisdom, and resilience. I loved reading the stories of these artists, business people, and activists about how their queerness has given them a great gift going out into the world. This is a deeply affirming book."

   —Joey Soloway, artist and activist

"Andrew's message and the collection of stories he has gathered are nothing short of inspiring. Words your friends and family can relate to on so many emotional levels. EVERYONE needs a copy. An outstandingly gorgeous read!"

   —Gigi Gorgeous, activist and author of *He Said, She Said*

"Throughout *The Queer Advantage*, Andrew Gelwicks and the people he is interviewing make clear that being fully oneself is an advantage, an edge, a benefit to one's individual life and our shared humanity. To be anything but one's full, glorious, gorgeous self would be less than whole and cheapen all of us. This is a book for anyone and everyone, bursting with dynamic conversations and revelations, and challenging all of us to own who we are, love those we love, and expect the best and most out of ourselves, our families, our friends and our society. It is well worth your time. Prepare for laughter, tears, reflection, and hope."

    —Chelsea Clinton, author, advocate, and vice chair of
      the Clinton Foundation

"From one once-confused Midwestern Jewish kid to another, Andrew Gelwicks has collected powerful personal stories and created an insightful guide to breaking free of confusion and frustration to be our best selves. This book is one that I'll keep coming back to."

    —Nate Berkus, interior designer and author of *The Things That Matter*

"The voices in *The Queer Advantage* will help us navigate toward the queer future that we urgently need. This important book arrives at the perfect time."

    —Casey Gerald, author of *There Will Be No Miracles Here*

"This book is for the birds—and I mean it in the nicest way. Just like the nightingale bird, the more people that tried to drown out their voices, the louder they sang. And now, they sing the most beautiful songs of all. Read this book! Hear the nightingales."

    —Leslie Jordan, actor

"The search for love, purpose, and identity is one that we all face, and *The Queer Advantage* is an empowering tool in helping us to find those answers within ourselves."

    —Bobby Berk, lifestyle and design expert, host of Netflix's *Queer Eye*

"Bold and powerful."

    —Martina Navratilova

the queer advantage

the queer advantage

conversations with LGBTQ+ leaders on the power of identity

andrew gelwicks

hachette
BOOKS

NEW YORK

Interviews have been condensed and edited for length and clarity.

Copyright © 2020 by Andrew Grant Gelwicks
Interior illustrations by Rooney

Cover copyright © 2020 by Hachette Book Group, Inc.

Hachette Book Group supports the right to free expression and the value of copyright. The purpose of copyright is to encourage writers and artists to produce the creative works that enrich our culture.

The scanning, uploading, and distribution of this book without permission is a theft of the author's intellectual property. If you would like permission to use material from the book (other than for review purposes), please contact permissions@hbgusa.com. Thank you for your support of the author's rights.

Hachette Go, an imprint of Hachette Books
Hachette Book Group
1290 Avenue of the Americas
New York, NY 10104
HachetteGo.com
Facebook.com/HachetteGo
Instagram.com/HachetteGo

First Edition: October 2020

Hachette Books is a division of Hachette Book Group, Inc.

The Hachette Go and Hachette Books name and logos are trademarks of Hachette Book Group, Inc.

The publisher is not responsible for websites (or their content) that are not owned by the publisher.

Print book interior design by Trish Wilkinson

Library of Congress Cataloging-in-Publication Data has been applied for.

ISBNs: 978-0-306-87462-8 (hardcover), 978-0-306-87461-1 (ebook)

Library of Congress Control Number: 2020940814

Printed in the United States of America

LSC-C

10 9 8 7 6 5 4 3 2 1

For all who have yet to realize their advantage

Contents

Preface

GROWING UP IS HARD. Growing up in a conservative part of Ohio and coming to the realization that you might be gay is *really* hard.

There were two sides to me. On the public side, in order to fit in, I would pretend to know and care who Ken Griffey, Jr., was, the pride of my hometown and star of the Cincinnati Reds baseball team. On the other, private side, I belted *Wicked*'s "Defying Gravity" at the top of my lungs, broomstick in hand, really hitting that incredibly high end note. These cherished moments with my mom's tablecloth draped around me as a windblown cape lifted me out of the darkness foisted upon me by social convention, where boys' and girls' roles were narrowly cast, never to stray from script. My struggle seemed more like a sad made-for-TV movie than a real-life coming of age in ostensibly placid suburbia.

No matter how hard I played in this tug-of-war, really digging my Mary Jane heels in, palms sweaty and blistering from the friction of the rope, day by day I kept getting pulled over to my private side. The green witch with the fabulous hat was winning.

My all-girl friend group, my affinity for Britney Spears, and my lack of enthusiasm for home runs and touchdowns slowly began to out me among my prepubescent peers. Later, reading *The Scarlet Letter*, it was apparent my life, against my best efforts, was turning bleaker; I was being emblazoned with a scarlet "gay."

By the time I was in middle school, an invisible miasma of negativity had settled around me. Like so many other boys and girls around the world—*we the different*—I was deemed "less than" my straight classmates by my detractors. Worse still, I internalized those dehumanizing beliefs about my sexual orientation. Those acrid, detracting beliefs others held were actually becoming who I was, and how I unconsciously thought about myself.

My parents, both liberal, successful lawyers, could not have been more supportive or nurturing. My older sister, equally encouraging, was a high achiever, and despite the issues I brought to the dining room table, we had a typical, Jewish, upper-middle-class household.

Yet while walking childhood's long corridor of carnival mirrors, I despised my gayness with every fiber of my being. Each day was another battle with mounting anxiety and depression over coming to terms with my true self. Perpetually feeling undercut by antagonists, I envied the boys around me who seemed unflustered, secure in a world without duality. I desperately longed for their seeming oblivion to any wrenching emotional struggle beyond deciding whether to take to the basketball court as one of the shirts or the skins.

It became clear that my genes, and lack of interest in stereotypical male roughness, were leaving me with a tainted social status. Despite being flayed with snide comments, I won a place on the Student Council, wrote a monthly column for my school's newspaper, and entered every writing competition. In spite of (or perhaps because of) my feminine flare, many of the school's most beautiful girls found me endearing. I nurtured these relationships, much to the irritation of the bullying boys who pined for them. The girls became not only my friends, but also my protectors.

Much of my everyday mental and emotional energy was depleted agonizing about how I was being perceived by others. I would study the way the football players carried their books and wore their backpacks, hoping to emulate them. If I raised my hand in class, I'd actively focus on the way my arm and hand were positioned, a slouchy, I'm-so-tough-I-could-care-less gesture. Any remotely stylish or colorful clothing accumulated dust in my closet. *Is the way I'm chewing my gum gay? If I slouch more, will that make me look straight?* I intentionally worsened my penmanship because "no straight guy had good handwriting." I watched YouTube videos on how to speak "straighter" and asked my parents to hire a voice coach to train me out of my high and fast over-articulation. (They said no.)

By junior year of high school, I had completely fallen apart. I began to strain under the weight of always feeling as if I somehow was operating at a deficit. The sneering I experienced from peers in the classrooms and hallways left me feeling trapped, governed by a calculus of inadequacy no matter what I did. I had run aground in an environment I saw as a zero-sum battleground, consumed in an enveloping despair. Every day, in every way, was simply *too much*. My parents were called in by my psychotherapist, who told them he could no longer continue to treat me unless they signed a waiver insulating him from litigation if I were to harm myself.

It was decided I would be sent to a residential treatment center in Salt Lake City, Utah. Into the heart of Mormonism my sixteen-year-old, sexually confused, Jewish boy self went, to hopefully find and save myself. This was not a gay conversion facility, but rather a place for me to learn how to accept myself in all dimensions. The ceaseless focus on changing self-defeating thinking and behavioral patterns was brutal work, but it was also a tremendously enlightening experience. I poured my life out to the nineteen other teenage boys I shared a house with. They, too, were trying to escape from the entrapment of their pained worlds, each dealing with his own hard-to-conquer struggles. We worked with caring therapists and staff members, learning how to grasp hold of that slippery goose called reality; learning healthy coping mechanisms for when we felt ourselves angling toward destructive thoughts and behavior.

By observing and dissecting the inner lives of others, I came to better understand and observe myself in a different way, through a decidedly different prism. By lifting myself out of the deep craters of depression I had been trapped in, which encased me in shadows that I had begun to welcome and cherish, I was able to see the world and its possibilities more clearly.

In this therapeutic environment I came to see that at a certain point, I had to leave behind the suffering imposed on me by others. The focus needed to turn to the suffering I brought on *myself*. I needed to relinquish my mental whip and swap my incessant self-belittlement for words of encouragement.

My entire life's trajectory shifted during those six months, as I was able to better grapple with and quiet many of my noisiest demons. Casting off the skewed repression others had weighed on me—and that I had absorbed—led me to a much greater place of self-acceptance.

For my senior year of high school, I returned to Cincinnati. I breathed new life into my school's moribund Gay-Straight Alliance, deciding I no longer wanted to cower in the shadows. Knowing I needed credibility for this organization, I asked the school's star quarterback, the straightest and most macho of the student body, if I could name him secretary to mooch off his celebrity status. When he said yes (and began to bring snacks to each meeting, which he would do throughout the year), I spent a weekend creating posters announcing the revamp of the club and naming the officials. The next week, I got to school, predawn, and taped them all over the hallway walls and lockers. When students began filtering in, there were no more questions and there was no more debate: *Gelwicks is gay.* I had taken a stand. And once I had taken that stand embracing my identity, the power that tormenters once held over me was taken away. There were no more snide comments, no more overt put-downs. I was in control.

My dad and I entrenched ourselves in the local PFLAG and GLSEN organizations, where I met and talked with openly gay teenagers in Ohio for the very first time. At the age of eighteen, I was finally able to talk to a friend about a crush without lying. It was empowering to find a group of adults and teens my own age who embraced me *because* I was gay.

I then found my footing in college, at Butler University in Indiana—joining a predominantly straight fraternity, no less. I found a group of amazing friends where I never once hid my true self. I was out, super-gay, and super-happy. No longer was I weighed down by society's expectations of who I should be.

I had even become self-assured enough in my gayness to out myself on a much wider scale, beyond the Midwest. I wrote an essay for the *Huffington Post* describing how in my sophomore year at Butler, I took a guy as my date to my fraternity's formal. Up until that point, my fraternity brothers had never actually seen me romantically with another guy. Until then, I was just gay in *theory*. But witnessing us dance together, they loved it, welcomed my date, and encouraged the relationship.

My summers were spent in New York City, where I managed to wrangle internships in the fashion industry at global operations such as Hearst Magazines and Michael Kors. For years, I had kept my interest in fashion as a career a secret. Once in college, though, where I was welcomed as my authentic self, I grew secure in pursuing something I felt passionate about.

While I was still adjusting to my life as an openly out person, it was exhilarating to spend months in one of the most exciting (and queerest) cities in the world. I was learning more about what I could expect in my new, gay life.

My first summer in the city, I was invited by a gay family friend to join a group of guys for a Memorial Day picnic in Central Park. He was well connected and highly regarded in the LGBTQ+ community in New York, and I was excited to meet young, professional queer men.

While the picnic itself was otherwise unremarkable, those hours together in the park impacted me in ways that still pay emotional dividends. This group of all gay men, complete strangers with no need to be nice to me, was warmly welcoming. It set into motion a chain reaction, one that continues as I write this, and foreshadowed many of the tight gay tribes I've met throughout the years. I realized I could gradually assemble a community of individuals who, although they might not have lived my exact story, nor I theirs, understood what it meant to be judged as "different." An invigorating sense of *belonging* now seemed within reach.

The gay community has been the foundation for me to build not only a vibrant social life, but also one that has deep roots, extending into my professional life—connecting me with people and opportunities I likely wouldn't have been granted access to otherwise. Society, which roundly condemns queer people, can also provide us chances to create a tightly knit chosen family.

Following graduation, I immediately headed back to my adopted city of NYC. I worked for GQ magazine, then *Teen Vogue*, and later began an independent celebrity styling business.

Three years into my life in New York and my career as a stylist, Bumble, the dating app, touted me as one of the "100 Most Inspiring New Yorkers." The campaign included a promotional interview. A young, effervescent woman started with the rote questions: where I'd grown up, what I did for a living, how long I had been living in New York.

Then came a seemingly simple question: *"What drives you to succeed?"*

For someone who started his LinkedIn account in seventh grade, had business cards by ninth (with my parents' home phone number on them), and now regularly works eighty-hour weeks without a second thought, it should have been a no-brainer.

But in that moment, there was only one real, plausible answer: *being gay*.

It was an odd response, really. What does my preference for Jude Law over Jennifer Lawrence have to do with my drive? In the city that doesn't sleep, I had never questioned what was behind my all-consuming need to keep moving ahead.

After the interview, I found myself back on the siren-blaring, eat-or-be-eaten streets of Manhattan. Over the years, the frenzy of the city had started to dissolve into white noise, a pulsating rhythm to my perpetually racing thoughts. With grand paradox, the louder and more haywire the city became, the more my mind was able to find a measure of serenity.

I walked the twenty blocks back to my Midtown styling studio with the question, and my answer, boring deeper into my psyche. What was it about my queerness that I felt had such an impact on me? Did my coming to terms with being gay—something I thought I had accepted years ago—*still* act as a fulcrum, allowing all other thoughts and emotions to rise up?

I now have an energizing career as a celebrity fashion stylist, am in a happy and healthy relationship, and have no ill feelings about who I am. Years separate me from those dark days of growing up, where I felt deep shame and embarrassment at being "other." The "It Gets Better" videos I had desperately sought out were right; it *does* get better—*a lot* better.

From a young age, we are told to use whatever assets we have at our disposal to get ahead. Some are born with trust funds, some with runway-ready looks, and others flourish in well-connected families. I had no such bounty given to me, wouldn't be asked onto a catwalk, and my family connections peaked with the county judge.

Was being queer *my* edge? Could my "difference," and all of the earlier negative energy associated with it, have been a good thing? Perhaps the best thing that ever happened to me?

For much of my life, it was my belief that my otherness was a weakness—something to *overcome*. The happy personal life and successful career I'd managed to create for myself was always *in spite of* being queer. Any accomplishments I'd racked up were because I managed to leap over that big, rainbow-colored hurdle.

In what world was I to think that being gay not only motivated me, but *advantaged* me? As this pebble of a crazy thought lodged deeper into my consciousness, I began to backtrack.

The gay slurs hurled my way on the playground and behind my back in the school halls had callused me, hardening me to the day-to-day harshness of reality, giving me a layer of emotional and mental protection.

The daily occurrences I experienced growing up, feeling uncomfortable and out of place, built up my social skills, and honed my adaptability. I can now walk into any room, even those where I feel entirely uncomfortable, and confidently assert myself, because I have been doing that since elementary school.

My deep sensitivity toward the emotions of my clients, colleagues, friends, and family was shaped by having so many deep feelings of my own, and easily sensing those of others. I learned to read people, gauging what they were thinking and how to make them more comfortable.

The hurt and sadness I felt led me to my diaries, where I learned to put thoughts onto paper. An entire lifetime of questioning myself, talking with myself, and thinking about why I am the way I am, was a tortured journey. But it gave me a deeper understanding of myself.

As early as four years old, I lived to dress myself creatively. My eye toward design, that began with wearing my mom's nightgowns, draped with her scarves, led to a career putting together looks for glamorous red carpet events.

Knowing I was considered inherently "less than" and "weaker" than my peers made me work *that* much harder, developing and honing my work ethic and drive. With these memories, I was able to see the clear lineage of how my strongest qualities and assets clearly could be linked to those early, often painful times surrounding my grappling with my queer identity.

I sensed that the only way to really come to a full understanding of this was to get out of my head—and into others'. I needed to talk to the queer people who are among society's highest achievers and see if *they* had similar thoughts and feelings.

I started reaching out to amazing achievers, asking how they did it and how they navigated their queer journey. I spoke to people in technology, theater, film, politics, activism, sports, and more. My focus was on queer people, irrespective of what playing field they excelled on.

Through the *Queer Advantage* project, I came to understand how some of the world's most successful people have achieved great heights with the help of their queer identity, *positively* impacting their careers and lives—and those of others.

The individuals profiled here took a leap of faith entrusting their stories to an unknown fashion stylist. They gave of themselves with tremendous poignancy and a generous spirit.

Not everyone has the same take on what the queer advantage is. If all fifty-one individuals profiled in this book were to sit down to discuss the topic, there would certainly be disagreements about what constitutes the queer advantage and how it applies to each of them.

Conversing with these entrepreneurs, artists, and thought leaders both intimidated and energized me. I was inspired by the reality that there are people like them in our society, pushing and pulling the collective consciousness to a higher level. It is within this collective consciousness that we are able to revel in our differences. Our ability to harness that difference is where we are able to find a great sense of power. And while our queer identity does not in any way define each of us entirely, it remains a significant and profound well from which we are able to draw.

The Queer Advantage puts before us different strategies for coping with the messiness and endless permutations of life's crazy circus. We can read about these trailblazers' ways of achieving, spot parallels, draw important connections, and determine how to apply the experiences of others to our own lives. As David Furnish notes within these pages, about supportive queer communities: "That's when you get an over-and-above advantage, of getting another level of community support that isn't necessarily available to everybody."

When we receive invaluable information, we each have the responsibility to integrate it into our daily lives and begin to dispel the noxious influences that have created stifling, straightjacketed limitations. This takes real, Herculean effort, but the results, as you are about to read, can be tremendous. Complex life navigation becomes vastly easier when we are able to see the playbooks of others, to help get *us* where *we* want to go. We sometimes protect ourselves by building walls around ourselves. But there are those who show us a better way. We can learn to build windows in those walls, to take in new vistas, and even climb out to seek the sunlit world awaiting us.

My own experience, and what I discovered talking with fifty-one highly successful people, is that being queer isn't an inherent advantage. It is something that gives you *potential*: the possibility of a precious, powerful edge. You have to make it work for you. This is achieved not so much by changing the perceptions of doubters, abusers, and tormenters. Rather, it springs from a shift in perspective that we make within ourselves. A shift that grants each of us the permission to bring the future—and all of our newly aware potential—into focus.

These conversations lay bare the truths of the queer advantage.

—Andrew Gelwicks, October 2020

GEORGE TAKEI

Actor, Writer & Activist

George Takei has achieved much in many areas, including acting, writing, and activism. He was born into a Japanese American family in Los Angeles in 1937. During World War II, the Takei family was interned at a camp in Arkansas and, later, a relocation center in California.

Following the war, the Takeis moved back to Los Angeles. George Takei went on to obtain undergraduate and master's degrees from UCLA in Theater. He further studied in England and Tokyo.

Takei's acting roles in television, movies, and Broadway have partnered him with John Wayne, Richard Burton, Alec Guinness, Martin Sheen, Jerry Lewis, Jamie Lee Curtis, and many others. He is most widely known for playing *Enterprise*'s helmsman Hikaru Sulu on *Star Trek: The Original Series*. His many stage appearances include the play *8*, written by Dustin Lance Black. Takei was interviewed in the documentary *Do I Sound Gay?* and was the subject of the documentary *To Be Takei*.

He has written a number of books, including his autobiography, published in 1994, *To the Stars*.

In 2004, the Japanese government conferred upon Takei the Order of the Rising Sun.

George and his husband, Brad, opened their front door together. It was one of those perfect Los Angeles days—warm, sunny, birds chirping, neighbors mowing their lawns. The house was a surprising home for a Hollywood icon, a pretty ranch nestled in the cozy suburbs. As I parked my car, I wondered if the neighbors knew that a true entertainment legend and civil rights trailblazer lived right next door.

As someone who admittedly doesn't know the difference between *Star Trek* and *Star Wars*, my appreciation for George Takei is different than much of the world. I became aware of him years after he shed the galactic star suit and exchanged it for a thoughtful and humorous social media account.

George was much more serious than I'd anticipated. He sat with perfect posture, both feet planted flat on the ground. His unnervingly deep voice, though I'd heard it many times before, struck a different chord in person as he detailed his time in internment camps as a young boy and how that experience shaped the rest of his life, both professionally and personally.

On top of a glittering stage, film, and TV career, George has been extensively involved in queer activism and has made significant contributions to equality efforts with the Human Rights Campaign and other organizations. His political efforts have embraced both California and national changes in the law, especially as related to same-sex marriage legislation.

As we sat in his living room, I marveled at the stories he casually told of organizing events with Jane Fonda, meeting Reverend Dr. Martin Luther King, Jr., and going head-to-head with Governor Arnold Schwarzenegger.

It was abundantly clear that his childhood and the teachings of his father had set the course for the rest of George's life. Beyond being a beloved actor, he was readied to create real social change.

You've spoken at length about your time in the Japanese American internment camps. You have said that experience in the camps gave you your identity.

About three weeks after my fifth birthday, soldiers came to our home. My parents got us up early in the morning, dressed us hurriedly, and my brother and I were told to wait in the living room while they packed. The two of us were gazing out the front window, and we saw two soldiers marching up our driveway carrying rifles with shiny bayonets. They began pounding on our door. My father answered the door, and we were ordered out of our home.

That was the frightening beginning to my internment. But my parents tried to protect us from the reality. They told us we were going for a long vacation in the country. The camps weren't built yet, so we were taken to the Santa Anita racetrack.

Later we were taken by train to the swamps of Arkansas. Our camp, Rohwer, happened to be the farthest east. And for this Southern California kid, it was a fantastical place. Right beyond the barbed wire fence was a bayou. Trees grew out of the water and their roots snaked in and out.

When I made the night runs from our barrack to the latrine, searchlights followed us. But I thought it was nice that they lit the way for me to pee. For my mother, it was invasive and humiliating. Two parallel stories: my parents' story and my real experience as a child.

You ask about my internment having defined who I am. As a preteen, I began to understand we were in something like a prison, and only bad people go to prison. I became very curious to know the reality of my imprisonment, and I started reading books voraciously. I couldn't find a thing about the internment, and the only person I could go to for information was my father. He was unusual in that most parents of my parents' generation didn't talk about the internment with their children.

But when I became curious about the internment, my father did talk. He shared his feelings, his pain. He said seeing the barbed wire fence and us playing nearby it tore him apart. *What kind of people are they going to turn into growing up like this?*

I said I was reading about the civil rights movement in newspapers and how they were struggling for equality. My father said the government made mistakes. I said, "Yeah, they did, but why didn't you protest it? Why didn't you resist it?"

He said, "They're pointing guns at me. If something happened to me, what do you think would happen to you, your mother, your brother, and your sister?"

By this time, I was reading civics books, looking for information on the internment. And instead I found out about the ideals of our system. *All men are created equal, equal justice under the law, this is a nation ruled by law.* And it wasn't, it was wrong, it was against the law. We were innocent, we were imprisoned with no charges and no trial. Due process is the central pivot of our justice system, and that disappeared. We were in prison simply because we looked exactly like the people who bombed Pearl Harbor.

So the internment defined my life as an activist and got me involved in many other campaigns. I try to bring that awareness to all of my LGBTQ+ advocacy. It's because of the unjust imprisonment that I experienced as a child and the guidance my father gave me to actively participate, not just be subject to whatever were the currents of the time.

When you realized you were gay, how did that impact your vision of your future?

After the internment, our first home for a few months was on Skid Row because we were penniless. We had freedom but we didn't have money. And then we moved into an all-Mexican American neighborhood. I was the only Asian kid and there was a cute boy, Bobby. Sweetest smile and long eyelashes. But the other boys didn't think so. All the other guys were getting excited about Monica. This was in junior high school, and she was prematurely bursting out in full womanhood. I thought Monica was nice, but the boys. . . .

Because of my incarceration as a child, because we were different, I didn't want to be different. We were punished for being different. And all the boys were getting excited about Monica so I joined in. I said, "Wow, Monica is nice." But I really didn't feel that. I thought other boys were much cuter.

I didn't know the definition of "gay." I thought I was the only one who felt that way. It was very lonely. But that was when I started learning to act what I didn't feel.

Did you fear others might think you were gay?

I was acting like I wasn't. By that time, I was pursuing an acting career. I was definitely aware of mannerisms. And I made it a point to not be like that. I sat like *this* instead of crossing my legs. And I learned to not walk like that boy who carried his books and minced. I was acting a part. I wasn't being paid for it, but I studied the part and I took on all the accoutrements of that part.

Do you recall your first impressions of a gay celebrity?

When I was teenager, there was a movie star, Tab Hunter, who I was smitten with. But then one of the scandal sheets of the 1950s exposed him as gay. And suddenly he disappeared. You never heard of him again. That was another underscoring: if it gets known you're gay, you won't have a career. I was a teenager aspiring to be an actor, and I knew then I couldn't let it be known that I was *one of those*.

Before you publicly came out in 2005, it's written that your sexual orientation was an "open secret." Can you elaborate on that?

As an adult, you make your peace with it and you're having boyfriends and being very quiet about it. I had a circle of gay friends and I went to gay bars and sometimes I recognized people. And the next day we were on the same set, we didn't talk about it.

When you're on set, at the beginning of the day, after makeup, before getting into your costume, you hang out at the coffee urn and chitchat with each other. I was chatting with Walter Koenig, a big actor who played Pavel Chekov on *Star Trek*. And suddenly he signaled me to turn around and look behind me. So I turned around to look, and the extras, who were sent to wardrobe to get into uniform, were coming in. And there was one gorgeous hunk who was wearing that tight Starfleet sweatshirt. He had a great build. My jaw dropped, my heart stopped.

It was Walter who told me to turn around, pointing out something I was about to miss. That's when I knew that he knew.

They kept quiet about it because they knew it would be damaging to my career. Like what happened to Tab Hunter. Everyone in the cast was friends, and they all knew.

When you came out in 2005, you said that you prepared yourself to no longer have a career.

The reason I came out was Arnold Schwarzenegger. In 2005, the California legislature voted to support the Marriage Equality Bill. This was a landmark event. On the East Coast, Massachusetts had marriage equality that came from the state courts. Ours was the legislature. They passed it, but the bill needed one more signature, from the governor of the state of California, who was Arnold Schwarzenegger. He campaigned for the governor's office by saying, "I'm from Hollywood, I've worked with gays and lesbians, some of my friends are gays and lesbians." That was his pompous campaign rhetoric. I thought surely he was going to sign it. But his base was the Republican right wing, and when the bill landed on his desk, he vetoed it. I was raging.

By this time, I was with Brad, my now husband. We'd been together for many years and we were watching TV at home when that story came on and they went to a shot of young people pouring out onto Santa Monica Boulevard, venting their rage at Schwarzenegger. And we felt the same way. I was boiling. But we were at home, comfortable, and there were all those young people out there demonstrating their true feelings.

Brad and I began a conversation and we decided it was time. I had to make my peace with the thought that I was not going to have a career. After *Star Trek*, all of us found it difficult to be cast in other projects. My feeling was, *If I'm not gonna get cast then I'm gonna adjust to that new reality*, and I was going to be active in the political arena.

In what ways has being gay positively impacted your life?

Being gay gives me another way of looking at people. Characters. Another sensibility. That's a unique thing that I bring to my work. Or in public service, I bring the vantage point of minority people, all different kinds, and gay people have their own unique concerns and sensibilities. So that's been an asset in my public service.

You have been part of minorities that have faced so much oppression. How have you remained optimistic?

Without optimism, you can't make progress. If you're a pessimist, you're already defeated. When Schwarzenegger vetoed the Marriage Equality Bill, a pessimist would have said, *Oh, they did it to us again. This society is homophobic and we're not gonna make any progress.* Then you won't make any progress.

But I said, *No, something's gotta be done about it. It's gonna cost me, but I'm gonna risk it all and I'm gonna come out.* That's an optimistic act. To say that I'm gonna be fully me, I'm going to be completely, 100 percent me, and I will try to do something about it.

I've been with Brad for thirty-three years now. We went to the Old Globe Theatre to celebrate our anniversary. Brad told one of the people there, who happened to be a city councilman, that this was our anniversary. He went up and whispered it to the MC and the MC announced that and led the entire ballroom in singing *"Happy anniversary to you, happy anniversary to you, happy anniversary Brad and George."* The entire ballroom burst out.

It was mind-boggling: a huge ballroom with about eight hundred people, singing in unison to a gay couple *"Happy anniversary Brad and George."* I would never have dreamed of anything like that at another point in my life, pre-2005. I was in my sixties when I came out. *In my sixties.* Most of my adult life has been closeted.

Optimism is what gets progress. Pessimism gets nowhere. We all are pulling at the same wagon. We're doing it collectively. No one person does it. And it's important to recognize that. We all have to work together in concert.

JORDAN ROTH & RICHIE JACKSON

Broadway Producers & Writers

Jordan Roth and Richie Jackson are a powerful force in the entertainment world.

Roth was educated at Horace Mann School in New York City, Princeton University, and later earned his MBA from Columbia University. He oversees five Broadway theaters and has produced numerous hits, including *The Rocky Horror Picture Show*, *Spring Awakening*, *Hair*, *Kinky Boots*, *Frozen*, *Mean Girls*, *Hadestown*, *Angels in America*, *The Book of Mormon*, and *Jersey Boys*.

Jackson is a graduate of Tisch School of the Arts at New York University. He is a writer, talent manager, and producer who has also worked to bring productions to Broadway. Jackson has been a guiding light behind movies and TV shows like *Nurse Jackie*. He is the author of *Gay Like Me: A Father Writes to His Son*.

Both men serve on boards and are active in philanthropic efforts to promote the LGBTQ+ community. Married since 2012, they are raising two boys.

The January morning of my meeting with Jordan Roth and Richie Jackson was drizzling, cold, and ferociously windy. By the time I arrived at their Times Square office, my carefully planned outfit was disheveled.

The couple arrived together, Jordan first and Richie right behind. From a quick glance, the men appeared complete opposites of each other: Richie, dressed in dark jeans and a blue Ralph Lauren sweater, with bald head and black-rimmed glasses; Jordan with long, full, brown hair, wearing an elaborate brown-and-orange ensemble, a chunky gold pendant necklace, and a shawl with brown leather fringes draped over his shoulders.

We sat at a large glass table in Jordan's office, with a perfect view of the *Frozen* marquee. Jordan and Richie sat perpendicular to each other, occasionally holding hands throughout our conversation.

A few weeks prior, I had spent the holiday break immersed in Richie's touching memoir, *Gay Like Me*, where he wrote to his newly out eighteen-year-old son about being gay. The book was thought-provoking and further deepened my conviction about the inexorable power of a queer advantage. Richie writes about how his queerness is part of his every move, thought, and decision—and how he *always* felt that positivity, even in the third grade.

Jordan talked slowly, choosing each word with great thought and precision. He brought up a provocative notion: in his work, Jordan created box office gold out of nothing. He took something that was in his head and brought it to life. What was the difference between that, coming out, and building the life you envisioned for yourself as an openly queer person? It was the manifestation of our true self that was such a powerful force.

| Jordan and Richie have grown into a powerful duo—a vibrant force of strength, self, creativity, and love. They feel it, imagine it, and bring their passion to light.

Richie, when you were in the third grade, you realized you were gay. And even then, you said you felt lucky, special, unique, chosen. Why do you think you had such a positive re-action, especially at such a young age, to understanding you were gay?

RICHIE: I didn't think anything was wrong with me. I grew up in a household where my parents never said anything negative about any group of people. They always valued what I had to say and what my interests were. It just never occurred to me that there would be a part of me that was wrong. And I always liked being different. I never wanted to be like anybody else. I never had one of those moments where I wished I was straight or was another person. I've only wanted to be me.

When I saw that I was different than everyone else in my class in the third grade, I felt so fortunate. I struggled with writing, I could not read; I had to be taken out of the third grade for special reading lessons. And so I had a lot of difficulties where I wasn't as good as everybody else in all the subjects we participated in. But there was one thing that made me better. And that was that I liked boys. I knew nobody else did, and that was one thing I had over everybody. I was more special than they were because I was gay, and I've always felt that way.

Jordan, did you have that same feeling growing up?

JORDAN: I knew I was different, and I struggled to articulate and identify the difference. I was different in a lot of ways. I wasn't very good at being a kid. All the kids seemed to know how to bound into rooms with groups of other kids and be okay, and how to run and play at recess and be carefree. I never had that sense of carefreeness. I don't know if that was specific to being a pre-gay child or just who I am, but that was my sense of where I was. I'm very aware that I have grown into myself.

I always knew there was something special about me, but I also thought that I was probably the only one who thought that. That tension of *different, special, different, special, worse, different, better, different* can cycle through an infinite number of times throughout the day of a seven-year-old mind. Or, frankly, a forty-four-year-old mind.

The difference always frightened me. It was a large concept of difference. It wasn't that I was just like everybody else except for this element. I felt *wholly* other.

There's sexuality and then there's gender. It felt to me that there was nothing worse you could possibly be than a "girly boy" or a "boyish girl." Any variation from what we come as children to understand as "that's a boy" and "that's a girl" was punished, reviled, and profoundly misunderstood. "What are you?" was the worst thing you could possibly be asked. And I was asked a lot.

How would you respond?

JORDAN: I don't think I would respond. It's not actually an invitation for a conversation. The fact of the question is the damnation. It's not the beginning of a conversation or an invitation to be known or seen.

I do think our gender, our sexuality, all of our identity, is active. It is a thing you have to invest in, process for yourself, create for yourself. And I don't mean "create" to imply an artificiality or fraudulence. I mean quite the reverse. It's an excavation and a formulation. For me, that active work wasn't formed enough then to even have had a conversation other than to just feel wrong.

When was the first time you realized your core identity was a powerful force?

RICHIE: I don't know if there was one moment. I always certainly felt different and I had more empathy than everybody I grew up with. All through grade school and high school, I just cared more. I always thought that was part of my gayness, my specialness. That was my strength—that ability to care about another person.

When I got to New York, I began to understand how you could make a gay life and what it meant to be gay. My gayness was the well from which everything I think, want, crave, and create comes from. I was experiencing it before I understood it. All of the things that are special about me come from being gay. Anything anybody thinks they like about me or that is a strength of mine is because I'm gay.

Do you feel the same way, Jordan?

JORDAN: I do now. What's so interesting to me is that in the early years, most of us associate all the bad about us with the gayness of us. Because we all have that feeling that gayness is *a great part of me* when you're talking about empathy. But that's *despite* this horrible thing, this secret; that if they knew, they would hate *every* part of me.

What I think is so shocking, in the best possible way, is that Richie's saying it never occurred to him that it was a bad thing. I had the reverse: it never occurred to me that it could be a *good* thing. Or that the good of me could come from that.

In my late teens, twenties, and early thirties, I was living in my gayness. And then in my late thirties and early forties, I have become much more expansive in expressing, excavating, and creating from all the parts of me. I actually look back on that early period of adulthood as much less free than I thought. I recognize now there was still a lot I was holding back.

RICHIE: But this is why we all have to talk about it. We need to change the way we talk about LGBTQ+ people. There are 4.5 percent of us. That's not a defect. That's not worthless. It's chosen. And if we start to talk about it like that—like the blessing and gift that it is—and we raise our LGBTQ+ youth to understand they have been chosen to have this incredible opportunity that is a blessing, we can help them along earlier.

How has being queer advantaged you in your career?

JORDAN: When I was younger, I was too narrowly defining myself. When I started producing, I was very young. Everybody who worked with me and for me was older. I was twenty-two when I did my first Off Broadway show and I was twenty-four when I did my first Broadway show. In both cases, I was the sole producer.

I adopted this uniform that was a putting on of authority and maturity, and a taking away of sexualness. Not sexuality, but sexualness. That was what I needed to do to make myself comfortable in the beginning of my career. And what I thought would make others comfortable, too, for them to think I could run this.

Yes, there's the baseline of gayness that is fundamental to who I am. But even still, there was a hiding and reserving of myself for what I thought was necessary for my career. As it evolved, and I had gotten to a point where I felt like I didn't have to fit into a prescribed idea of *This is what this role looks like*, I could actually define it for myself and say, *This is what I look like in this role. This is what this role looks like on* me. That was when I really could start to wholly express myself.

My gayness is the fertile soil from which that grows, but it is not all of it. It is the earth that I stand on.

Jordan, you used to have a shaved head, and wore suits with untucked white button-down shirts. You said, "My uniform served me very well until it didn't." Is this along the same lines as that?

JORDAN: Yes, that's exactly what I was talking about. That was the comfort and armor I needed to do the work I wanted to do, and be in the position I wanted to be in. Did I need it, or did I just think I needed it? But it served me because it bolstered me to do the work I wanted to do, until it started to feel constricting and restricting.

I really believe I have grown into myself. We will sit down three years from now and I will have grown into myself even further. And so I don't reject or resent what I was doing then. I don't take it to be not who I was. I don't think I could be doing what I'm doing now if I hadn't done that. But I can't do that again. It served me until it didn't.

How has being queer advantaged you in your career?

RICHIE: One of the ways being gay is an advantage for me in my career is that there's risk to our life every day as LGBTQ+ people. Getting from point A to B can be harrowing. We constantly have to be on guard. There's a vigilance to being queer. I'm used to risk throughout my day as a gay person, so risk in my career has never bothered me. I'm used to it, and it never rose to the level of risk involved with being an LGBTQ+ person trying to find safety in this country. Taking a chance on this or that didn't have the risk that other things have felt in my life.

JORDAN: The ability to see what doesn't exist is core to any creative pursuit. It's the ability to see what doesn't exist and manifest it. Either writing on the page or convening a group of people as a producer. There is something fundamentally, uniquely gay about that. Because we all have done it for ourselves. We all have seen that which is not yet, and manifested it.

When we talk about coming out as a manifestation of self, that is another way in which coming out is a constant process. You don't just say it once and the entire world knows. You make a decision every time you say, "My husband and I," or any of the various ways in which we come out every day. The manifestation of self as the act of coming out is also a thing we have to continue to invest in, in order to continue to grow into ourselves. Imagining something that doesn't yet exist, manifesting it, and bringing it into existence is a personal pursuit and a creative pursuit. That is the creative work of art and the creative work of self.

Richie, in your book you talk about double consciousness* as it relates to Black Americans. How would you describe the queer double consciousness?

RICHIE: Every LGBTQ+ person has to have double vision. They have to keep the clear-eyed, keen view of how America sees them and treats them. And in the other, they have to keep their own sense of their beautiful, gay self. You have to make sure the view of how you're treated doesn't poison the view of how you think about yourself.

There are two distinct views. One is keeping you safe and making sure you're not living in a fantasyland, thinking that rainbows and #LoveIsLove mean everything is okay. You have to be an alert person.

In the other view, you have to protect your queerness, nurture it, invest in it, rely on it, and make sure nothing seeps into it that will poison the way you feel about yourself and your beauty as a queer person. Because that is where your divinity is. That's where your answers are.

Does this queer double consciousness give you an edge in your professional life?

RICHIE: Anytime you get to look at things from another point of view is an advantage. That's why I think being different is always an advantage. The entire structure of the world is built for straight people, and we're seeing it from a different angle. So if you bring that to

---

* A phrase coined by W. E. B. Du Bois in his essay, "The Souls of Black Folk," describing how one's identity can feel divided into different parts based on having a knowledge of how the dominant society views you, and how you might view yourself, and that those views are not the same.

bear on your creative projects or businesses, that's always going to be an advantage.

What advice do you have for young queer people beginning their careers?

JORDAN: Understand that bringing your entire self to your work is what will make you extraordinary at the work. The goal for all of us is to do the work that only we can do. And that will only happen if we bring *all* of ourselves to that work. Such that there is nobody else who could do this work in exactly the same way. Because there is nobody else who has *all* of what I have in me, and *all* of what you have in you.

TROYE SIVAN

Musician & Actor

Born in South Africa in 1995 and raised in Australia, Troye Sivan is among the most beloved pop stars of the digital age.

Sivan attended a small, modern Orthodox Jewish school near his home in Perth and began making videos online when he was twelve, quickly shooting to Internet stardom as a singer and vlogger. He lived out his youth online, and at the age of eighteen dropped a YouTube video titled "Coming Out," sharing his queerness with his millions of followers. Within two years, Sivan had signed with a major music label, walked the runways at Paris Fashion Week, been named one of the most influential teens by *Time*, and released an EP that debuted at number five on the U.S. *Billboard* charts.

Since then, Sivan has released two certified platinum albums, *Blue Neighborhood* and *Bloom*, which each have been streamed over a billion times. He was nominated for a Golden Globe for Best Original Song for "Revelation," from the 2018 film *Boy Erased*, in which he also had a supporting acting role.

I had just finished interviewing Drew Elliott, MAC Cosmetics' global creative director, and we were sitting on his couch chatting. He asked who else I was hoping to speak with. One of the names I rattled off was pop phenomenon Troye Sivan.

"Oh, you should definitely talk to Troye. He would be great. Want me to text him for you?" Drew asked casually.

"Um . . . YES!"

Drew whipped out his phone, shot off a few sentences, and within minutes received a response from Troye: *I'm down!*

A few days later, I was on the phone with the megawatt musician. He was as charming, sweet, and thoughtful as I had hoped.

One point he made in particular stood out, and has been on my mind often since. I had never given much thought to the significance of how when growing up queer, we often sought refuge in our own minds. With nobody else to talk to, we were left to figure out what was happening to us, and around us, by ourselves. Deep, maddening, and complex conversations with ourselves—at a very young age—about who we are, why we feel this way, and what this all means.

As a child, I hated those conversations. I found it exasperating. I felt trapped in my mind, often comparing my thoughts to a prison. Troye, though, brought me out of that. He offered up that those conversations were really a miraculous, highly beneficial experience. We were forced to dig deep into our psyches, giving us an attunement that extended far beyond others who never had to question who they were. For Troye, that very act of introspection manifested hit songs, chart-soaring albums, and fans around the world.

The *New Yorker* noted in 2019 that Sivan's "pop songs translate the gay teen experience into recognizable rites of passage." He is redefining what it means to be an icon and pioneer within and outside the queer community.

You came out on YouTube before you signed with a record label, and before you had established yourself as a musician. What was your thought process on coming out before your music career had taken off, versus going the usual route of establishing yourself and *then* coming out?

I had been out to my family and friends for a long enough time and I felt really secure in my personal life. I knew I had a great family and friends that supported and loved me. To me, that was the most important thing. Career, music, and opening myself up to the public was something that came secondary, once I felt I had a strong enough foundation. I had heard horror stories of people kept in the closet by executives, record labels, or management. I didn't ever want anybody to have that power over me: to keep me in the closet or pull the rug out from under my feet.

For me, not coming out was not an option. I knew it was going to happen at some point, so I decided to take that moment and take back the power—so I could come out on my own terms in a way that felt comfortable and genuine.

Throughout your career you've collaborated with artists and songwriters who are both straight and queer. Have you noticed a different synergy working with someone who also identifies as queer?

I find that synergy both in work and also just in my life. Queer kinship is a very, *very* real thing. I've been lucky enough to travel all over, and I can meet a queer person from the other side of the world who I have never met before, and really have very little in common with, except for the fact that we are both queer. And there's this mutual understanding and vibe that is special and something I'm extremely grateful for. I'm very thankful and proud to be a part of a community, and I consider myself really lucky to be queer. It's a special human experience that can bring people together.

I have always written extremely personally, and that's the only songwriting that's of any interest to me. A lot of those experiences happen to be about love, relationships, or sex. And so to have someone in the room who is queer and I know I can trust is really important.

Early on, I definitely had a couple of sessions where I had to come out to the producer. And you're not really sure how they're going to react, or if they are going to shut down and switch off for the rest of the session and become uninterested. I've had that happen to me before. Or are they going to be totally cool with it and we're going to write a great song? So finding my people within the writing community was really important to the music I create.

You've talked openly about how when you were growing up, you were hyperconscious of gay "tells"—your mannerisms, the way you walked, talked, danced. As you learned to loosen your

grip on those concerns, and started to embrace your identity, did you notice a difference in the music you were creating?

Definitely. Childhood and adolescence as a queer person is not talked about enough. Oftentimes, we end up getting sort of desensitized to the experience. But then I'll be sitting with queer friends, or talking with my therapist, and something will come up that has lingered. Some sort of insecurity or weird internalized homophobia that I really thought I was beyond, or simply hadn't thought about in years. It always takes me by surprise to remember how charged those emotions are. So for me, a lot of my adult life as a queer person has been deprogramming and unlearning a lot of things I taught myself or was taught as a little kid.

I'm constantly learning more about myself and experiencing the world as a queer person: your body, sexuality, femininity, style, the way you present yourself to the world. All of these things can be a really loaded part of a queer person's life without them even necessarily realizing it. The ultimate goal for me is complete freedom to express myself—however I please and however I feel is natural. It's a work in progress to get to that point and I hope to stay on that journey.

I'm constantly asking myself questions: *Why do I feel that way? Why am I nervous to wear that? Why am I attracted to that person?* I'm having those conversations with myself. I've found the more open and free I am, the better music I create and the happier I am in my personal life.

Do you think there is any connection between your ambition, drive, and work ethic, and being queer?

Definitely. I often think back to feeling like an outcast and not really understanding myself. For me, creative expression was where I turned to in those moments: writing songs, making things, consuming media from all around the world online. Those were the places I turned to when I didn't know what the hell was going on with myself, and didn't know where I was supposed to be and who I was supposed to hang out with. I think the normal devices people lean on when they are growing up were different for me as a queer person. I never felt like "one of the boys" in my year and I never really felt like a cool kid. There was nothing I could have possibly done.

I did one of the X-Men movies when I was thirteen. Even that scored me nil cool points at school, because it was creative and it wasn't sport or some sort of academic achievement.

That kind of adversity and struggle has followed me into my adult life in a really positive way. It's become just wanting to get the work done. It's not about anyone else and it's not social status or trying to get into the cool parties. For me it's just about the actual creation as a form of therapy. It's always been my therapy and I don't think I would've needed that therapy had I been your average bloke going around the school. I don't think I would have needed to recoil into my bedroom and start making stuff and expressing myself and thinking about the way I feel.

I'm super-grateful that I've had all the experiences I've had in my life—tough and easy. They have shaped me as a professional, a creative, and as a friend.

Have you felt the need to work harder because you're queer?

I've always had a weird relationship with work because I love it so much and I think I would be doing it regardless if I was making any money from it or if I was successful or not. I know I've done that because I'm queer.

Being queer and being creative are intensely linked for me. Maybe just the amount of work I do has been directly linked to being queer because, even if I wasn't doing it professionally, I would need to do it just for my own sanity. When I'm maybe working harder than somebody else, it's not because I'm trying to prove anything to anyone, it's just because I feel I have to for myself.

How has being queer advantaged you in your career?

I'm a very privileged, rare case. I don't take it lightly that it's not common for somebody to come out and it helps their career. I think we are just starting to see that happening now, for the first time.

I definitely feel like being queer has, at the very least, creatively been a huge advantage for me, and made me much more introspective and thoughtful. I think queer people spend a lot of time in their own brains, talking to themselves, having very intense conversations with themselves, and figuring a lot of shit out. Especially at these young ages when our brains are forming and I think that is a really beautiful thing. Through it comes a lot of incredible art, drive, and sense of belonging amongst the LGBTQ+ community at large.

There are so many advantages to being queer and it's made my life infinitely more interesting, inspiring, and colorful. My family would say the same thing, which I think is something that's really beautiful. I don't think for one second my parents, siblings, or anyone in my life would change a single thing about me. That's special and I can't wait to be a queer parent someday. We now get to benefit from the hard work of the people who came before us, and the people who have fought to make this possible for us. And now that it is possible, I plan on really enjoying it.

CLIFF HOPKINS

Marketing Strategist, Broadway Producer & Philanthropist

Cliff Hopkins graduated summa cum laude with an English degree from the University of Massachusetts in 1992. His first job was working for President Bill Clinton, managing the awareness campaign for the HIV/AIDS crisis.

Later, after entering the private sector, Hopkins rose through the ranks of a number of companies, including MCI/Verizon, AOL, and PayPal. He was the global marketing director at Google. Hopkins has also been head of marketing for Instagram. He now works for the travel company Elude.

Business Insider named Hopkins one of the top 50 most innovative chief marketing officers in the world, and the *Financial Times* ranks him as one of the top 100 LGBTQ+ executives in the world.

As a theater producer, his work has won the Drama Desk Award and was nominated for a Tony with *The Prom*. He helped produce *The Prom*, *The Inheritance*, *Slave Play*, and *Broadway Bounty Hunter*.

Hopkins has made significant philanthropic contributions, serving on the boards of The Trevor Project and the San Francisco AIDS Foundation.

He and his husband have been together for twenty-five years.

Cliff Hopkins invited me to Instagram's New York City headquarters, where he was the tech company's chief marketing officer at the time of our interview. The labyrinthine office was just what one might hope for—colorful glass walls and hip furniture; bustling with young people that have that inherent, built-into-their-bones sense of coolness.

As I sat at the front entrance, I expected a young assistant to greet me and whisk me off to Cliff's beautiful corner office. Instead, I was delightfully surprised to be greeted by Cliff himself.

As Cliff guided me out onto the main floor, everyone's gaze was on him. It was the kind of power I suspect supermodels have when they step into a restaurant—straight men gazing with lust, women with envy, gay men appreciating cheekbones. Perhaps it was his high-ranking title, or perhaps it was just that he exuded the kind of warmth that made people gravitate toward him, but the fact that he seemed completely unaware of his charisma made me like him even more.

Cliff took me over to Instagram's kitchen, which looked straight out of a futuristic movie. He handed me a LaCroix, and instead of taking me to his office, we sat down at a conference table in the middle of the shared-space floor. The atmosphere was energizing and had a creative buzz. We began to talk.

What was your coming out process?

I knew I liked boys when I was around eleven years old, and I started coming out to people early in high school. Despite some teasing, most of my family was pretty supportive. I didn't struggle with my sexuality that much.

When I finally came out to my mother and we had that explicit conversation, she cried. She said, "You're my son and I love you." But my mom was crying because she had that reflexive instinct many parents have, especially as a single mother, wanting her kids to have an easy, stress-free life. She said, "I'm crying because life is going to be hard for you. People are going to be prejudiced against you and you may not be able to achieve your full potential." And those words, *"You may not be able to achieve your full potential,"* seared into my mind. I decided right then and there that I wasn't going to allow being gay to preclude me from achieving my full potential. In some ways I'm glad that conversation happened, because it pushed me to not let being gay, and being different, stand in my way.

Before you had that conversation, had the thought even crossed your mind that being gay could potentially inhibit you from achieving your goals?

It did. You know how children start to try to make sense of things? Such as, *What is my identity? Who am I? Do I have friends? What are my interests?* It's not a linear process. It's fluid.

When most people in the world think of identity, a lot of their identity is having somebody who is the opposite sex, and ultimately getting married and having kids. So I did fret about, *Does this mean I won't be able to have a family?* Or a sense of belonging because I'm different, because boys can't be married. Back then, it was not even conceivable. It was more about my own sense of family, belonging, happiness, and whether this would be a curse.

After that conversation, and once that thought was in your head, did it change anything inside of you?

It changed my sense of ambition. I decided that if I couldn't have a traditional marriage and a traditional family, being successful in my career would be something I could control and could achieve. What I could do was show that I could do really well in school, I could go to college and do well, and be very successful in the world. If you compare my career trajectory, and simply my career itself, it far outshines pretty much everyone in my family. I know that might sound harsh. But especially economically, I've achieved the most financially compared to anyone in my family.

Has any bullying you experienced as a child stayed with you?

Yeah, it's all still there. I remember the first person. It was in sixth grade and he said, "Cliff, you are so *fairy* nice." I remember it as clear as if it just happened right now.

It does show up sometimes, even in the corporate world. If I am dealing with straight male colleagues who are higher in rank than me, it sometimes can be a trigger—particularly if they get mad, frustrated, or upset. I have this reflexive instinct to want to please them. I want them to like me. I've worked on it over the years, but the demons are still there.

Do you feel that bullying also added to your sense of ambition?

Straight white men in general—and now I'm stereotyping, but there is truth in stereotypes—who have a lot of inherent privilege, don't think as hard about how they come across. Women are much more attuned to how they're speaking, what they're saying, do they cut people off, because of all the baggage they have as underrepresented minorities in corporate America—especially as you go up the food chain.

As a gay man, I can relate to that because there's always some amount of self-editing that comes on at an early age. *How do I position myself to these people so they see me for who I am?*

You've amassed great success, and yet here you are saying that, even now, you still feel like you have to edit yourself sometimes.

I've worked at Instagram for almost four years, and the straight men I work with are incredibly supportive. I've never once felt discriminated against because of being LGBTQ+. It's more in my own mind, my own narrative, when times are stressful and things aren't going well. I just feel that. They're not putting it on me. It's my own demons, this extra burden to try to make things better and appease.

I'm the head of marketing for Instagram. If the issue is around the question of whether we have the right marketing strategy or if the campaigns we're running are working, I feel a little bit of added pressure to be the best little boy in the world. And to have the best answers and know everything, to show them I've got this.

Can you describe the difference between coming out in your personal life versus your professional life?

Bill Clinton became president in January of 1993. As somebody who was switched on and paying attention to political events, I felt inspired by this young guy who was a Democrat. This after growing up in my most formative years under twelve years of Republicans, when I saw my gay brothers dying of HIV/AIDS, and Reagan and

H. W. Bush not even uttering the word. It was a horrifying, scary, frightening time to be a young gay person.

When Bill Clinton came in, I felt a renewed sense of hope I hadn't felt before. I went to work for his administration, and he, unlike his predecessors, did want to do something about HIV/AIDS. His view was *We should model the right behavior.* And so the federal government was required to teach its employees about HIV/AIDS and try to educate people about it, as well as address the stigma that many people felt in the workplace.

They were looking for volunteers to learn how to teach this course. So here I am, twenty-three years old, my first job out of college, working for this new president. And then getting the opportunity to raise my hand and become a trainer, and learn how to teach my colleagues, in my department I was working in, about HIV/AIDS and about how to deal with colleagues fairly.

So with that being the backdrop, it was sort of easy to come out, because it was being talked about so publicly and I was on the forefront.

How has your queer identity impacted your skills as a creative and business professional?

Marketing is part art, part science. But in Silicon Valley, where it's metrics mania and data, data, data, to be successful as a marketer you have to get the science part. Particularly with digital marketing, it's about the numbers and making sure your campaigns are cutting through, and there are quantitative measures you can put in place to measure that.

I have always felt almost differently where, as a gay person, yes, I'm creative, but I had to pay special attention to make sure the science part was there. And that people didn't dismiss me as, *He's the artsy, creative gay, but he can't do math.*

I also paid extra attention to the people I hired. For example, I hired our head of analytics, who has a PhD in statistics. I can bring him into a meeting with anyone at any level, including the CFO of Facebook, Inc., and he can go shoulder-to-shoulder with him on any number problem. That has helped me along the way tremendously, to be able to deal with the finance people and to have a team that really prioritizes knowing and measuring impact.

Have you had to work harder because you are gay?

Definitely. It goes back to that conversation with my mother. I've definitely worked harder and pushed harder—first one in, last one out. Going above and beyond is what's gotten me here.

Being gay has forced me to dig deeper and have more ambition, to prove doubters wrong. It pushed me to be much more thoughtful and intentional about my choices and what I wanted to do, what I wanted to achieve, and how I wanted to be perceived.

ALANA MAYO

Hollywood Film Producer

Born in New York in 1985 and raised in Chicago, Alana Mayo attended Columbia University. At the same time, she interned at Tribeca Films and worked for film directors Lee Daniels and Warrington Hudlin. She graduated with degrees in English and Film Studies.

Mayo headed to Los Angeles and began working for Warner Bros. Studios and 20th Century Fox (now 20th Century Studios) as creative director, spearheading movies such as *Get Smart* and *I Love You Phillip Morris*.

As vice president at Paramount Pictures, Mayo worked on *The Big Short*, *Annihilation*, *Selma*, *Jack Ryan*, the Academy Award–winning *Fences*, and other films. She is a behind-the-scenes power player in Hollywood, serving as the production and development chief for Michael B. Jordan's Outlier Society production company.

You grew up in Chicago. When you were coming to understand you identified as queer, did that change your perception of what your future might look like, and what you might or might not be able to accomplish?

No, actually. One of the greatest privileges I've always had is being raised with the understanding from my parents that my individuality was valid, worthwhile, and to be celebrated, as long as I was being a good person and was following the values I was raised with. Which was really just to be a kind person who cares about and helps other people.

I didn't feel it would be limiting. My experience with coming to an awareness of my sexuality was more of just a personal understanding of how I defined my sexuality—who I was attracted to, and how that could and would manifest in my personal life.

I was raised in a fairly dogmatic religion that does not allow for homosexuality. There were a lot of things I planned to do with my life that I knew weren't acceptable to the religion I practiced growing up. But the thing I was most certain would never be accepted was being anything queer. That was what I focused on. I never thought of it as potentially limiting other areas of my life.

I'm also Black, and also a woman, and there were any number of things that put me at the margins of my community. I was very accustomed to being "one of one" in various rooms, whether it was school, work, or friends.

You've said in past interviews that you are "contrarian by nature." What do you mean by that?

I really enjoy being considered an "other." I don't enjoy the challenges that can come with that, but the idea of feeling like I am an individual, and no one will *really* get me except for a few people, and that I'm gonna have opinions, beliefs, mores, traditions, and ways of being that are uniquely my own, I love that. I've always felt that.

I have a very big family and I'm very close to all of them. But I was always the weird one within it. And I was always described by other people in my life as marching to the beat of my own drummer. That can come with insecurities and pitfalls, but I always really loved that and leaned into that.

Do you think that's helped you in your work?

One hundred percent. If I identify as anything, I identify as bisexual. I wasn't the biggest relationship person in general, and most people only knew of my heterosexual relationships.

When I met my [now former] wife, Lena Waithe, we were very serious very fast and we started dating very quickly. A lot of her friends were saying, "Is Alana gonna be okay with people knowing about your relationship?"

I said, "I don't understand. This is my relationship. This is who I love. I don't care what anyone thinks." And I say that with the full understanding, being in the privileged position I come from, where I had the luxury of it not threatening my safety physically or emotionally. I had the luxury of knowing I have a community, support system, and people who would help me navigate that kind of transition in my life. I had the safety of being stable in my economic life, so I knew it wouldn't threaten my professional existence. I'm very grateful for being a person who has felt different for the majority of my life and so this new relationship, which added a profound difference to my identity, was never something that felt like a threat or uncomfortable.

In your rise through entertainment, which minority status has been a bigger obstacle for you: being a woman, being Black, or being queer?

All of them at different times. I have been in a management position where I've managed teams of people, and in those instances, being a woman—and being a young woman—is always very challenging. The male privilege that exists in most spaces I inhabit professionally is profound, oppressive, ever-present, and difficult to navigate and manage. And my womanness, and however I define and express that, is also very important to me.

When you are from a cultural background that the vast majority of people you work with aren't, or may not have any exposure to or even a desire to have an exposure to, it is challenging. You're always explaining yourself. And it's even more difficult when your job is to create and tell narratives.

As a queer person, I find myself micro-aggressed almost as much as, if not more so, than any of my other identities. We have so much further to go and I find myself constantly having to correct people. Constantly having to make people aware of why it's not okay to say something; making the argument for why pronouns are important and not a silly effort. The micro-aggressions there are consistent and, frankly, not even that micro.

The answer is they are all challenging and they are all hard in different ways and at different times. The intersection of those identities is where I live. I never feel more one thing than another. The only thing I probably get some benefit and privilege with, if there is such a thing, is "straight passing." I don't necessarily have to tell people who haven't met my [ex-]wife that I'm a queer person. So maybe there's less discrimination there?

Do you think there is any link between your ambitious work ethic and that of being queer?

One hundred percent. There are two sides of it. There's the one of *I'll show you*. And the underdog feeling of *there not being that many of us in positions of power, and if I have a position of power, I will show you that I'm as capable as the next person.* Not that I ever want to represent any community of people, but you now know a badass queer person. An exceptional queer person. A tenacious queer person.

I get to be a person who's very proud of and interested in my identity. And interested in the advancement and opportunity that are not yet available to other people and communities I belong to.

For me, it's very important to try to be successful to create opportunities for other queer people, for other Black people, for other women, for other people who identify as all of the above. Because it's not a good thing for me to be one of one.

I'm very proud to be in a position to hire people. It's important to me to be able to hire people who identify in the same way I do. So part of it is wanting to amass and retain a certain amount of power and privilege so that I can do that for other people.

How has being queer advantaged you in your career?

In two ways. I'm really grateful that the queer community in Hollywood is "ride or die." It's small but, in my experience, an aligned and supportive community. There are people in my professional life who would not have thought of me as a queer person who, when I started dating my wife, called me and took me to lunch. They said, "I had no idea you were queer. Let's go have lunch and let's talk about what you're doing with your life and career." I think there's something really cool and special about being a part of a community that, once they recognize a person who might have this shared experience with them, have an instinct to look out for and embrace them.

I happen to work in an industry that right now, in this weird way, has made a very hard shift away from *not* having any interest in telling the stories of a lot of communities and people, to really *wanting* to tell the stories of a lot of communities and people. That's due to the incredible and intrepid work of some amazing artists and creatives—generations of them—who are insisting on inserting themselves into narratives in ways that hasn't happened before. I feel so lucky to be here at precisely this moment, because, regardless of the time and environment in which I was working, the opportunity to make sure there are queer characters and stories is something I would have wanted to do. But *right now*, to be working at a time where that door is maybe still cracked, but way more open than it ever was before, is just *unbelievably* exciting.

CHRIS MOSIER

Triathlon & Duathlon Champion

Chris Mosier was assigned female at birth in 1980, grew up in Lake Zurich, Illinois, and attended Northern Michigan University.

Mosier began competing in and winning various races, excelling in the triathlon (swimming-biking-running) and the duathlon (running-biking-running). In 2009, Mosier competed in the triathlon as female.

In 2010, Mosier began his gender transition. For two years, he had competed in the Nautica NYC triathlon as a woman, but the third year he entered as male.

Mosier won a place on Team USA in 2015 for the men's duathlon team and went on to compete in the World Championships. He became the first out transgender athlete on a United States national team and challenged the exclusionary policies successfully. The rules that were developed as a result included new guidelines for the International Olympic Committee (IOC).

ESPN featured Mosier in 2016 as its first openly transgender athlete. He received positive media coverage, including in the *New York Times*.

Mosier is now a triathlon coach and is married to his wife, Zhen Heinemann.

What was your experience growing up in Lake Zurich, Illinois, as you began to feel that the identity of female, the gender you were assigned at birth, didn't align with how you felt inside?

I didn't understand how other people were placing me. I started to see that what I wanted to do and how I wanted to express myself didn't align with the way my family and the adults around me thought I should be expressing myself.

An early life example was when I was four years old. It was hot in the summer and I was playing outside with the kids in the neighborhood. My aunt would pull me aside and say, "You can't run around with your shirt off like this. Little girls have to wear a shirt." I didn't understand, because all of our four-year-old bodies looked the same. That was one of the first moments where gender—or the concept of there being a difference between myself, my brother, and the boys in my neighborhood—first came on my radar.

Growing up in the Midwest, as you started to have these inklings of doubt and misunderstanding, how did you envision your future?

I didn't. There was a disconnect between the way I felt and the way I perceived my peers were feeling, so I felt out of place. But I never had an idea or an understanding of that being related to my gender identity, my sexual orientation, or identifying as queer. Trans wasn't a concept I understood even in high school, in a way that I thought might fit me. I also did not identify as queer in high school. I didn't have the language, terminology, or understanding to put my finger on it. I just always felt like me.

I felt really comfortable for the most part just being myself, and not putting much thought into my identity. Part of that was purposeful. I made myself so busy in high school and college as it started to creep on my radar, that I didn't have time to think about who I was as a person. I didn't have time to think about my identity. I didn't have time to be in relationships.

I went from sport to sport to sport in high school. I was a three-sport, all-conference athlete in volleyball, basketball, and softball. Sport was how I made friends and how I found community, regardless of how weird people thought I was on the outside. I didn't conform to gender norms.

I avoided this idea of "figuring it out." But I didn't have an understanding of what my future would be either, because I didn't see a future for myself. I never had dreams of growing up and getting married. I never envisioned myself with a partner. I never thought about what my career would actually be.

Even in college, I didn't have a long-term vision for myself, in part because I couldn't picture what I would look like. This is actually the first time I'm saying that out loud: I couldn't have that picture of myself in the future, because what I was seeing in the mirror was not lining up with the way I thought I would grow up to be.

If there were visible transgender people in the media, do you think you would have connected with them? Or were you perhaps in a state of denial?

All of that. We all come to process and understand ourselves in our own time. Even when I did understand and meet gay, lesbian, and bisexual people, I didn't feel closely connected to them, based on my own experience at that point. I don't think I was ready to accept or understand my identity as a queer person.

But I also don't think I had been presented or faced with that reality yet. I was dating men at the time and felt very comfortable dating men. I never entertained the possibility of dating anyone else. I do think seeing a reflection of myself in someone else, whether it was in the media, sports, business, or at my university, who I could relate to, might have opened me up to that experience of understanding myself earlier.

The way I did come to understand my identity as a trans person was by seeing representation I thought fit with parts of my experience. There wasn't a single person where I felt, *I'm just like that person.* But there were people who identified as trans and had similar experiences as I felt, whom I learned about on YouTube. Just seeing those people helped me understand my own identity. There's power in representation and in visibility, which is the driving force behind what I do, and why I'm so public as an out trans athlete. I know the power in seeing those representations and feeling validated, and helping others understand who they are.

How old were you at this point when you started connecting with other people's stories?

I was out of undergrad. I was working a full-time job in New York City. And even in New York I didn't know any trans people in real life. My partner at the time was a woman—my first relationship with a woman—and she was much more advanced in understanding the queer community and identity than I was. She opened me up to understanding, in a very gentle way, *Hey maybe you should explore your gender identity a bit. Here are some books to read and videos to watch.*

Even with that support, it took me seeing people who I related to, to make a difference. At that time, I was around twenty-six years old when I first started to see these representations. My only understanding from the media was these caricatures of trans people. It was Jerry Springer and Maury Povich. A lot of times it was people cross-dressing or in drag. And many times, it was poor representations of trans women and they were the butt of a joke. So even in the media, I wasn't seeing trans men.

You began your transition in 2010, but it wasn't until 2015 that you qualified for the men's duathlon team. What was happening during that five-year process?

Sport was the area I was most concerned about transitioning in. It was also the area I found was the easiest for me to transition in my life. When I came to understand my identity in 2008–2009, I chose not to tell anyone about it. I chose not to act on it or to start a transition of any kind, because I was terrified I would lose my ability to compete in sports.

At that time, I had been running races in New York City and I was just starting triathlon. I had done really well in my first race and thought, *This is my sport and maybe there's a future for me as a competitive athlete in triathlon.* Being a professional athlete was always a dream when I was a kid.

I chose not to do college sports because of my growing discomfort with being assigned on a women's team. I didn't know that at the time, but in hindsight, the sole reason I didn't pursue college athletics was that I didn't want to be on a women's team and what that meant.

Even though I didn't have the words to express that to anyone at that time. I was terrified to switch categories. The policies that did exist would prevent me from competing. I didn't see anyone who looked like me in sports.

I finally decided my discomfort with the rest of my life outweighed those hours I was competing or practicing in sports. I decided to transition. But in those first years, it meant a lot of coming out to people. The organizations I was a part of and the sports I was playing didn't have policies on the books for trans people. In many cases, I was the first trans person a lot of the national governing bodies and local organizations encountered. I would write to them and say, *Here's my situation. Can I switch categories so I can start competing with men?* The response I would get was *I'm not exactly sure what to do here and I'm copying five of my colleagues on this.* And then they would contact other people. Suddenly I was on an email string with twenty people in the organization, outing myself to all of them, just trying to figure out if there was a place I could play.

It was a real challenge in the beginning as I switched categories. As I started to compete as male, my confidence grew. I stopped worrying about what people thought of me at the starting line. I had felt so much discomfort lining up with women. A lot of these races are segregated at starts, so women start at a different time than men. Or there's some sort of differentiating factor, like pink swim caps versus blue swim caps. I always felt like I did not belong competing with the women, and I made a lot of stories up in my head about what other people might be thinking about me.

I had started living in this perpetual state of stress and fear about what might happen to me in sports. And when I came out, and when I started competing as male, I found I very quickly inherited male privilege. I also saw the sexism in sport. No one thought I would be competitive against men, which made my time in sport much easier, because no one challenged me lining up with the men. With that, I felt this great sense to prove myself and to work extra hard to show I belonged there. Which I think really helped me achieve my goal of making Team USA.

Was that the driving force pushing you to succeed?

It was one of them. I started to do really well in men's races about three years into my transition. I was just starting triathlons in that year before transition, so I was new to the sport. I think I would've been improving no matter what, but I started to place more frequently.

I remember winning my first race overall and thinking maybe this was an option for me. That was a special moment because most people told me it couldn't be done; that there was no way I could be competitive against men.

I think that's part of the reason why I was so widely accepted. People thought I would be a middle-of-the-pack guy; that I wouldn't be a threat. *Go ahead, have fun.*

When I first got it on my radar that making Team USA was possible, I wanted to try to compete in 2014 and get my paperwork in on time. (My paperwork being the clearance I needed to take testosterone, to compete at that level.)

I didn't get the paperwork, so I didn't get to compete in the 2014 championship. I had a full year to think about it, set my intentions, and think about what it would mean—not only for me, but for my community—to accomplish that. I knew early on, when I first came out publicly in 2010, that I was doing this not just for myself but for other athletes to see themselves in sports.

I could've started to compete as male and never told anyone I was trans or not have made it a headline. But I chose to be out in public because I thought it was really important that other people see *me* doing it, so they knew *they* could do it, too. And that was part of my plan when I came out publicly in the *Advocate* and a *New York Times* article in 2011.

But in 2014, I had the idea that what I was doing now was much larger than just my own achievements. I would be in a position to challenge the International Olympic Committee policy on transgender athletes and have my making Team USA impact athletes across the world and their ability to make the Olympics.

I also like to prove people wrong. So I was personally motivated to show I could do it. But it's much larger than me. I wanted to prove that, not only was I able to work hard enough and was a good enough athlete, but also that trans people do belong in sports and that we can be competitive.

Do you ever feel you are treated differently from other athletes?

I'm treated with respect because I am a good athlete. What helped me come out in sport was that people loved and appreciated me as a great athlete, a great teammate, and a great competitor *before* I told them about my identity.

When I told them who I was and let them in, it went much easier than it did at work or in other parts in my life. I don't think I'm treated any differently, and I think one of the cool things about sport is that it's an equalizer. We value diversity on our teams. You wouldn't field a whole team of quarterbacks in a football game, right? You need different players with different specialties and different positions to contribute to achieving your end goal.

There's something about that sort of mentality within sports that I think makes it easier for me to be accepted. It helps to be good at what you do. My investment in making sure other people are successful around me enables me to be accepted by other people.

Has being queer advantaged your career?

Absolutely. Being queer has helped me in so many different ways. My identity as a queer person and a trans person has helped me position myself as an expert in policy. I've been able to use both my personal experience as an athlete and my experience with policy to be the go-to person when it comes to this topic.

I also think it helped me with confidence in navigating professional situations as well as personal situations. I know exactly who I am and I'm very clear about the person I want to be and my mission every single day.

JONATHAN MILDENHALL

Marketing Executive

Born in 1967, Jonathan Mildenhall was raised in northern England by a single mother in public housing.

Mildenhall's career began at the London advertising firm McCann Erickson. Coca-Cola later enlisted him as vice president of global advertising strategy and creative, where he was the force behind Coke's "Open Happiness" campaign. The campaign led to the company's strongest profit increase in two decades and won thirty Cannes Lions awards. He then spent three years as chief marketing officer at Airbnb.

Mildenhall has made the most influential lists, from *Forbes*, to the *Financial Times*, *Adweek*, *Business Insider*, and *PR Week*, and was awarded Creative Marketer of the Year at the Cannes Lions International Festival of Creativity. Since 2018, Mildenhall has been the chief marketing officer of his own marketing consulting firm, TwentyFirstCenturyBrand. His clients include Peloton, Nextdoor, Uber, Pinterest, and WeWork.

Before you came out, was being queer something you were ashamed of?

I was always very popular at school, and I used to have this incredible duality. I would sit with the bookish kids in class, and then I'd hang out with the rebels during lunch break. I was always very popular with girls, and yet at the same time, there was a mannerism about me that was definitely not totally straight. But when I came out to those people closest to me, they were really shocked.

And yet other people who were slightly more distant to me, said, "Yeah, of course we always knew." Sometimes when you're so close to something, you don't want to see the truth. I did feel, in my teenage years, an intense shame about my sexual attraction for guys. I tried *really hard* to be heterosexual. And I had a number of long-term female relationships because it was easier, and that would be my pathway towards having children.

Why you were trying to suppress it?

There were no role models. This was in the 1980s. There was no Internet. There was no way you could find anything to help you understand what you were going through. Your education on sex and sexuality in the 1980s was what was taught in class or what happened behind your friend's couch on a Friday night. There was no way to get educated. It was so limiting. Self-awareness, cultural awareness, role models—there were none of the things we have now. You felt different. You felt ashamed. You felt lonely. You felt isolated. And you just wanted to be like everybody else.

Were you bullied?

Yeah, I was. I was born in a white project, so there were no other Black people. I am the middle child of five boys and I am the only Black kid in my family. My two older brothers are white and my two younger brothers are white. I was also the only Black kid in my school up until the age of twelve. I was bullied because of the color of my skin.

I do remember one evening, I was walking along the track to pick up my mum from work. There was this older girl and her friend who came over and kicked the shit out of me. I got beaten up badly. She was calling me all of these names, like *puff*, which is the English equivalent of faggot.

By the time I got to the gates to meet my mum, I had a black eye, I was bleeding, and my school uniform had been ripped. I couldn't tell my mum I had been beaten up by a girl, that I'd been beaten up because she thought I was a puff. I felt this intense shame as I manufactured a story that I had been beaten up by a load of guys. The irony of that tale is that girl grew up to be a lesbian. She saw in me something that was true to her, and she was desperately trying to struggle with her own sexuality, and she took it out on me.

Did the bullying have an impact on your sense of ambition and motivation?

Definitely. Because I was born in a project, I didn't know what middle-class was until I was about fourteen and I started hanging out with some middle-class people. As I started to get a glimpse of what middle-class looked like, I was like, *Fuck your lot who have all ridiculed me and beaten me up because I'm different. I'm going to use my difference to get out of this hellhole.* There was definitely this sense of *Screw you, I'm going to show you, I'm going to be successful.*

I was very conscious and I used that tension as a springboard. Because when you're a young Black kid in any city in the world, you have two choices: you either get weighed down by a chip on your shoulder, or you get bollied up by the fact that you're going to be different and you're going to succeed against all odds.

Now I use my sexuality and the color of my skin as a totem of my difference. I still want to prove to those people who put me down and tried to make me feel small. I'm still motivated deeply by making them feel that actually they never had what I had—which was this incredible energy, incredible character, this creative intelligence that pulled me away from them.

When you eventually came out to your family, did your ambitions change?

Yeah, and this was a huge moment for me. I was the first ethnic minority to be taken on by a top London advertising agency, back in 1990. McCann Erickson took a massive bet on me because I didn't go to university, I only went to a polytechnic. I was Black and I was working class. That was huge.

The first weekend I moved to London, I fell in love with this German guy. I didn't dare think in 1990 I could tell the advertising agency that placed a bet on me that the bet was even greater because I was gay.

Every weekend I'd be in gay clubs. I'd be dancing on podiums, wearing hot pants and cheap jewelry. And then Monday morning everybody would say to me, "What did you do this weekend?" And I'd say, "Oh, my girlfriend and I went to Ikea." I started this lie every Monday morning. Eventually, I'd been living with this guy for two-and-a-half years and everybody thought I was living with a girl named Danielle, because that was my professional narrative.

I hated this duality. I hated being inauthentic. The only way I could think of addressing it was to leave the company and get another job in an agency on the other side of town. This was before the Internet and social media. If you left one side of town and started working in another, chances were you were not bumping into everybody. And so I got a job at a company called BBH. I made a pact to myself that if anybody asked me about my sexuality, I would tell them.

By this time I was twenty-five years old. One day I was on the phone with my client and my boss walked into my office. She sat opposite me and started rapping her fingernails on the table as if to say, *Hurry up.* She was very formidable, so I thought, *Oh God, I fucked up.* I put the phone down and I looked at her and said, "How can I help you?"

She looked at me with this piercing look and she said, "Jonathan. You're gay, aren't you?" And I was like, *I've been outed, I'm going to get fired.*

This is what people can't appreciate: twenty-eight years ago, you felt like you were going to get fired for being gay in an advertising agency—arguably one of the most progressive workplaces on the planet. I said, "Yes I am."

And she said, "What's the name of your partner?"

I said, "Frank."

She scribbled "Frank and Jonathan" on an envelope, gave me it, and said, "It's my birthday on Saturday and I expect you both to be there. I expect you both to be dressed fabulously and no excuses. Whatever else is on your calendar is not as important as my birthday."

She marched out of my office and that was how I came out to my boss. She drew it out of me. But then I came out to the industry because my boss had invited me to a party that had all of the top talent and leadership of all the cool agencies in London. And she proudly introduced me as her account director and his boyfriend, who had been living together for three years. I came out on such a stage that there was no going back.

When you were interviewing for that very first job, were you actively trying to act "straighter"?

Without question. I had programmed myself. I came from a working-class background, I had different color skin, I knew I was gay, but I wasn't going to tell anybody. I programmed myself to speak with a more neutral accent, to use fewer hand movements, to be more forth-right in the room, to have more physical presence. I rehearsed my interviews in the mirror, and I was very disciplined in terms of showing up in a very narrow-cast but forthright way, so that the judgments against me would be minimized.

Did you think there could be a "gay, professional Jonathan"?

That's why it was such a significant party for me, because my boss brought me out and put me on that stage and because so many of the people were really positive about my relationship. The first time I came out professionally, I was with my partner and everybody adored him. I got home that night and I remember looking at him and going, *I can genuinely live the integrated lifestyle I want. There is no more "Jonathan on the Weekends" and "Jonathan Monday through Friday." I'm going to really enjoy the awareness of integrating myself so that I can find my true, authentic self.*

Has being gay helped you in your career?

It has given me license to be very creative. There is a creative license that gay men and women have, particularly gay men, in all sorts of fields. There is a creative flair that is almost expected, and I lean into that. I feel there is a sense of social freedom I have been able to stand on as a result of being gay.

There is definitely an energy I bring to a social room that is more effective because I'm gay. I feel I can straddle the masculine energy of the room and the masculine intellect of the room and the feminine energy of the room and the feminine intellect of the room.

I also think that people are, even today, curious about my sexuality. I've got a career in North America, I'm Black, I'm gay, and I'm British. There's a whole lot of "exotic" there that Americans are intrigued by. I can say things about the state of American society, or the way I might have been treated, and I think, *If I was a young, Black American, I wouldn't be able to get away with this, because people would say, "Look at the angry Black guy."* I use that example because I use my sexuality, my accent, and the color of my skin to disarm people with incredible vulnerability and honesty.

I am very lucky that I have that combination. Because I've seen young Black people not be able to say the things I say in a business meeting. And I've seen straight guys not be able to say the things I say because people would see them as being overly emotional, and soft with their feelings. And I've seen women not be able to say the things I say because people would say, "She's being bossy." I've seen these different groups get compromised and I've got it all.

BILLIE JEAN KING

Former World No. 1 Professional Tennis Player & Founder of the Billie Jean King Leadership Initiative

Billie Jean King was born into an athletic family in Long Beach, California, in 1943. She attended California State University, Los Angeles, and turned tennis pro in 1959.

King won thirty-nine Grand Slam titles, including twelve in singles, sixteen in doubles, and eleven in mixed doubles. She was inducted into the National Women's Hall of Fame and the International Tennis Hall of Fame. She has received the Federation Cup Award of Excellence. *Life* magazine named her one of the 100 Most Important Americans of the 20th Century. She also received the Presidential Medal of Freedom.

King has spent decades fighting for female and queer equality in sport. From the 1960s on, she strongly criticized the treatment of women within tennis, particularly as to them receiving lesser prize money compensation.

In 2008, King published her memoir, *Pressure Is a Privilege: Lessons I've Learned from Life and the Battle of the Sexes.*

She is partners with former tennis champion and World Team Tennis commissioner Ilana Kloss. They are part-owners of the Los Angeles Dodgers.

Despite my lack of interest in anything related to sports, I have a general awareness of select superstars such as Shaquille O'Neal, Serena and Venus Williams, Kobe Bryant, Tom Brady, Maria Sharapova—and Billie Jean King. Along with my understanding that Billie Jean is considered one of the best tennis players ever, her fame extends beyond the courts. She has been a pioneering and unstoppable force for women's and queer rights.

In 1973, King played former No. 1 tennis champion Bobby Riggs at the Houston Astrodome in what was known as the "Battle of the Sexes." Riggs claimed that women played a decidedly inferior game to men. It was one of the most widely televised athletic events in history, viewed around the world. King defeated Riggs, a decisive win for the fledgling women's liberation movement. (Emma Stone played Billie Jean King in the 2017 biopic *Battle of the Sexes*.)

That same year, King became the founder of the Women's Sports Foundation and the founder and first president of the Women's Tennis Association. She was instrumental in starting World Team Tennis with her former husband, Larry King. She has worked to bolster many organizations, including the Sports

Museum of America, the Women's Sports Foundation, and the Elton John AIDS Foundation.

King has been named Sportsman of the Year by *Sports Illustrated* and one of *Time* magazine's Persons of the Year. The *Sunday Times* of London named her Sportswoman of the Year and she was voted Sports Personality of the Year by the BBC.

This dizzying array of achievements left my mind spinning. A key piece of information that consistently arose through my research, though, was how Billie Jean King's career was practically ruined—despite *everything* she had achieved—when she came out as gay. It seemed to me that, as a woman who had suffered so greatly for opening up about her authentic self, she might not be interested in participating in a project whose sole purpose was to showcase the many advantages queerness created. Luckily, my fears were unfounded.

Billie Jean King agreed that our best selves can only be achieved when we embrace our full, authentic self, which is why she created the Billie Jean King Leadership Initiative, to work on bringing this topic to the forefront of corporations.

How has being queer positively impacted your life or career?

It took me until I was fifty-one years old to be comfortable in my own skin. For too long I was afraid to be my authentic self. Since that time, I've been able to focus on using my voice and the opportunities before me to advocate for others. And I've met some incredible people along the way. Being the New York Gay Pride marshal in 2018 was truly a full circle moment for me and gave me an opportunity to celebrate and appreciate how far our community has really come.

What advice do you have for young queer people entering the workforce?

Everyone should be able to bring all of themselves to the workplace and feel like they don't have to hide or cover. You can only be your best when you embrace your authentic self. Thankfully, companies are becoming more inclusive. A key focus of our work at the Billie Jean King Leadership Initiative is to foster constructive dialogue with CEOs and companies on how to embrace those who may look or live differently than ourselves.

American history will regard you as one of the most significant figures in women's rights and in queer social justice. After all you have achieved, has that lessened any anger or resentment you've felt for all of the battles you had to fight?

Anger is usually not a good motivator for me. What has been important in my life—and what is still important today—is for me to make sure I am on the right side of history. You are never going to "win" every time. In fact, I see failure as feedback. I learned very early not to take things personally and to keep moving forward.

You have received innumerable awards and honors. Was your ongoing struggle with sexual orientation a central impetus driving you to such heights?

My whole life, my sexual identity has been a driving force. But it is my lifelong commitment to achieving equality for all that has always been the driving force in everything I do.

HOWARD ROSENMAN

Film Producer

The films Howard Rosenman has produced have spanned both commercial and critical success, including *Call Me by Your Name*, *Father of the Bride*, *The Celluloid Closet*, *Sparkle*, the original film version of *Buffy the Vampire Slayer*, and *Common Threads*.

Rosenman grew up in Queens, New York, in a Jewish household. Graduating from Brooklyn College, he then attended Hahnemann Medical College. His studies were disrupted when he left for Israel to serve in the Six-Day War in 1967. While in Israel, he met his mentor, legendary composer Leonard Bernstein.

It was Bernstein who encouraged Rosenman to leave medical school and pursue a career in the arts. He ultimately did, and later became assistant to Katharine Hepburn while she performed *Coco* on Broadway, about the life of Coco Chanel.

Rosenman is the cofounder of Project Angel Food in Los Angeles, a meals-on-wheels program for people living with life-threatening diseases. The nonprofit was created in response to the HIV/AIDS epidemic, and then expanded to help others with life-threatening illnesses. Every week, Project Angel Food delivers twelve thousand meals across Los Angeles.

It was a busy lunchtime when I sat down with Rosenman at a dishes-crashing, frenetic restaurant in Los Angeles. Although I was familiar with Howard and his decades-spanning work, I'd become especially enchanted through an article he wrote for the *Hollywood Reporter*. In the essay, he described the "magic" of being gay in the 1970s in New York and Los Angeles. He concluded the piece with "If I wasn't gay, I never would have had the career that I have."

As he spoke, I found myself hanging on every word, fascinated and envious. What he'd accomplished, the people he'd met and collaborated with, the places he'd seen, and the projects he'd created felt otherworldly and incomprehensible.

He casually rattled off stories about pool parties with Rock Hudson, Tennessee Williams, Gore Vidal, Tab Hunter, and David Hockney. How he once casually dated Andrew Cunanan, the man who murdered Gianni Versace. (It was startling to learn that after Cunanan's death, the FBI approached Rosenman with alarming news: found with Cunanan's body was his hit list. Among the top targets was Rosenman, along with media and entertainment moguls David Geffen and Barry Diller.)

As we talked, I found that beneath his Hollywood roughness was a deeply caring, thoughtful, and passionate person. Beyond the glitz, glamor, and celebrities, Rosenman was a man who had experienced tremendous pain and suffering, much to do with AIDS. I was convinced I'd misheard him when he said he had lost 2,700 friends to the disease, in addition to having his own scare in 1983.

What was evident, though, through looking at his dazzling career, was that on top of a steely resilience, Rosenman was spectacularly gifted at networking. He has an uncanny ability to work a room, meet the right people, and then bring those people together to create big, moneymaking and critically acclaimed cinema. All of these skills, paired with the cultural savvy he noted that many queer people have, have made him a formidable force, spanning decades of some of Hollywood's most spectacular work.

Growing up in Brooklyn, as you came to understand you were gay, how did that impact your vision of your future?

I knew I was gay when I was four. I didn't think I was going to have a future. I thought it was so secret and internal that I couldn't tell anyone. It was hard. And my father was rough on me. He was very macho, and I was an effeminate kid.

In school, the teacher gave each of us clay. Everybody made a clay pot, and I didn't. Use your imagination. So they sent me to the school psychologist. It was a progressive school, and the school psychologist sent a letter to my parents. I didn't know what was in that letter. But before the letter, my father had always been tender with me. Suddenly he changed his whole demeanor and started being very tough.

In 2001, my parents moved to Israel, as did my sister. That same year, my mother was on her deathbed in Jerusalem. She called me over and said, "Get me my pocketbook." Inside there was a yellow letter. She said, "Read this and you'll understand everything."

Dear Mr. and Mrs. Rosenman,

Your brilliant young son is in the throes of a homosexual crisis. It's incumbent upon you to take him to a psychoanalyst to determine whether he has enough heterosexual fabric to make a heterosexual adjustment, or whether he's truly a homosexual. Yours truly.

That was from 1949. Thirty years before the American Psychiatric Association changed the designation of homosexuality from psychotic to normalcy. The school psychiatrist was very progressive and was trying to tell my father *If your son is gay, love him.* But my father took it all wrong.

It shaped my whole life, because I became very rebellious. My father would say *red* and I would say *blue.* My father would say *do this* and I would say *fuck you.* Later, that turned me into a producer. All of that rejection and bullying hardened my skin. I get rejected a billion times a day. I wake up every morning and gird my loins for war. Years later I reconciled with my father.

In 1967, you took a leave from medical school to serve as a medic in the Six-Day War, as part of the Israeli Defense Forces.

The war was over so quickly that I was transferred to the hospital. Leonard Bernstein, the composer, came to Israel to visit the volunteers. He took one look at me and said, "Oh my god, I know a guy who looks exactly like you. He was my waiter at a discotheque in New York."

And I said in Hebrew, "Maestro, I was your waiter." He kissed me on the lips and gave me four tickets to his concert. I took my parents and cousin.

At the party afterwards, Leonard asked me if I wanted to be a gopher* on the documentary they were making about him, conducting the Israel Philharmonic Orchestra in Judea and Samaria. I became his gopher—and more.

---

* A gopher is a personal assistant.

He would say to me, "You should leave medical school and go into the arts. You'll never bow to the mistress of science." I didn't know what the fuck he was talking about. He took me on vacation to Italy with his wife and children. He traveled with an entourage.

I came back to Israel, worked on another documentary, and then went back to medical school. While I was assisting on an amputation, I'm listening to Lenny saying to me, *You'll never bow to the mistress of science*, and I decided to take a leave of absence.

I came to New York and called Lenny. "I'm here," I say.

He says, "I'm married with two kids. But I'll introduce you to my best friend." So he introduces me to Katharine Hepburn and I became her assistant on the musical *Coco*, about Coco Chanel. And then I'm introduced to Alan Jay Lerner, André Previn, and then Stephen Sondheim. That was my entrance.

Do you think some artists took an interest in you and helped you along because they suspected you were gay and wanted to be supportive?

Some of them took an interest in me because I was good-looking, not because I was gay. They thought they could seduce me. Which they did.

You've said that life in New York and Los Angeles in the 1970s was "magical" for gay people. But there was also such a tremendous amount of homophobia in entertainment. Wouldn't it have been stressful?

I had a leg up because I knew these very powerful people, and I was smart. I also had a girlfriend in New York named Kitty Hawks, daughter of film director Howard Hawks. She was *the* girl of 1970. We were in the newspapers all the time. So when I came out to Hollywood, everybody had known about me because they kind of knew I was gay, but there I was with a girlfriend. And in those days, it was interesting, exotic, and alluring to be able to be that way.

There was a whole network of people in New York that were like that: Oscar de la Renta, Calvin Klein, and all these people that had *other lives*. But everybody knew they were also gay. A certain strata of society knew; the outside didn't really know. The cognoscenti knew, but they didn't give a shit.

You've mentioned before that gay people during this time had a huge impact on culture. What did that impact look like?

When I came to New York in the winter of 1967, men couldn't dance with other men—even at gay bars. They had to dance in a circle with a woman in the center. In every gay bar there was a fat man on a stool, a Mafioso, because the mafia owned all of the bars. If two men touched each other, he would shine a flashlight on you. If they shined the light on you three times, the police were called. I had a boyfriend in the police force who told me this. Whenever I saw the second flashlight, I was out of there.

After Stonewall, there was an attitude of *Don't fuck with us.* And I had a very Israeli attitude about it anyway: *Don't touch me or I'll kill you.* Six months later, the laws were changed in New York so men could dance with other men. From that time on, to be gay and good-looking, you had the world by the fucking balls. Everybody wanted that.

If you were a talented architect, designer, composer, musician, theater director, everybody wanted you. Fire Island became the center of the culture. I fucked everything that moved. Do you know who Patient Zero is?* I had been with patients one through nineteen. The only one I wasn't with was Patient Zero. I'm HIV negative.

At one point though, you thought you did have it. You were given a false positive.

I was diagnosed in 1983. I went to Israel to die. After a while, I still hadn't died, so I came back to California. In 1987, when it was available, I was given the test.

After I was told I was negative, I made a deal with God. I had an epiphany that if I had this second chance, I would concentrate on the work itself. I don't give a shit about getting in the newspapers, I don't care about going to the parties, I don't care about Barbra Streisand. Out of that came my best work. The diagnosis made me humble. I was an arrogant prick and out of my mind. That changed the whole course of my career and life.

At what point in all of this did you decide that you were no longer going to keep your gayness a secret?

I never kept it a secret. *Ever.* I was very open about it and very comfortable in my skin. I was masculine, good-looking, had a lot of friends that were girls. None of that means anything today, but then it did. So I never hid it. In fact, I used it.

---

*Flight attendant Gaëtan Dugas was incorrectly regarded as "Patient Zero" in the AIDS crisis but was found to be one of several early cases that occurred around the same time.

Did you feel like you needed to work harder because you were gay?

To get into the straight world. At the time, there were agencies that were notorious for not liking gays. But I always allied myself with great power. For instance, I ran Sandy Gallin's Sandollar Productions. Sandy managed Barbra Streisand, Dolly Parton, and Michael Jackson. All those people would together throw off $300 million a year.

How has being queer advantaged you in your career?

I don't mean to generalize, but when you are gay, you have a certain kind of cultural savvy; that outsider thing, which was very well developed in me because I was bullied by both my father and the kids at school. I was very honed to pick up on special talent. I was like a heat-seeking missile.

Because you were marginalized, do you think that has given you a lens from which to have a unique perspective on projects that others might not have?

Yes. No straight man in his wildest imagination would make *Common Threads, The Celluloid Closet,* or *Call Me by Your Name.* No straight man whatsoever. They may now say they would, but they wouldn't.

When I was on the Oscar track for *Call Me by Your Name,* heads of film studios would come up to me and say, "Why didn't you bring this to us? We would have loved it." And I always take very good notes. So I would whip out my phone and say, "Really? But I came to you in 2015, and you said you only wanted commercial movies and movies that will win awards." I said that a lot. *A lot.*

Do you think there's a connection between your resilience and ambition and being queer?

No. I've never really thought about it. When I came home to Long Island from Israel, after the war and after having worked with Leonard Bernstein, I told my father I was leaving medical school, that I was gay, and that I was no longer religious. The trifecta.

My father said to me, "You're too much of a schmuck to make it in the world of the goyim. You'll come crawling back to me for money."

I said, "Really? The next time you see me I will be in the back of a fucking limousine." And the next time I saw him I was in the back of a fucking limousine.

JENNIFER FINNEY BOYLAN

New York Times *Columnist & Author*

Jennifer Finney Boylan was born in 1958. Raised in Valley Forge, Pennsylvania, she studied at Wesleyan University and Johns Hopkins University. She began her transition from male to female in 2000.

In 2014, after working at Colby College, Boylan became an English professor and the Anna Quindlen writer-in-residence at Barnard College in New York. She has written sixteen books, including her bestselling autobiographies, *She's Not There: A Life in Two Genders* and *Good Boy: My Life in Seven Dogs*.

Boylan is a regular columnist for the *New York Times*. She has served as a consultant for a number of television shows, including *Transparent* and *I Am Cait*. She has appeared on *48 Hours*, *The Today Show*, *The Oprah Winfrey Show*, *Larry King Live*, and many other programs.

Boylan served on multiple boards, including the Kinsey Institute for Research on Sex, Gender, and Reproduction.

Jennifer Boylan has a cozy office at Barnard College's New York City campus. It was a rainy Friday afternoon when we sat down together in-between her classes and student meetings. Boylan wore a red button-down shirt with white polka dots, dark-wash denim jeans, and brown closed-toe sandals. Dozens of books lined the walls of her quiet space. She sat on her brown, broken-in couch opposite me. As we talked, she ran her hands through her hair, shifting it from one shoulder to the other.

I am an avid reader of Boylan's *New York Times* column, where she approaches a myriad of social issues, personal musings, and political hot topics. Her writing is sharp and smart, interlaced with a cutting wit. I found her in person to be quite the same.

With two writers having a conversation, it seemed appropriate that we ended up talking about writing. Or, rather, the process of writing and how it related to our identity. When anyone begins writing—a term paper, a complicated text message, a book—we start with a first draft. Then, after review and consideration, we edit. It never occurred to me that the same tactics applied to us as humans in our quest for personal revision. And even more specifically, transgender people.

Our first draft is often (thankfully) very different than our final draft. There are errors, changes of ideas, character revisions, new plots. Boylan made the case that we have multiple shots throughout life to get it right.

On the subway back downtown, I thought about editing. As queer people, many of us go through extensive revisions of ourselves. When I came out as gay, I took my first stab at a deep edit. My wardrobe shifted, my social group varied. Things about myself I had kept hidden, I brought to the surface. And this revision of self continues to this day. Finding new layers of myself and revealing them to the world as I see fit is an exciting experience. One that leaves me feeling a bit more optimistic and hopeful.

By the time the subway screeched to a halt at my stop and I stepped back out onto the dizzying Manhattan streets, I was able to pinpoint the various versions of myself. They've led me here, to my current draft I am very happy with, but that I know will not be my last.

You once said, "I'd arrived at early adolescence having inherited my mother's buoyant optimism. In spite of the nearly constant sense that I was the wrong person, I was filled with a simultaneous hopefulness and cheer that most people found annoying. . . . This legacy of cheerful wit became the thing that sustained me and also, at times, burdened me. . . . In spite of a sense of ever-present exasperation with my own body, I was rarely depressed and reacted to my awful life with joy, with humor, and with light." Where do you think you got that optimism, and how were you able to keep that during such difficult times?

I wonder how much of our sense of self, and our view of the world, is something we inherit. Is there something genetic about it? My mother had one of the hardest lives of anybody I know. And yet she was the happiest person I knew. When we were kids, we thought it was superficial and that she was out of touch with reality.

Is optimism and hope a blindness to the realities of the world? Does that mean you're just not awake enough to understand how truly sad and oppressive life is? Or is it in fact an act of great courage? Is having a sense of humor and buoyance not a kind of blindness, but a higher vision and ability to see into something transcendent and bigger than ourselves?

So did I inherit my optimism from my mother? Sometimes I think so, because I've always had that. There were times when I was incredibly depressed and crushed with sorrow, but I was always very hopeful and had a sense of humor.

My mother's phrase was "Love will prevail." I have that faith, too. Whether I inherited that, or whether I came to understand that this was a glorious way to live in the world, I can't tell you. But a thing I have inherited is that we have to believe in love, forgiveness, raising hell, kicking ass, and being happy warriors. An awareness of how hard life can be should inspire us to the light and to have a sense of humor and to be hopeful. Otherwise, you're just going to get crushed by your sadness. Which isn't to say I haven't been crushed by sadness. But I've always managed to float like a cork.

When you came out at age forty, did you notice a difference in the work you were able to do?

The biggest difference for me was not going from male to female. The biggest difference was going from someone who'd had a secret, to someone who didn't have a secret. Having a secret is like having an invisible Tyrannosaurus rex on a leash: it has to go everywhere, it's hungry, must be constantly fed, and has to be maintained. A lot of your psychic energy goes into making sure other people don't perceive this thing in you, and that you don't perceive this thing in yourself, if you can avoid it.

The funny thing is then you come out and everyone says, "That's impossible. I had no idea." And you're thinking, *You didn't see it because I spent all of my life making sure you didn't see it.*

So, suddenly, I was free. There was some euphoria in being publicly female, but the glorious thing was not devoting every moment of my waking life to making sure people didn't know the truth about me.

Was there a shift in your writing?

My writing pre-transition was full of hysterical energy. It was very wound up, self-obsessed, nervous. Even in the fiction I wrote, you could read that this was an author who was very entertaining, but was keeping something hidden on some level. There was some truth that was being hidden from the reader, and instead of truth, you got very outrageous, funny situations. I think most comic writers are driven by some private discomfort.

After transition, I hope my writing is able to go to a deeper place. I don't want to say it's less entertaining, but it's less about the jokes and more about the truth. Before transition I wrote fiction. After transition I wrote nonfiction. When I was male and hiding, I was writing stories that were on some fundamental level not true. And once I came out, I was writing the truth.

Do you think there's any connection between your drive, resilience, ambition, and work ethic and being queer?

The biggest thing I have (certainly as a writer, but also in other ways) is belief in *revision*. If you don't get something right the first time, your life isn't over. To be willing to admit that any belief you have might be wrong, to be willing to have your mind changed, to be open to new knowledge.

What is being transgender if not a kind of cosmic way of believing in the power of multiple drafts? Being trans made me understand you get a lot of shots in this life. It's never too late to become yourself. It also helped me understand when I was forty that my life wasn't over. That it was possible to start my life over as a woman and to take the goodness of my earlier life with me. So then I came out as trans.

And then when I was fifty, it was possible for me to understand that the woman I'd been in my early middle age was different from who I was going to be in the years to come. I was able to revise my sense of the world and my sense of self again, to become a different kind of woman.

Now I'm in my sixties, looking down at the approaching hills of old age and seeing my sense of self change again.

How has being queer advantaged you in your career?

For one thing, it's given me a sense of fierceness. When you get beaten up for who you are, when you get told that who you are and what you are is an impossibility, when you are teased and bullied and hated just for the sheer fact of who you are, it lights a fire in you. A fire to set things right. A fire to get your revenge and, at least in my case, to get your revenge by succeeding. No matter how low they brought you, you know that by the sheer fire of your imagination and creativity and your *refusal* to die, that you will have the last laugh in the end.

I'm a big crybaby also, especially since transition. I hope that means my heart is more open. It's said that one of the things estrogen does is that it removes this protective shield you have between the world and your heart. So certainly since I came out, the world gets through to me now and I spend a lot of time in tears. I also spend a lot of time laughing my head off. Just having the ability to experience both the gloriousness and the sadness of life has made me able to live more fully.

Being queer has made me more sympathetic to people who are different, all across the board. It's given me occasion to interrogate my own privilege and consider just how hard other people's lives are. Because I know how hard my life was and it makes me more able to understand the burdens that other people carry in silence.

In the end, being queer has meant I was different. When you're a child or adolescent, being different is such a curse. All you want to do is to fit in. And then you realize that all those people who fit in are *bores*. They will spend their whole lives being bores and being nothing. And that, as a queer person, the very thing that caused all those tears is now your glorious gift. And it enables you to turn the thing you always thought was your curse into your *superpower*.

It is hard to see difference as a superpower. But in some ways, it's been shown to me again and again that whatever it was that I was given was a gift. I think about the people I grew up with for whom life seemed to have been a lot easier. For some of them, I think, *You don't know how lucky I was to be so unhappy. Because I never would have wound up where I am now.* And the other times I think, *Were they really so happy?* If I can open my heart to them, maybe I will understand that their lives were hard, too.

Being queer gives you X-ray vision. Superman has the ability to see through walls and bricks. Being queer gives you the ability to see into people's hearts, just like you have radioactive blood. You can see into other people's hearts and know how much turmoil there is, and to respond to them with kindness, sympathy, and love.

JIM OBERGEFELL

Lead Plaintiff in Obergefell v. Hodges, which legalized same-sex marriage in the United States

James Obergefell was born and raised in Sandusky, Ohio. He went on to study German and Education at the University of Cincinnati and Bowling Green University.

Obergefell taught high school German, then became a realtor and IT consultant for a number of companies.

He met his husband, John Arthur, in Cincinnati, and they lived together for two decades. When Arthur was suffering from ALS, Obergefell was his caretaker. By 2013 Arthur was bedbound, and the men decided to marry. They were flown in a medically equipped plane to Maryland and were married onboard. When they returned to Cincinnati, Ohio refused to recognize their marriage and they initiated a lawsuit.

Though Arthur died in October 2013, *Obergefell v. Hodges* was argued before the United States Supreme Court, pushing for the fundamental right to marry under both the Due Process Clause and the Equal Protection Clause of the Fourteenth Amendment.

In 2016, Obergefell prevailed in the landmark case. He was cited by President Obama for his bold display of leadership.

It was June 26, 2015, and I remember standing outside on a corner in the West Village in Manhattan, talking to my dad. Hordes of people passed by me, decked out in Pride paraphernalia, glitter everywhere, rainbow flags waving. My dad had called to make sure I fully understood the significance of what had just occurred: same-sex marriage was now legal in all fifty states, through the 5-4 *Obergefell v. Hodges* decision. He also wanted me to make a special note that the very man who brought this case to the Supreme Court was from Cincinnati, Ohio, just like I was.

Five years later, I was sitting in that Ohio man's living room in his cozy Columbus apartment. Jim Obergefell, a name that will live on in history books, was barefoot, his legs curled up on the couch, and wearing a navy blue sweater and jeans. He was a nice Midwest boy through and through. Polite and soft-spoken, we gossiped about *Gossip Girl* and other guilty-pleasure television shows we were bingeing over the holidays. It was Christmastime, and his tree was immaculately decorated in the corner, the lights reflecting off the ornaments onto the many photos and paintings on the walls.

As I'd driven up to Columbus that morning, sipping my Dunkin' Donuts coffee and listening to Lady Gaga, I ruminated on the phone call I'd had with my dad five years earlier and why—or rather, *how*—I did not grasp the life-altering, tectonic plate-shifting magnitude of what Jim Obergefell had accomplished.

Up until starting this book and tackling the question of what our queer advantage is, I had never *truly* had to think about my lawful rights as a gay man living in the United States. I wasn't thinking about marriage in 2015, and hadn't begun my professional career, where I'd run the risk of being fired for being gay. I had never spent the much-needed time to comprehend queer history. Others were doing that for me. I wasn't an activist. I didn't march in rallies and pin rainbow buttons on my shirt in protest.

But the more I learned through speaking with people and reading about our history, the angrier I became. And specifically on that morning drive to Columbus, I became angry at myself for having taken for granted my entire life what people like Jim had risked everything for.

Thankfully, Jim was nothing like me. He hadn't brushed away the thought of equal rights. Instead, he had used his queer advantage of compassion and determination to go out and change something he knew was wrong.

As humans, we all want to feel that we matter; that we are of value, and that we offer value to others as well. Jim realized that he, John, and their relationship mattered and deserved to be appreciated.

As you came to understand you were gay, how did that impact your vision of your future?

I'm the baby of six in a Catholic family. All of my siblings were married. So for me growing up, my future was always *I'm gonna get married and have kids.* Needless to say, I would marry a woman. So, when I was two years out of undergrad, I was engaged to a woman.

When that relationship ended, it was a sense of relief that I didn't drag her into something that would've been really bad and painful for her. At that point in my life I thought, *Marriage and kids are out; that's not gonna be part of my world.* But it was okay, because I had that incredible sense of relief that I hadn't dragged an innocent person into a marriage that wasn't completely true and honest.

My father was the first person I told in my family. My mom had passed away years before and my dad and I had become pretty close. I was twenty-six and I thought he would approach it from the mindset of me not being able to have a family. He was a mid-sixties, blue collar, Catholic man. I was petrified. But his response was "Jim, all I want is for you to be happy." I felt so incredibly lucky in that moment. He proved me wrong.

When did you meet your husband, John?

It was the spring of 1992 and I was twenty-six. My friend Kevin and I went to a University of Cincinnati campus bar. He saw his friend and introduced us. It was John.

I was still closeted, and John scared the daylights out of me because he was a gay man and comfortable with that. I thought he was going to say something or know right away.

We met a second time at the same bar. This was after I'd come out, and during that conversation, John made some comment along the lines of "Well, you'd never go out with someone like me."

I said, "How do you know? You've never asked." And he didn't.

So then the third time we met was when I was back in Cincinnati for the holidays and my friend Kevin invited me to his New Year's Eve party. At that time, John was one of Kevin's housemates. I went to the party and never left.

When you and John eventually decided you wanted to get married, he had already been diagnosed with ALS. Was the goal to actively try and change the law? Because at the time, it was not legal in Ohio.

No. It was purely that we wanted to *exist*. It wasn't that we were trying to change the law. Within the first two years of our relationship, we both talked about how we would love to get married, but we didn't think it was ever going to be something we could do. We had friends who went through commitment ceremonies, but we both agreed that we didn't want that. We didn't want it to just be symbolic. So we assumed it was never gonna happen.

On June 26, 2013, after the *United States v. Windsor* decision, it was the first time in our twenty-one years together that we could get married and actually have it exist in the eyes of the government.* So I proposed.

That was the only thing we wanted. We just wanted our relationship to matter, to exist, to be. And because of Edie Windsor, at least at the federal level, we would exist. We had no plans to do anything other than just get married, and let John die a married man.

At that point, same-sex marriage wasn't legal in Ohio, and John was bedridden. What were those initial steps in figuring out how to go about the marriage ceremony?

The first thing I did was I reached out to John's favorite aunt. She had told us years before, "I think you represent marriage more than any

---

*The United States Supreme Court held that Section 3 of the Defense of Marriage Act, which denied federal recognition of same-sex marriages, was a violation of the Due Process Clause of the Fifth Amendment.

other couple I know. If you can get married, I want to do it." So she went to the Internet and clicked the "ordain me" button.

I got in touch with her and asked, "Does it still stand?"

She said, "Absolutely, tell me when and where."

Then it was the challenge of *We want to get married, but where?* The courthouse was just six blocks from us, but because it wasn't legal in Ohio, I couldn't take John in his wheelchair there. Where were we gonna do this?

I started researching the states where we *could* get married. My big thing was wanting to make sure I kept John as comfortable and as safe as possible. He was completely bedridden and couldn't do anything. So if we were gonna go to another state, I wanted to make it as least disruptive as possible.

At this time, John and I were both working at Fidelity Investments. One of our coworkers asked if we had looked into Maryland yet. When I researched Maryland, I discovered it helped in one major way: it was the only place that did not require *both* people to appear in person to apply for the marriage license. One person could do it and, in essence, sign an affidavit saying, *I am applying for this marriage license with the other's approval.* I thought, *Well this is great. I can go get the marriage license myself and then John and I can go back together and it will just be a day trip.* So that's what we decided to do.

But then it was a matter of how we would get there. I didn't want to put John in our wheelchair minivan or in the back of an ambulance. And I couldn't take him to the airport and fly on Delta. So our only real option was a charter medical jet. And then I found out just how expensive those are.

I went on Facebook, thinking somebody might have a connection to a pilot or charter company or something that might help mitigate the cost. People said, "We're here, we want to help. Please accept this money." Our family and friends covered the entire $14,000 cost.

So you fly to Maryland, get married, and come back to Ohio, even though you know Ohio doesn't recognize your marriage. What happened next that led to filing the lawsuit?

A friend of ours was on the editorial board of the *Cincinnati Enquirer*. She had been pushing the paper to come out and support marriage equality. When she found out we were doing this, she asked if we'd be willing to have her write a story. We got married on a Thursday. That Saturday, her story came out.

Friends and neighbors were at a party and they ran into a friend of theirs, Al Gerhardstein, who's a civil rights attorney. Our story came up in conversation. He hadn't heard about it and they told him to look it up. Al called them later and asked if they thought John and I would be willing to talk with him.

We had no idea what he wanted to talk about but said, "Sure, why not?" So Tuesday, five days after we got married, Al came to our home. He pulled out a blank Ohio death certificate. And that's when that abstract understanding of the state constitutional amendment became real for us. And it hurt because we hadn't thought about this. Here I was realizing that when John died, his last record as a person would be wrong. It broke our hearts and, more importantly, made us angry. He asked if we wanted to do something about it. After talking about it, we decided we did. So we filed suit.

Up until you're presented with the blank death certificate, you had no plans to fight the Ohio amendment?

None whatsoever. Never in our wildest dreams would we have conceived the possibility of suing the state of Ohio. Al made it okay for us to consider it. I was losing John to ALS and I didn't want to lose our marriage. I wanted it to exist. John felt guilty he had gotten ill and that I was his caregiver. He felt like he ruined my life by getting sick. Even though he could do nothing for himself, he gave me the okay to take time away from him to meet with our lawyer, to be in court. That was his way of thanking me for taking care of him and his way of saying, *Our marriage matters, our relationship matters, and let's fight for it.*

What gave you the confidence to take on the state of Ohio?

Nothing more than loving John and wanting our marriage to matter. That's really all it was. And after hearing what Al saw as our legal argument, it made perfect sense. We knew the state constitutional amendment simply was wrong. But for Al to be able to explain it from a legal perspective, and explain what our argument would be, made it even more clearly wrong.

How has being gay been a positive dynamic in your life?

It has made me more empathetic, more easily able to understand how other minority groups feel, and how fighting for a group that's discriminated against is important. I grew up in Sandusky and 30 percent of my classmates were people of color. That was normal to me. But coming out as gay and living through those direct attacks—and understanding how unequal we were—helped me understand how unequal life was for my friends who were people of color. It helped build my sense of empathy, my willingness to speak up on another's behalf, and to fight.

Do you think that kind of awareness or empathy helped when you were up against this massive legal battle?

From the start, I knew our fight was the right thing to do. Because of my experience as the named plaintiff, people think I must've been attacked and had horrible experiences. But I didn't. Again, I seem to have, in some ways, this lucky life where my experience was nothing but support. And I think part of our story is something people can relate to. Because whoever you are, you love somebody, and everyone has lost someone they've loved. Because our story was one of love and loss, and fighting for someone you love, I think it helped protect me from some of the ugliness. People could connect to that and they could see themselves in our story.

When we started this fight, it was very personal. It was about us, it was about our marriage. After John died and as this case started getting *bigger* and *bigger* and *bigger*, it was understanding how important it was to so many other people across the country. It became so much bigger than just us. And I knew that on a very logical, rational level from the start. But emotionally, over time, it just became clearer. People would come up to me and give me their condolences, and talk about how they really appreciated it, and how important it was to them. It was a two-way street, where they were showing me empathy but they were also building empathy in me.

SALLY SUSMAN

Executive Vice President &
Chief Corporate Affairs Officer, Pfizer

Whether moving through the executive suites of corporate America, working the corridors of power in Washington or Brussels, or leading a humanitarian relief mission, Sally Susman is motivated by the many hats she wears: business leader, engaged citizen, and influencer.

Born in 1961, Susman is the daughter of former United States ambassador to the United Kingdom, Louis Susman. She was raised in St. Louis, Missouri, where public service was ingrained in her life from an early age.

Susman previously worked for the Senate Commerce Committee and United States Department of Commerce on international trade issues. She later held senior communications and government relations roles at the Estée Lauder Companies and American Express. At Pfizer, the world's largest biopharmaceutical company, she is currently executive vice president and chief corporate affairs officer, leading reputation management and directing the company's communications, public affairs, philanthropic, and patient engagement activities globally. The 2008 ABC series *Cashmere*

Mafia character Caitlin Dowd was based on Susman. The *Financial Times* has included her in its list of top 100 LGBTQ+ executives in the world.

It was the 1980s when you first fell in love with a woman and realized you were gay. When you came out to your parents, your dad told you that, in addition to not having a spouse or children, you wouldn't have a career. How did your perception of your future change when you realized you were queer, coupled with what your dad told you?

It's a moment in my life I'll never forget. I was sitting in my parents' bedroom and telling them I was gay, and seeing my father, the man I admire more than any guy out there, just crumble with sadness and say these things. He certainly wasn't trying to be mean. It was just what he believed true at the time, based on his experience as a lawyer in St. Louis, Missouri.

I didn't know if he was right or wrong, but I knew I had to have my life, and not being out wouldn't be a life worth living. Whether or not I could make a living, I didn't know.

After telling my parents in St. Louis, I went back to Washington, D.C., where I was working at the time on Capitol Hill. I originally was only out in an underground network of other Capitol staffers who were gay. It was incredible, because we ended up forming a powerful alliance of friends. "Friend" doesn't really begin to describe it. These people were like me—young but driven—and placed around Washington in powerful positions. As a young person in Washington, I was able to get more things done because I had this underground network that was this *powerful* family of people.

Then the AIDS epidemic was upon us, and being closeted became more difficult. People were dying, our hearts were breaking, and we were scared. Activism took hold. When I left Washington and took my next career step in New York, it was very clear to me that I wanted to come out. I began the process of telling colleagues, and then I got a promotion to take a position in London with American Express. I needed to tell my boss because I needed a visa for my partner.

I was overwhelmed with how well the world responded to us as young, gay people. They wanted to be helpful. But there wasn't much that American Express could do because there was no marriage or reciprocal right. It was a tough period because my wife's ability to stay in England was always somewhat in jeopardy.

The fact that I had been forthcoming with my employer opened up new levels of respect for me as an individual, and it was liberating for me to not feel I had to hide or lie. I was put on committees working on how a big company like American Express would handle the domestic partner benefit. In the very early stages, it ended up being an asset. You were stronger in your relationships, you were seen as courageous, and you were *trusted* as being an honest person.

I then went back into government and worked for President Clinton. Again, being an out, gay person was helpful. There was no sexual politics around me, no guy was going to harass me, you become known as someone who is not going to put up with a lot of ridiculousness. And some of those male-female gender dynamics that pervade the workplace, I felt insulated from.

When you came out and were openly gay in the office, you flourished. What were the factors that led up to you deciding you felt comfortable enough to vocalize that part of your life?

After American Express in London, I came back to New York. I came to a crossroads when I applied to the Estée Lauder Companies. I was going to work for a very visible company in a different way—and also a company that has a family in the center. I wasn't just going to be on a team, as I had been in the past. I was going to be the spokesperson of the company.

In the context of the interview, I was asked, "What does your husband do?" And you come to a point in your life where you don't want the job any longer if you have to go back in the closet. I told him what my wife, Robin, did. And in that moment, Ronald Lauder was very gracious and basically gave me the job on the spot.

I realized how much more power I had because I was playing with my whole heart and speaking with my full throat. The work I do is primarily communications work. I'm essentially trying to convey a message. And a message needs two things: it has to be a relative message and come from an authentic messenger. When someone is closeted, they become a very inauthentic messenger. I found that by coming out, I was practicing what I was preaching through everyone I was advising, to say *You need to be fully forthcoming.* I felt that gave me a lot of power.

Queer people know well what it feels like to be otherized. When operating in the business sphere, do you still find difference to be an advantage?

In addition to the otherness that gay people feel together, we have this incredible bond. American business has really struggled with diversity at the most fundamental level. African Americans are deeply underrepresented in companies; Asians are seen as good in technical jobs but not in leadership roles. And a gay person—not every gay person, but a lot of gay people—has a fine sense for what it means to be left out, or what it feels like when you walk into a room and people stop talking. Having experienced those, you become much more attuned to them, and can become an agent to combat those subtle forms of discrimination and prejudice when they worm their way into the business and office.

Do you think there is a connection between your ambition, drive, work ethic, and resilience and being queer?

There's a connection between those qualities and a number of things in my life. I have hardworking parents, so that was a family trait. I'm a Midwesterner, so we pride ourselves on that bootstrap mentality. But without question, being gay was an accelerator on my ambition. Because back in the eighties, I was suddenly scared. Would I have the ability to have a lifelong partner? Would I be able to have a home? Would I be able to have a job I felt proud of?

I couldn't take things for granted. I wasn't going to be taken care of by any husband. There was no house for me in my hometown of St. Louis, where I wanted to live. I was going to need to make my own way in the world.

Have you had to work harder because you're gay?

I *wanted* to work harder because I was gay. I don't know if I had to, but I wanted to because I was going to prove it. It wasn't that I wanted to prove my dad wrong, but looking back at that conversation I had with my parents in my early twenties, I feel that moment set the plan for my life.

I didn't know it then, but I was going to be damn sure to get those things. Even for gay people to have families and children, it all has to be very thoughtful. No gay couple gets drunk in the back of a Chevy and ends up with a family. Gay people put more thinking into their families than anybody. *How do we do it? Adopt? Inseminate?* One of the things I'm so grateful for is that it created a mindfulness about my life that I'm not sure I would've otherwise had.

I grew up in a nice, upper-middle-class neighborhood. Everybody's life was on remote control. They were going to get married at the Jewish country club. They knew where they would send their kids to school. They knew what hospital they would get old in. I didn't know any of that. I had to think a lot about where I was going to put down roots and how I would form my career. I'm grateful for that.

How has being queer advantaged you throughout your career?

The way I've been advantaged by being openly gay is that it set a tone going into all of my work environments of being honest, courageous, unafraid, and open. Those are assets I didn't realize would be so powerful. I couldn't have predicted that. I didn't come out because I thought that was how this was going to roll, but now that I'm at a point in my career where I can see things in the rearview mirror, I see that at every turn, I got a little bit more benefit of the doubt for authenticity. I also got more visible assignments in some way, because people knew I could handle stress and pressure. It advanced me in some ways and held me back in none.

D.J. "SHANGELA" PIERCE

Drag Superstar & Actor

D.J. "Shangela" Pierce was born in Paris, Texas, in 1981, the only child of a mother in the U.S. Army. Of African American and Saudi Arabian descent, the aspiring entertainer got his first break as an assistant to his longtime idol, actress and comedian Jenifer Lewis.

Pierce rose to prominence in 2010, competing in season two of *RuPaul's Drag Race*. Though eliminated in the first episode, he solidified himself as a fan favorite and came back for season three as well as a season of *RuPaul's Drag Race All Stars*.

Lady Gaga personally requested Shangela for a supporting role in the 2018 adaptation of *A Star Is Born*. During awards season, Shangela became the first drag queen to walk the Oscars red carpet.

Gaga is not Shangela's only celebrity fan: in 2019, Ariana Grande featured Shangela's voice on the song "NASA" from her fifth studio album *Thank U, Next*.

Pierce's other acting credits include *Glee*, *Bones*, *2 Broke Girls*, and *Katy Keene*, as well as the HBO series *We're Here*, which follows Shangela and two other drag superstars as they travel around America.

In 2019, *New York* magazine named Shangela one of the 100 Most Powerful Drag Queens in America.

When in drag, Shangela uses she/her pronouns. Out of drag, Pierce uses he/him pronouns.

You grew up in a small, rural community and are the grandson of Southern Baptist Christians. You're half-American, half-Saudi Arabian, and gay. I'd love to hear more about your childhood.

For the younger part of my life, my mom was in the military and traveled often, so I was raised by my grandparents. My grandma is a very strong Southern Baptist Christian. She's in church on a Tuesday, Wednesday, Saturday morning, and a Sunday afternoon. I was with her all those times.

It's great to be brought up with some type of spirituality and faith. But at the same time, sometimes the messages you're hearing aren't pro-homosexual. It's *Homosexuals are going to hell, homosexuality is a sin*. I would internalize those and I was having a lot of conflict. I didn't see a lot of people around who looked like me, who were out and proud—even on television and film. So you start to think, *Am I wrong? Am I bad? Do I not belong?*

But one thing that always pushed me forward was my desire to do well. I wanted to be someone my grandparents could be proud of. I wanted to be seen. I pushed through and I didn't let negativity hold me back. Even with being bullied for being gay, I still auditioned for the cheerleading squad. I became the first male cheerleader at my high school since 1963. I became the first in my family to go to college. And that's what got me to the big city and, honey, I never looked back.

Do you still think back to those bullies?

I don't think back to the bullies themselves. What I like to look back on is the resilience I had. I'm thankful for the people in my life who saw I was struggling and said, "Hey, you're okay and you're gonna make it."

My tenth grade English teacher was named Ms. Gifford, and we had to do a report on *The Adventures of Huckleberry Finn*. She said to make a creative project that tells your experience in reading the book. Instead of writing a book report, I wrote a song called "Rolling Down the River," like Tina Turner's "Proud Mary," that I rewrote to Huck and Finn rolling down the river.

I proceeded to get up in front of the class and perform it with full-out choreography. Even though some people in class laughed, my teacher loved it. And she invited me back for four other class periods to perform it again. It was that kind of stuff that makes me look back and smile. People who saw *Yeah, he's a gay kid—probably one of the few like him around here—but there's gonna be a bigger world for him.* They didn't hold me back, they didn't tell me to cut it out. They pushed me forward and told me to explore every part of my creative self.

So when I think about where I am now, I think back to those teachers. I'm so grateful and thankful for them for not trying to dim me, but guiding me in the right way. I think back to my cheer coach who was like, *You're the only boy on my squad ever, but let's make this work. Get out there with the girls and go for it.*

When I think of Shangela, I think of not just her confidence, but also her positivity. Has that positivity always been an inherent part of who you are?

I'm thankful to still have that excitement about life and the things I'm doing, but also just to be able to live in that positivity and that space. It's not an everyday thing. We all have struggles, challenges, and hardships. Hell, I broke a leg in 2013 from a death drop gone wrong.* I laid in a hospital bed for three weeks while a titanium rod was being put in my leg, two screws in my knee, and two in the ankle. Those were dark times. I thought, *What am I gonna do? How am I gonna pull myself up?* But it is that innate positivity I have, and also because I've learned that wallowing in the hardships doesn't get you anywhere. You'll stay down there.

I could've been a pig farmer, but I wasn't. I pushed myself and I looked for the silver lining in life because with a smile and with joy, that's the only way you can *meet* joy. If you want to see positivity in front of you, you have to radiate it yourself. If you're a nasty person at all times of every day, then that's what you're gonna attract to yourself. And that's not what I want in my life. So, when those times come that I'm feeling down or something negative happens, I have to figure out a way to change the channel in my own way of thinking to get to a better place. Because that's where I ultimately want to be. That's who I am.

---

* A "death drop" is when a dancer falls backward into a pose on the ground.

94

I'm thankful those are the kind of images I've seen around me. But it's also a learned behavior, too. I've *learned* that in life, if you don't have a smile, you're not gonna meet a smile. And I want to see lots of smiles.

You said once how you felt like your life is a Cinderella story. But from where I stand, you *made* this life happen—you built it and worked for it. Where did you get your work ethic?

I said it best in my sugar daddy speech. *I don't have a sugar daddy, I never had a sugar daddy. If I want a sugar daddy, I could get one, 'cause I'm what? Sickening!* I built myself from the ground up.

I go back to what I've seen in my family. We're a family of workers. My mom served in the army in Desert Storm and Bosnia. I remember when her job was filling vending machines. Late at night at the power plants throughout Paris, she would go around and restock all the machines with Coke cans, chips, and candies. I would watch my mom wheeling that dolly and realizing my mom works *hard*.

That's what I learned in life. If you want something, you have to work hard for it. And I'm not afraid to work for it. That's why I got to where I am, because I wasn't afraid to tour 184 cities, sleep two hours a night, and hop on a plane. And if the plane was delayed, get in drag in a taxi going across London while I'm shifting around in the backseat.

On season two of *RuPaul's Drag Race*, I was the first girl voted off. People said, "We liked her, but she's gone. That's it for Shangela." But I didn't think so. I went out there and I started booking myself. I didn't have an agent, I didn't have a manager. I had myself, I had a telephone, and I had email. I would figure out a way to book myself. I was doing everything. I was trying to make myself what I dreamed I wanted to be. I knew I could be what I wanted to be because no one could hold me back as long as I said it could happen.

I wrote a song called "Werqin' Girl" and I thought, *I guess I can't go back to being a bum now, because I have a song that says I'm a working girl.*

Can you attribute any of your ambition, drive, and work ethic to being queer?

Yes. Being a part of the queer community makes you a more resilient person. Being someone who doesn't fit into the mainstream *forced me* to be more resourceful, and to have a thicker skin. Life will try to eat you up and spit you out. But if you can withstand the chew, honey, you're gonna be fine. You have to be able to stand between those teeth and say, "I'm not going down." Even if I was swallowed in the body of a whale, I would figure out how to get out. That's the kind of attitude I have in my life.

I never saw any actors on TV or film who were gay. For a long time I thought I couldn't be an actor because there were no gay actors. I'd have to pretend to be straight. And, Lord knows, I wasn't gonna pass that test! I learned how to be a better actor from being a queer person as well, because we learn how to navigate in and out of different rooms and with different communities.

How has being queer been a positive dynamic in your life and career?

Ooh I love being gay. *I love being gay.* You can write that one down. *I love being gay!* It's made me a more colorful person and I love my life. I love being able to walk with every color of the rainbow behind me and have it radiate through me. That's what I love. I'm so proud we have Pride, and times that we come together and celebrate. I'm so happy that we have a rich history. I love being Black. I love being gay. Although our communities have had a struggle and we still are facing adversity, that gives us a greater purpose in life. And as much as I would hope that we don't have to go through those challenges, I know it has made us a more resilient and bonded community.

SAM LANSKY

Writer

Born in 1988 and raised in Portland, Oregon, Sam Lansky spent his adolescence in New York City; his teenage struggles with addiction and subsequent recovery were the subject of his 2016 memoir, *The Gilded Razor*, which Lansky is adapting as a feature film with Oscar-winning writer-director Dustin Lance Black (see page 136).

A graduate of the New School, Lansky wrote for *New York* magazine, *Esquire*, the *Atlantic*, and *Out* before joining the masthead at *Time*, where he became the West Coast editor. He now plays a vital role in the magazine's TIME 100 and Person of the Year projects, as well as contributing profiles and criticism.

Lansky's debut novel, *Broken People*, was published in 2020.

It was late on a Saturday night when I finished *The Gilded Razor*, Sam Lansky's memoir. I sat upright in bed, turned the last page, and closed the book. The candle I'd lit hours earlier flickered next to me on my nightstand. The flame grew, down at the end of the wick, on its last breath, and then was engulfed by an abrupt wisp of smoke.

I had confined myself to Lansky's world for the past thirty-six hours, fully invested in his story of addiction, trauma, men, family, treatment programs, and self-discovery. Our adolescenses were completely different. He grew up in Manhattan, I in the suburbs of Ohio. He came out at eleven, me at eighteen. His parents' supervision was dubious, mine teetering on helicopter. But a nerve had been struck. The book incited me to reflect on my former demons: depression, anxiety, suicidal ideation, and my own stay in a residential treatment center.

Although struggles such as these never fully leave us, it was clear both Lansky and I had made it to the other side. His narcotic addiction had been reined in, and I had gotten hold of my overwhelming unhappiness. Now we both were thriving in big, vibrant cities, he in LA and me in NYC, working in creative and dynamic fields, and living authentic lives.

Sam and I met in Los Angeles at the San Vicente Bungalows. A suave valet greeted me on arrival, ushering me inside. The beautiful hostess placed a sticker on the camera lens of my phone (no photos allowed!), and I was led through the courtyard to where Sam was waiting.

He was wearing Gucci loafers and carrying a backpack. I found him disarmingly friendly as we ordered our green teas and got to know each other.

Midway through our talk, when we landed on the topic of mental health, I told him a bit about my own struggles, and the personal connection I felt with his story.

Our conversation took various paths, including a difficult one regarding body image. Body dysmorphia, and the fixation with appearances, is a fun-house distortion, a terrible mental space in which to be trapped. Both Sam and I noted our own difficulties, and the prominence of this issue within the gay community.

In *The Gilded Razor* you wrote, "I had no sexuality crisis. No struggle with my own self-identification. And so being gay changed nothing more than who I was attracted to." But then on the next page you write, "Full of self-loathing, when the weight of my budding sexuality was too much to bear. I felt dirty and disconnected. Shame descending all over me." That's quite a contrast.

It is, but it's not. When we use "sexuality" as a word, we often use it to describe sexual identity—whether you're gay, straight, queer, or however you identify. I used sexuality in this context to mean the experience of coming into your own understanding of *what it means to be a sexual adult*. Not necessarily in a way that is all about identity.

My journey into my sexual identity as a queer person was not vexed in any way. My parents were really supportive. I grew up in a progressive community and school, with a lot of other queer kids and people with whom I could talk and process.

My problem was much more elemental. *Oh my god, I am a sexual being.* Regardless of to whom I'm feeling sexually attracted, *what does it mean that my body is capable of this? What does it mean to be a person who feels desire?* That sense of reckoning with what it meant to be a sexual being who wanted sex, who wanted to express an experience of pleasure or desire, was very complicated for me. Whereas identifying as gay was not.

I give a lot of credit to my parents. My mom told me that she knew when I was three years old that I was gay. And she deliberately worked to facilitate a normalizing environment for me where I wouldn't feel like there was anything that was wrong with that.

I went to this very progressive arts magnet middle school with mixed grades. I started when I was ten and was in classes with fourteen-year-olds. Developmentally, that's an ocean of difference of life experience, maturity, and sophistication.

As a very young person, I was exposed to more adult conceptions of sexuality and identity. I had all of that working in my favor to where I was able to come out at eleven. I wrote a letter to my parents and told my friends at school. Being able to do that without pushback allowed me to have a more authentic journey of self-discovery than I would have been able to if it happened later.

Would you attribute any of your addiction to your sexual orientation?

Yes and no. It's statistically proven that LGBTQ+ people suffer disproportionately more from addiction and mental health challenges than the population at large. That's obviously not an accident.

As a gay teenager, how was I going to connect with my community? How was I going to figure out what it meant to be gay? As a teenager living in New York City, with dubious supervision and a strong need to figure out who I was, I had a lot of questions. *Where do I fit in as a gay dude moving through the world? How do I meet other queer people? How do they teach me what it's like to be a gay man in the world?* The ways I did that were through partying and sex. That was the best blueprint I had that was available to me.

We are all forever doing the best we can with what we have. And what I had was Craigslist and dudes who wanted to use drugs and hook up. If there had been other avenues available to me to find points of connection with my community, would I have sought them out? I'd like to think yes, but knowing me, probably not.

It's also possible there were other avenues, and I just wasn't seeing them due to immaturity, a willful ignorance, or an unwillingness to do anything other than the most immediately gratifying thing. What

I felt then, I think, was that as a young gay man, *this is my right*. My *right* is to stay up all night, sleep with strangers, and ingest any variety of substances. I couldn't tell you where that came from.

It feels like it would be unfair to blame society, because that could've been my own need to justify my own behavior. I did not feel tortured about being gay. I felt fucking lonely. Was I lonely because I was and am an addict, and addiction is the loneliest disease? Was I lonely because I was the only openly gay person in my school? Was I lonely because the only way I could connect with other queer people was under the influence, usually leveraging my body? I don't know. For better or worse, rightly or wrongly—I'm going to go with wrongly—that was the path I chose.

You did a profile on Ryan Murphy for the cover story of *Time*. In the article, you noted how Ryan's difficulty of coming to terms with his sexuality at a young age fueled his ambition. Does that resonate with your own experiences?

For me, it's almost the opposite. For some people, feeling downtrodden or otherized by their queer identity would lead them to work even harder. I always felt my precocious queerness was like a superpower, and it made me special, and I just wanted to be *more* special.

I reveled in my difference. For the most part, I wanted to celebrate what made me different. I knew I had something other people didn't. And part of that was being queer and being able to bridge the communication gap between men and women.

I read this book when I was in rehab called *Coming Out Spiritually* by Christian de la Huerta. It was about the tradition of queer people in spirituality and different faith practices and our historical relationship to God. I learned that in certain indigenous communities, queer people were the shamans. They were *revered* as leaders because of their ability to possess both the masculine and feminine, and the ability to act as mediators between men and women. The ability to see both sides was seen as divine. It was like a superpower.

For that reason, I maintain that queer people are magical. And I really believe that. I'm not being glib. I think we're special. Even before I read that book, or even had the full context of that, I always felt really anchored in my specialness. What fueled my ambition was a sense of already being special, and just wanting to be more special.

You mentioned that being gay helps you bridge the gap between men and women. What do you mean by that?

In my own life, there has been something very powerful about developing relationships of texture and intimacy with women that I think men don't typically get to have outside of a romantic partnership. That's been really special to me. But I am still a man. I still possess the masculine within me.

Maybe it's less about bridging the gap between men and women out in the world, and more about bridging the gap between the masculine and feminine in myself. In cultural and social systems that are relentlessly and ruthlessly binary, people are always wanting you to choose to be one thing or another. I'm very much a man, but I am also very in touch with my feminine side. I have the ability to process and experience the world, and talk about my emotional life, in a way that I more closely associate with how women do.

I don't want to say that only women are allowed to do so or that straight men can't or shouldn't. But I feel as a gay man, it's perceived as *permissible*, whether it should be that way or not, for me to have all of that. And that feels like a form of power. That feels like a form of queer privilege, ultimately, to be able to move through the world, to move through conversations, being able to have it all.

How has being queer advantaged you in your career?

Part of it is about emotional security and comfort. The comfort other people, who are not queer, feel around you as a queer person. Men experience you as nonthreatening because you aren't competition to them. Women experience you as nonthreatening because you're not trying to have sex with them or police their freedoms and bodies in the ways that straight men sometimes do.

When I show up to an interview or meeting, as a gay man, I think there's a sense of safety people feel. I'm not saying that is how the world should be. But I think it's how the world is. And I've been able to capitalize on that, to some extent.

I'm also very observant. Is that because I have a weird self-protective survivalist thing, so someone doesn't beat the fucking shit out of me? Or is that just because that's in my wiring? It's hard to say.

There is a queer advantage, but there's also a queer liability. I've had to overcome obstacles as a queer person, but I've also benefited from the queer advantage.

After I got sober, my addiction shifted to food and I spent the early part of my twenties in a much bigger body than the one I'm in right now. I felt really invisible and I felt very ignored and rejected by gay society at large. I felt like, *If only I were in a smaller body, I would probably have lots of people wanting to help me up and give me a leg up through the world.*

Part of me wants to hang that on the shitty, shallow culture we live in as a whole and in its totality. But I'm also not afraid to say that I think gay men especially have a finely tuned eye for aesthetics. We frequently want things to be beautiful and we want things to look a certain way. And we reject or dismiss things that don't.

In my personal work, a lot of what is very alive for me in this stage in my life is beginning to dissolve some of that bitterness I felt at the front end of my twenties where I felt like I represented no value to other gay men. It did not matter that I was smart, that I was funny, that I was a good writer. It did not matter that I had any of the traits that I had and hopefully still do have, because I did not look the way that young gay men were supposed to look. And therefore, my self-worth was effectively negated. That was really painful and difficult for me.

I don't judge anyone for wanting what they want, or prioritizing the values they prioritize, but I didn't feel desirable enough to be deserving of anyone's help or mentorship.

People in bodies of all sizes are a part of diversity, too. I wish there had been a greater sense of openness or community for me in points in my life where I was really vulnerable and needed that.

Instead, I was twenty-two, sober, fat, and couldn't go out. I was profoundly lonely. That's why the work that I do, whatever shape it takes, is about making connections. Connecting with people on a really deep level. Whether that's interviewing a really famous person or writing a story that people can lose themselves in. Where they can feel connected to me and see some of themselves reflected back at them. That desire for connection probably comes from a lot of places, and being gay is definitely one of them.

It was very painful to go from feeling like I had relationships with gay people—even if my only perceived value was partying and hooking up—to having no value and being alone, when I was actually doing the difficult work of turning my life around.

Since you've lost weight, have you felt a shift in the way you're treated?

Of course. This is something I argue about with myself constantly. Even by moving through the world in a smaller body and experiencing the rewards of that, I feel complicit in a system that I fucking hate. I wish we lived in a different world. And I wish it wasn't like this.

I deeply worry for gay men and our bodies. So many of us have so much embodied shame. We suffer from addiction disproportionately. We suffer from disordered eating and body dysmorphia disproportionately. We trash our bodies in so many ways. So much of our psychic baggage is expressed bodily. We don't talk about it, and it worries me.

Have you had to work harder because you're gay?

This is probably very "*Velvet Rage* 101," but I do think there is a part of me that has always wanted or needed to be the best, so that I would be unimpeachable or inarguable. If the fear is that nobody wants to publish this book about a gay kid who's a drug addict and teen terror, the book better be fucking gorgeous. Every sentence better gleam. I think that definitely could be informed by my sense of knowing it is a little bit harder for me to be taken seriously, or that people have more judgments or preconceptions because I am gay. So yeah, I've worked harder to prove myself. And whether it was a world that made me do that, or whether that was my own interpersonal need to be or feel exceptional, I don't think I can say.

I used to have a really glib and judgmental take on some of the ideas we're talking about. I used to think the reason I was never bullied—because I wasn't, even though I've been out since I was eleven years old—is because I was different, better, more special than the other gays. All the other little queens might allow themselves to be victims, but I would not. And that was something I wore with a lot of pride in a way that I think, looking back in retrospect, I wish I never let myself feel that way. It was uncharitable and self-aggrandizing.

But it helped you survive.

I've always been a pretty good reader of people. I've always been really, really strategic. In school, I knew on a pretty reflexive level that if I was allied with all of the popular girls, I would be untouchable. They were armor. And I was always able to identify ways to gather the necessary power for survival, and leverage that.

The deeper wounds for me are all *informed* by being gay—but not *about* being gay. The wound was not being gay. The wound was that as a teenager, it felt like gay men were primarily interested in me for my youthful pliability. And then in early adulthood, I had no perceived value because of the way I subsequently looked. Those are the wounds.

It wasn't about being rejected by family or community for being gay. It was about other stuff that is a part of that, but also, on some level, extraneous to it. If I had the misfortune of experiencing what I know a lot of other queer people, including a lot of gay men, have experienced, having been rejected for being gay, I feel like I would have a very different set of issues around that—a lot more pain, and it would have fractured my confidence in different ways.

I have other shit. That's not my bag exactly. But I will reiterate that I think queer people are magic, and I do want to have it both ways. I'm very like, *Love is love, let's have all the rights. Let's have all of the options and opportunities and flexibility that are afforded straight people. Let's be protected and let's be like everyone else.*

And there's this kind of radical and contrarian part of me that's like, *No. Fuck that, we're not like them. We are different, and arguably better.* I don't want what makes us different and special to be eroded in our continued quest for equality. Fiercely protecting and celebrating what is special and distinct and unique about queer people as a whole is super-important. And they're not mutually exclusive. I think we can have both.

What advice do you have for young queer professionals beginning their careers?

Shine brightly. Shine the fuck on. Feel your strength. Move through the world undeterred. I spent a lot of my early career feeling insecure about who I was and wanting to be more like other people; to play by the rules. I wish I had embraced my authenticity more and doubted it less in my career. If you have the job, you have the job because they have seen you and think you are good at it. Don't second-guess the version of you that you're putting forward. Be who you are and trust that that will be rewarded. Trust yourself, trust your instincts, be authentic, and shine.

JEREMY BERNARD

Former White House
Social Secretary & Author

Jeremy Bernard was born in 1961 and raised in San Antonio, Texas. Bernard went to Hunter College in New York, though he dropped out before graduating. He moved to Los Angeles, where, while waiting tables at a restaurant, he met gay rights leader David Mixner. Mixner took Bernard under his wing and brought him on to raise money for Bill Clinton's first run for president.

After later working for a wealthy cable executive in the 1990s, Bernard started a consulting firm, B&G Associates, with his partner at the time. Years later, they raised millions of dollars for Barack Obama as he ran for president. Bernard went on to become the White House liaison to the National Endowment for the Humanities and senior advisor to the United States ambassador in France.

In 2011, President Obama appointed Bernard as White House social secretary, making him the first male, and openly gay person, to hold the position. He served in the role until 2015.

In 2018, Bernard coauthored *Treating People Well: The Extraordinary Power of Civility at Work and in Life*. That same year, he was appointed president of the Mayor's Fund for Los Angeles, where he has lived for over thirty years.

When you moved to New York City in 1985 to attend Hunter College, you had a really tough time, especially in dealing with your sexuality. Going from Dallas to Manhattan, what was it that made it *more* difficult?

It was overwhelming. Ed Koch, the mayor of New York, put on so many restrictions. The AIDS epidemic was coming to fruition, so it made sex really scary and there wasn't a feeling of security in New York at the time.

I did have a couple things that worked in my favor, though. My Shakespeare professor was great. I started talking to him one day, and I actually came out to him—it was the first time I had come out to someone. I was telling him what a horrible fear it was for me, and he told me how he had been with the same person for thirty years. He was the first person I felt safe enough to tell. He and his partner introduced me to a whole group of people—all gay—and it was an eye-opening experience. I realized there was a real vibrancy, and possibilities. They were all successful!

Someone who brought you into politics and was a big mentor to you was David Mixner, an influential civil rights activist and political advisor. How did you first get involved in politics?

I was lost. I was trying to figure out what I wanted to do. Did I want to be an actor, a writer? But I had grown up with politics and had always found it interesting.

I was actually working here, in the restaurant we're sitting in right now. It was a different restaurant at the time, but they used to have all these political events. David came in several times and I was sometimes his waiter. We would always talk politics. One day, he was walking out and he goes, "If you want, I can call around about getting you a job. Do you know Bill Clinton?"

I stupidly said, "Oh yeah, my parents knew him during the Mc-Govern days. He kind of turned into a jerk as governor of Arkansas."

He said, "Oh, well, I'm in his cabinet." That's how it all started.

David, who is gay, encouraged you to come out. What was his argument in trying to convince you it was the right decision?

He talked about the relief, and how it is physically and emotionally better. But that you also owe it to your family to be honest. David and another mentor told me everyone comes out in their own way. "You don't have to be in front of them when you tell them. Send them a letter and let them deal with it, whether it's a day, week, or whatever." That made it more plausible. It was 1992, and I was working on the Bill Clinton campaign with David when I sent the letter via FedEx.

When my parents got it, they called me immediately. My dad said, "Everything's cool, we don't live in the Dark Ages." My mom said my dad wasn't surprised but that she was, but they both love me. It was a great relief, but it took me, even after that, a while not to feel like I had let them down.

You later started your own consulting business, and in 2007, started working with Barack Obama as a political advisor.

We had a couple of Senate candidates we would raise money for, but our main client was Obama. I first met him when he was in LA, as a senator from Illinois, and first started going around. He came to my former boss's office and we talked politics. So when we met again in 2007, he remembered me.

Did he know you were gay?

Yeah. For me, at that point, it was part of my identity and something I was proud of. It was a huge change.

You said before, "Never in a million years did I think I would have this job." Why did you think you could never become social secretary?

If the young Jeremy living in New York could have seen me getting out of the motorcade, and being on Marine One with the president, he wouldn't have believed it. Being gay was a deal breaker if you wanted to be in politics.

And then there was another aspect of not thinking I knew how to do the job. I remember telling Mrs. Obama, "I don't know how to do flowers."

She said, "No, I need someone with political sense." So it was a combination of those two fears.

Do you think Obama and Biden came out in support of gay marriage at the right time or could they have done it sooner?

When I met Obama in 2007, no one thought he had a chance of becoming president. He came to California for the State Convention down in San Diego, and in those days we could throw something on the schedule without getting it "on the schedule." So we threw on a quick meeting at the hotel with regular people from the gay and lesbian community. They were asking questions and one of them was, "How can you be against gay marriage when you come from a mixed marriage?"

He said, "The fact of the matter is, I can't. I'm not opposed. But if I say that I *am* for gay marriage, I lose the primary to Hillary Clinton, no doubt. Just know, if I become president, you will be very happy with what is done in my first term." He had a lot of people, including some I knew from the Human Rights Campaign, who were saying not to come out for gay marriage until *after* the election.

The day we pre-announced the legalization of gay marriage in the United States, I was standing with the Obamas in the Blue Room and it was just us. I said, "Mr. President, this is one of the proudest days of my life."

He put his arm around me and said, "You know we love you and I've always been there." It was amazing to be there and to see that side of it. It's one of my fondest memories.

Were you surprised by all of the media attention you received by being the first male, and gay, social secretary?

I was working in Paris at the embassy when they first suggested I come back and interview for the position. I thought all of the West Wing interviews went well, but I couldn't tell how it went with Mrs. Obama.

When she came in, she hugged me and goes, "Look at you! You've lost weight since you've been in Paris." We chatted for a little and then started talking about the position. And she has a great poker face. She's very professional.

We talked for about an hour and fifteen minutes, and I remember leaving and calling my mom and saying, "I truly have no idea how my interview with Mrs. Obama went."

I was in Los Angeles when I got word that I got the job. When they released the news, I was on a flight back to Paris. The plane stopped in New York and the lady sitting next to me starts talking and says, "I know who you are." It was exciting, but at the same time I was trying to stay under the radar.

How has being gay advantaged you in your career?

I'd be naïve to say it didn't help me. There's a part of wanting to prove one's self. Once I was open and had come out of the closet, I was more comfortable with myself. I was able to start doing things I never would've been able to do before, like public speaking. It's made things easier in my career. I'm different and proud of it. It was empowering.

What advice do you have for young queer people beginning their careers?

I have benefited by going with my gut. Even though I had uncertainties about Bill Clinton's campaign, I really believed in his change and his whole attitude. And then in 2007, I went for Obama against what people thought was common sense. You have to go with your gut and what you believe in.

ADAM RIPPON

Olympic Figure Skater

Adam Rippon was born in 1989 and raised with five siblings in Pittston, Pennsylvania.

He is one of the world's most accomplished figure skaters. Over the years he won numerous international competitions, including the World Junior Championships, the Junior Grand Prix Final, the Four Continents Championship, and the United States National Championship. In 2018, at Pyeongchang, South Korea, he won a bronze medal in the Winter Olympics. This feat was the first time in American history that an openly gay athlete had medaled in the Winter Olympics.

His autobiography, *Beautiful on the Outside*, is dedicated to his "haters," and he thanks them for providing much of the fire within him. The memoir received critical acclaim for its comic slant, and also for providing granular details on the brutal regimen required to rank among the world's best in a competitive sport.

Rippon has been recognized by various publications, including *Forbes* (30 Under 30), *Out* magazine (Power 50), and *Time* (100 Most Influential People).

He won the athletes' competition on *Dancing with the Stars*, and has often served as a commentator for televised skating competitions.

The 2018 Winter Olympics came through as usual, a blizzard of high-flying snowboarders and death-defying skiers. In that same gust of winter winds, another force emerged.

From the outside, Adam Rippon might appear to be your typical all-American boy: handsome, tall, athletic, charming smile, and cheekbones that could cut glass. The world very quickly realized that Adam, the talented figure skater, was anything but typical.

I had heard murmurs of his name leading up to the Olympics; the boy wonder with the fabulously over-the-top personality and sharp wit. And the jaw-dropping, can-you-believe-it fact that Adam, the face of American athletics at the Winter Olympics, was gay! On and off the ice, this athlete was ablaze with energy and attitude, skillfully maneuvering complex turns and high leaps around his competition—as well as the United States executive branch.

After weeks of brilliant skating, Adam rode the American media circuit. As I watched him woo the likes of Reese Witherspoon, Ellen DeGeneres, and Whoopi Goldberg, as well as strut the red carpet at the Oscars, I felt a distinct sense of jealously. Sure, I'd love to buddy up with stars, but what I most responded to was Adam Rippon being completely himself.

When we spoke, I was hoping for wisdom he might have for living authentically and unapologetically. Speaking with Adam was engaging, easy, and inspiring. He spoke openly about needing to be *that* much better in order to not be known just as "that gay Olympian," as well as demanding to be treated as nothing less than what he was: an Olympic champion.

As you started to come to terms with being gay, did that change your vision of your future and what you might or might not be able to accomplish?

It wasn't until I met another person who was flirting with me, and I was flirting back, that I thought, *This isn't going to be something that I just keep to myself forever.* Because that's what I thought was going to happen; that I would keep this secret to myself forever. When I was twenty-one, that's when it all changed for me. It was the first time I had to see my future differently, because I didn't see my present the same way I had seen it before.

In those moments, I was not so much thinking *What are other people going to think?* I was thinking *I've never felt this way before and I've never felt so* myself. It felt like something I didn't have a choice about. It was something I *had* to do.

Did you feel being gay would restrict you from accomplishing anything you wanted to do?

When I decided to come out publicly, I knew I could be putting myself in a situation where I might be judged differently. But when I really thought about it, I truly felt in my heart it was the right thing to do for *me*. It felt like something I could not keep inside.

I didn't realize how much energy I put into making sure people wouldn't ask me about being gay or even perceive that I was gay. I put so much energy into that. It wasn't until I was out in my personal life that I realized I was so mentally exhausted by it.

You've spoken at great length about your experience with bullying. With years separating you from that, and everything you have accomplished, how often do you think back to those bullies? How do you perceive them now?

When I think about the times I was teased, or I felt like people were treating me differently, I don't look at it and get angry. I look at it and think, *They really didn't know better.* I feel bad for those people. In the moments where I needed to come out to my friends, my family, and then publicly to the judges, those were the moments where I truly owned who I was. Maybe they were projecting things they felt about themselves onto me, because I was an easy target.

Of course when it was happening, I wanted to say, *Go fuck yourselves and die.* But then I was like, *You know what? It's really out of my control. They don't know any better.*

You didn't come out publicly until your early twenties. What was the impact coming out had on your work and career as a skater?

The impact that coming out had on me and my career was huge. It was huge because I was owning who I was for the first time. I *truly* owned it. I didn't worry about what other people thought. I didn't worry about how I might be judged differently. I felt so confident and so comfortable in my own skin. I felt confident, I felt smart, I felt like I wasn't hiding anything.

I became the monster I always wanted to be—that powerful person who took charge of the things they wanted, and went after them without any sort of hesitation.

You only have seven minutes to prove your worth at a skating competition; to say, *This is why I deserve to be here.* In those seven minutes, I wasn't afraid to bare everything I had, and for people to know who I was, and who was going after these titles and medals. I felt so much comfort and so confident in my own skin after coming out. It was the most liberating thing that ever happened to me as a competitor.

You once said, "I knew that I was opening my big mouth, and that if I wanted to be taken seriously, I needed to back it up with solid performances or it would just be 'there's-that-homosexual-with-the-big-mouth.'" Can you walk me through that mindset and how that affected your training?

It made me train harder. I've always loved entertaining people, and when I competed I had to remind myself it was not a competition, it was just a show. I would focus on that. Then when I was doing all those interviews at the Olympics, I enjoyed doing them so much, making people laugh. It was the best experience.

But I knew I was at the Olympics, and when you're an Olympian you have one job. And it's to show up, perform, get medals, and then go home. My job wasn't to have comedy hour every interview. It was to be an Olympian. And it was great I could make people laugh, but if I really went out there and I didn't skate perfectly, I was a joke.

I was ten years older than my teammates, so it was already funny that I had made it so late in my career. I knew I needed to show up. If I hadn't shown up, everything I said would've been a joke and you could roll your eyes and say, "Adam Rippon's just a class clown. He doesn't matter. We don't need to listen to him. He had one job and he couldn't even fucking do it, so what's the point of watching or listening anymore?" I knew I never wanted that, and I also knew that the Olympics was something I had waited for my entire life.

With it came a lot of moments that were life changing. But I needed to focus on why I was there and the moments I had been thinking about for twenty years. So when I stepped into those moments, I needed to be as prepared as possible. By the time I got to South Korea, I was ready for anything and ready to be perfect.

You said before, "My whole life is political." What do you mean by that?

In some parts of the world, being gay is a punishable act. And in a way, living out and speaking out for gay rights, for other gay people, and for other people in the LGBTQ+ community, is a political act in itself. But for me and for a lot of other people, it's our daily life.

In this community, we owe it to each other to stand up for each other. I'm the oldest of six kids, and I've always felt this big brother sort of gene in my body, and I've always felt I needed to stand up for other people.

I also know what it feels like to feel that nobody is standing up for you. And it sucks. I didn't want that for anybody else, and that's why I wanted to use my own voice. But I think when you use your own voice, especially in today's political climate, it feels almost like a politicized act. Because right now, everything is politicized. And it's not just policies—human decency is politicized.

You've been very outspoken and have taken risks, such as coming out before the Olympics and then declining a meeting

with Vice President Pence. It's brought out a lot of haters. Do you think you have a unique ability to channel negative energy to propel yourself forward?

I'm lucky because I'm quick and I adapt to situations quickly. There are times where I felt so out of my element and I couldn't handle what was going on. But I just took a step back, and I sometimes had to disassociate myself from what was going on. When I was able to do that, I could think, *What would I want someone else to do in this situation?* I realized there were a lot of people who weren't going to like what you do, especially when you speak out *against* something or *for* something.

But at the end of the day, what did it mean to me? A lot of the things I spoke out about were really important to me, and that's what mattered. And then it didn't really matter what other people thought about it. Even if there were people saying they didn't agree with me, it was okay because I didn't agree with them.

I don't think it was the hate that fueled me. I would go as far as saying it was the *strength of people behind me* that motivated me. More so than the people who were talking shit about me.

In every profile of you, the writer notes your work ethic and drive. Do you think there's any link between your ambition and being queer?

I think there's a huge marriage between the two of them. One, I think sports was always an escape from the doubts and feelings I had about myself. So I threw myself into it. And I threw myself into it so intensely that it was the only thing I focused on because it was the only place I felt nobody was judging me for being myself.

I also felt when I got older, and when I was an out athlete, I had this responsibility to be a really good role model (even if at the time I came out, not many people were watching or cared what was going on). I still felt this responsibility to be a role model to my ten-year-old self who felt so uncomfortable in their own skin, who felt like they were going to have this secret for their entire life.

And when I felt that, that was motivation enough to go into every practice, into every competition, and never settle for anything but my best. Being queer pushed me to be my best because I didn't want to be anything other than that for the people who have come before me so I could be an out athlete. So, in a way, it sort of relieved pressure I was putting on myself, because I could channel it into doing this for other people. It's sometimes easier to do things for other people than it is for ourselves.

At least from an outsider's perspective, sports can seem excessively masculine and heterosexually driven. Do you feel that other athletes treat you as an equal?

They do because I demand that of other people. Growing up, there were times where I had friends call me their "gay best friend." I remember having a conversation with them saying they needed to decide if I was their *best friend* or if I was their *gay friend*. I hate that saying. Is it because you're not good enough to be their actual best friend? It's so demeaning.

Even when I was at the Olympics, there were of course tons of *The gay Olympian Adam Rippon*. Well, at the end of the day, I'm still a fucking Olympian. It wasn't because I was gay. If it were the gay Olympics, I probably would've gone a lot earlier and gotten more gold medals. But it wasn't. It was the actual Olympics.

I was like, *That's okay because I can go to the Olympics and be the gay Olympian and I can open my mouth and I can say all this fucking bullshit. But at the end of the day, the next people who go to the Olympics who are gay will just be Olympians.* And that's what I hope. I hope they're just Olympians. Because I spent a lot of time talking about being one of the first openly gay athletes to represent Team USA at the Winter Games.

The "being gay" is something I can't control, so it feels almost redundant that it would be something I talk about. But it's important to talk about because if I was one of the first in *2018*, which seems insane to me, then it's important, and we need to bring that up and highlight that.

Do you think you've had to work harder because you're gay?

I've had to work harder because I'm not as talented as a lot of the people I competed against. But I think I also worked harder because I didn't want to let anybody down. And when I thought of that, I thought of other gay people who were in the closet when they competed in all different kinds of sports. I think there's a sense of regret to athletes who come out post their athletic career. I think they regret not being able to come out and be openly themselves.

And for a lot of those athletes, they don't have the luxury I had where I'm an individual athlete. I felt the responsibility that if this bigmouthed, gay figure skater could go out and open his mouth, in a way it sort of opens a few doors for other people who are on teams.

And I think it helps that I have a sense of humor and that I'm quick. Because if somebody said anything, I was able to say something that would bring them down to my level and level the playing field. When people want to exclude you, it's because they don't feel you can connect on any sort of thing. But I think there's some innate human reaction to humor and laughter that brings everybody to the same level. We all level out when we can laugh together.

That was sort of my superpower as a person, rather than an athlete, that I didn't allow anyone to treat me differently. When I was at the Olympic Village, everyone was excited to see me, and hang out with me, and to take a picture. Because they thought I was funny, and on that level, I could relate to everyone.

What was the biggest difference between coming out in your professional life versus your personal life?

It was way easier professionally because I had already done the hard stuff. I was twenty-two when I came out to my friends, and I had this huge amount of fear and worry that they weren't gonna want to be friends with me. Or they would be mad or upset because I had kept this secret from them for so long. There was this weight on me, and I felt like I was going to lose those people. I didn't know how they would react. I was really fortunate that they all didn't care.

By the time I came out professionally, the people who I loved and who were close to me, it didn't matter to them, and so the opinion of another person at that point didn't matter.

What advice would you give to young queer athletes beginning their careers?

The first thing I would say is being gay isn't special. It's not anything that makes you better than or worse than anybody else. With that in mind, don't worry about the preconceived notions that people might have of you. We all have this superpower to control the way people treat us.

When you demand that respect by treating them like they're your peer already, people will treat you like their peer. Don't give people the opportunity to question you, or for you to ask permission to be yourself. Because when you ask permission to be yourself, you're also giving permission to someone to tell you why they don't agree with you. But when you don't ask permission and you just *are*, they don't even have that opportunity to say that they might not agree, because you didn't give it to them. So don't give it to anybody. Don't give anybody the opportunity to tell you that you're less than.

I would also say that being LGBTQ+ is amazing. Because when you're an athlete, you have this athlete community around you. But being a gay athlete, you also have this community of people who rally behind you as well.

Focus on your sport and that's all you need to worry about. Because at the end of the day, what you're judged on is the quality of your work.

LEE DANIELS

Director, Producer & Writer

Lee Daniels, born in Philadelphia, Pennsylvania, in 1959, has had a wide-ranging career. After dropping out of college and moving to Hollywood, Daniels got a job working at a nursing agency. His entrepreneurial spirit took over, and he started his own agency. By the age of twenty-two, Daniels had over five hundred nurses working for him.

Eventually he sold his nursing agency and took a job as a production assistant on Prince's film *Purple Rain*. From there, he went on to become a talent manager and casting director, eventually producing, directing, and writing.

In 2001, Daniels's production company, Lee Daniels Entertainment, made its feature film debut with *Monster's Ball*, earning Halle Berry her Oscar for Best Actress. Daniels has also been responsible for films such as *Precious*, *The Butler*, *The Woodsman*, and *Shadowboxer*, as well as the hit television shows *Empire* and *Star*. His productions have garnered nominations and awards globally, including the Academy Awards, Emmy Awards, Golden Globes, Cannes Film Festival, and Toronto Film Festival.

Daniels signed an overall development deal with Fox Television in 2015, and received a star on the Hollywood Walk of Fame in 2016.

When you were a kid, your grandmother said to you, "You are a faggot. You have to remember, as long as you are strong, as long as you are fearless, as long as you are honest, you have nothing to worry about." How have you interpreted that throughout your life?

She was a very wise woman. I think she was afraid I would wither if I wasn't open about who I was. She saw something in me I certainly didn't see. She also told me I was going to make a mark on the world, which I didn't understand at the time. I didn't know what any of that meant. She saw I had a spark and she did not want that spark to die. It wasn't until my teens, after she had passed, that I understood those words of encouragement. She wanted me to protect myself and, at the same time, be the man she knew I could be. That information she gave made me grow an armor of self-defense.

Growing up in Philadelphia, you thought you would end up in jail because that was what you saw around you. How did living in that world, coupled with understanding you were gay, impact your vision of your future?

I knew there was not an option. I knew that what I thought was a dream needed to be accomplished. There was no room for error. I knew jail meant death. Even staying in the place I was in, the environment I lived in, meant death. It was life or death. I didn't have time to think. Again, I was inspired by my grandmother's words.

You later moved to Hollywood. After you started your own nursing agency, a producer from *Purple Rain* came into your office. He hired you as a production assistant and continued to

hire you after. What do you think he saw in you that made him want to support you and nurture your career?

Hope. When people see my work, or when they get to know me, they see hope.

Throughout your career, you have worked with and mentored many queer people. Have you seen a certain set of skills or perspectives queer people bring to the table?

We all have a third eye. We have a *knowingness* that is inherent, and that makes us who we are, as queer people. It's almost psychic.

When you look at some of the great fashion, art, music, film, literature, there's a queer person in the mix, in a very big way, making that happen. Whether or not we choose to tap into it, it's a gift we all have. It's that twinkle in our eyes.

Do you think there's a connection between your ambition, drive, and work ethic and being queer?

Absolutely. I've grown up in a society that was not embracing of my kind until recently. All of that has to do with my rejection from the world and from society, which has made me the creative that I am.

How has being queer advantaged you in your career?

With my sense of resilience. Knowing I wouldn't take no for an answer. Because I was always being told no, and always being rejected. So that gave me the inner strength to succeed. My queerness gave me a strength that was superhuman.

MOJ MAHDARA

CEO, Beautycon

Moj Mahdara, an Iranian American Muslim, grew up in Erie, Pennsylvania, and Lexington, Kentucky.

A graduate of the University of California, Irvine, Mahdara has been an entrepreneur for most of her adult life. While in her twenties she founded two branding agencies, along with Exopolis, a digital interactive studio. Their clients included Apple, Microsoft, BlackBerry, Gwen Stefani, Pharrell Williams, and U2, earning the company $30 million in annual revenue.

In 2014, Mahdara was introduced to an event called Beautycon. The following year, she became CEO of the LA-based company and invested her own money into the brand, as well as brought investors in, including talent agency CAA, Hearst Media, Demi Moore, and Rachel Zoe.

Since taking over the reins of what the *New York Times* deemed "the Super Bowl of the beauty industry," Mahdara has grown the company into a global brand, with mammoth business-to-consumer cosmetic summits around the world, selling out to crowds of fifteen thousand avid beauty fans.

Mahdara and her trailblazing work have been covered extensively in the *New York Times*, *Forbes*, the *Wall Street Journal*, *Vanity Fair*, the *Hollywood Reporter*, *Marie Claire*, *Fast Company*, *Refinery29*, and *New York* magazine, among others.

I was late to meet Moj Mahdara. I didn't realize my usually trusty maps app had led me to the complete wrong end of La Cienega Blvd. As someone who prides himself on being prompt (if not chronically early), I was panicked. To make matters worse, I was wearing my brand-new pair of black leather loafers, which I hadn't broken in beforehand. Sprinting in my black sweater in the sweltering Los Angeles heat, feet bleeding, and panting heavily, I made it to Moj's exactly twenty-one minutes behind schedule.

The beauty gods must have been looking down on me that day because, as late as I was, Moj was running even later. As my panting subsided, I was afforded a moment to take in the large and quiet office space. I was in the very heart of Beautycon, a revolutionary, out-of-the-box juggernaut that has brought together digital influencers of all varieties: beauty trends, social media, and commerce. Except for two female employees excitedly debating how a hairstylist managed to perfect her braids, the office was silent. Every inch, save for the occasional splashes of pink and the massive bulletin board of photos of beauty influencers, was a crisp, clean white.

Moj Mahdara proudly defies the upside-down standards of beauty. She rarely wears makeup herself, has short (though stylish) jet-black hair, tattoos, and when I met her, was wearing an oversized T-shirt.

She had just wrapped up a meeting with Beautycon's chief financial officer when I stepped into her conference room, but she was ready for her next appointment. I was immediately drawn to her unapologetically ambitious nature and how she had coupled that with a deep, fiery desire to build a successful and culture-shifting empire.

In an industry like beauty that is often criticized for being fake and superficial, Moj has managed to create a space that is built entirely on authenticity. And it is exactly in that authentic living where she, and the people who attend and participate in her events, thrive.

You describe yourself as a "brown, gay, butch woman." But in the beginning of your work with Beautycon, when you were approaching investors and shareholders, you grew your hair out and wore button-down collared shirts. What was the process of trying to convince these financers to invest in you and your brand, while at the same time hiding your authentic self?

The Beautycon audience is one of the most expressive, self-possessed, creative, and brave audiences. I'm forty-two—I'm not in my twenties. I did not grow up in a time where celebrating your anything-ness was something you would do. My audience—Gen Z, content creators, influencers—have all of this self-expression and creativity. At some point I thought, *How authentic am I really being if I'm not being myself?* If you look at pictures of me, I look now more like I did when I was in my late teens/early twenties, than when I was in my late twenties/ early thirties. My late twenties and early thirties was trying-to-fit-into-a-businessman-kind-of-world Moj.

You've taken many of the traditional beauty and business models and turned them on their heads, making them unique to Beautycon. How has being an "other" contributed to the way you approach consumers, now that you are in a position to influence the masses?

I'm very empathetic to feeling "other" and not belonging. I'm empathetic to what it feels like to go to a beauty counter and feel not marketed to or addressed. I understand what it feels like to love yourself, but also feel like you're still trying to fit in with a certain framework in society.

That hurt creates a lot of empathy, and it creates a lot of passion to think about things. I have an always-evolving state of mind around these topics. I don't understand anything at 100 percent, or even 50 percent—gender, transness, being a parent.

The human condition is super-complicated, and getting more complicated as time goes on. I'm interested in how we're all so similar, but at the same time so unique. It's that headiness I have around it that drives the creative, programming, tonality, and concepts around Beautycon.

I'm super-interested in what the zoo would look like if you opened up all of the cages and everyone ran out. I always think about peacocks when they grow out their feathers. I feel like Beautycon is that space where people come to really turn it up and turn it out. The unexpected is my favorite thing; that you can live in an environment where you can break the mold of clichés. We're so busy having our minds made up about each other, and that's a huge missed opportunity in life.

Most people walk out of a Beautycon experience feeling like they learned something about themselves through the lens of learning something about somebody else. That's a very sexy thing to get to do, because you're imprinting people's experiences on a commercial basis. You're talking about a $700 billion industry. I love the ability to do that through commerce.

In beauty—especially with a company like Beautycon—can you describe the power of authenticity?

People who are queer are authentic, not out of choice, but out of survival. It's that societal mark on us that we're somehow different that brings us together to our community and tribe. For us, I feel authenticity is very earnest, because what else is there? When you get past living in the closet, you're really committed to that self-expression, which becomes your passport to freedom on a lot of levels.

I like how heteronormative culture is now adopting this concept of authenticity. Different cultures and different tribes within society are now adopting authenticity: women, people of color, body acceptance. Self-expression is power. I don't know what else is more powerful than self-expression.

You've said before that the fear of being mediocre motivates you. Do you think there's a correlation to that fear and growing up queer?

When you come from a background where both your parents and society want you to be extinct, you either die or you fight for survival. When your spirit is threatened, your real self shows up. And my real self really, *really* wanted to thrive. So I refused to give up. That refusal has poured into all of my work, and everything I do, and wanting to be really good at what I do.

Aside from that drive, how has being queer advantaged you in your career?

By being queer, you're a supercharged personality within society, so you're also connected to other people through that lens. It's like a secret society of relationships, and people who want to talk about ideas.

Being queer gives you access to other people who are pushing the boundaries of the rules written around society.

What has been the biggest difference between coming out in your professional versus your personal life?

Coming out in my personal life was all about my parents and their disappointment, frustration, anxiety, and alienation. I came out, but then had to deal with the next decade of their coming out to their friends. Considering how conservative they are, and that I'm definitely the only gay person they know, they've done a good job.

My mom didn't even believe gay people were in Iran. She thought this was something that happened to me by being in America.

I didn't say the words to them until I was twenty-eight. They had been accusing me of it for years and I told them I didn't want to talk about it. They would give my sisters a hard time about why they weren't more focused on work like I was. My sisters prioritized dating and personal lives, whereas I was focused on my career. I buried myself in my career because I didn't want to tell them anything else about my life.

Professionally, everyone knew I was gay. They were like, *She looks gay, so she's gay.* I just didn't talk about it.

What advice do you have for young queer people beginning their careers, either in beauty or entrepreneurship?

Like anything, you have to work hard and learn your craft. And some people are not going to like you. But I don't think anyone's promised likability. When you're queer, you have to understand you're promised more unlikability than others. But most of the gay people I know turn up and are very charming people. Because you make people like you by being really charming.

Someone once said to me, "I'm not as good with people as you are."

And I said, "I'm really good with people as a function of compensating for the fact that my presence makes them uncomfortable."

It's a way of survival, and I don't know that many people understand that. Look at Drew Elliott, who was just named global creative director of MAC. When he steps into the room, he turns it on. Do you think if Drew had been raised in a society where it was all Drew's and Moj's he would be like that? Not at all. Because it's a lot of work.

You have to understand that you're starting from behind, which means you've got to over-deliver. Not just on intelligence or intellect, but also on emotiveness. You have to work that much harder for people to really consider your work.

We're better at certain things because of it. I'm better at it because I know I'm not entitled to it. I'm not going to get it for just showing up. I have to claw for this. My muscles are way stronger at this stuff.

DUSTIN LANCE BLACK
Writer, Producer & Civil Rights Activist

Dustin Lance Black is a unique hybrid of Hollywood heavyweight and prominent civil rights activist.

Born in San Antonio, Texas, in 1974 and later moving to Salinas, California, Black was raised in a Mormon household by his mother, who was physically disabled from polio. He attended UCLA School of Theater, Film, and Television, where he graduated in 1996 with honors.

In 2004, Black was tapped to join the writers' room of HBO's *Big Love*, utilizing his personal knowledge of Mormonism.

After working on multiple films, Black won the 2009 Academy Award for Best Original Screenplay for his biopic *Milk*, about gay rights activist Harvey Milk, starring Sean Penn.

Black is a founding board member of the American Foundation for Equal Rights (AFER), which successfully led the federal cases for marriage equality in California (ending Prop 8) and Virginia.

He is married to British Olympic diver Tom Daley (see page 279). They have a son together.

Thousands of miles from where I sat at a kitchen counter in Los Angeles, the ringing of my FaceTime call broke through the quiet of a London flat. In his zone of writing, Dustin Lance Black had lost track of time and I'd managed to interrupt him. He was seated at a table, wearing a black turtleneck and surrounded by notecards for a project. There were yellow paint swatches on the wall behind him, though he noted, "Someone told me yellow is creative, but I think it makes me look sick."

I had just finished reading Lance's heart-wrenching memoir, *Mama's Boy*, when we connected. The book was powerful, detailing his childhood as a painfully shy boy, overwhelmed with turmoil over his budding sense of his gayness, and the messages he was receiving from the Mormon Church.

Throughout the years, I had been familiar with Lance from *Milk*, and for his power-couple relationship status with Olympic champion diver Tom Daley. It wasn't until I picked up his book that I recognized the complex and wide arc of this man's life.

After winning his Oscar in 2009, with all of Hollywood vying for Lance's attention and offers flooding in, he did something highly unusual: he took a break. He pressed pause on his meteoric film career and doubled down to oppose Proposition 8, which was promoted to ban same-sex marriage in California.

While that might seem an odd trajectory for a writer in Hollywood, it became abundantly clear to me in reading his memoir that this man was able to see things before others could. To understand Dustin Lance Black, you had to understand where he came from. And where he came from was the upbringing of a remarkably strong, fiercely independent, and vivacious woman: his mother, Anne. Disabled by polio, crippled by poverty, and taken advantage of by men, Lance's mother still did—quite literally—anything and everything she wanted. Get married?

Done. Have children even when doctors said it wouldn't be possible? *Had three of them.* Defy the tenets of her religious background and accept her two gay sons? *You bet.*

It was that innate tenacity, bred into his bones, that fought against the self-loathing Lance felt growing up, when every message he received indicated that because of his homosexual thoughts, he was destined to be ripped from his main source of comfort—his family—and be sentenced to eternity in hell.

We talked about the power of difference and how once that difference is harnessed, it can lead to gold.

What was your thought process as a young boy coming to the realization that you were gay, growing up in a conservative, Mormon, military family?

I was six years old. I didn't know what my attraction was. Just on an emotional level, I had the desire to be close to my older brother's friends who were boys. But within months I learned, first from my church, what the word "homosexual" meant. The minister declared that homosexuality was akin to murder.

I was quickly taught what homosexuality meant in the context of Mormondom. It meant never going to heaven, which meant eternal separation from your family. And, for a six-year-old kid, that was terrifying—particularly because I would soon be left with just one parent anyway.

We didn't have any money, so family was all we had. I was terrified of losing that. Shortly after, when we were in the military, I would start to tune into other words that meant the same thing. I was clever enough to know that *gay, faggot, cocksucker, pansy, turd burglar,* and all of these colorful military terms meant the same thing as *homosexual*. It was pretty obvious I wouldn't make any friends if anyone found out those words applied to me. And at that point, I knew they did.

This was 1980, with the words of anti-homosexuality activist and singer Anita Bryant still hanging in the air. I soon had a deep understanding that I was an enemy of the state; that this was illegal. So at six years old I was going to have no friends, no community, I was going to hell, and I would be on the wrong side of the law.

Those moments when young people deserve to have their first butterflies of attraction, crushes, or maybe even love, only lasted moments for me. Because I realized that if anyone found out my stomach was filled with butterflies over the boy down the street, I was going to be in serious trouble. My butterflies turned to terror. And that's incredibly debilitating. Your butterflies should turn to terror when that other person leans in for a first kiss. Not because you think you're going to be locked up, lobotomized, and sent to hell.

As you came to understand you were gay, how did that impact your perception of what your future might look like and what you could accomplish?

I was convinced I could hide forever. I was very shy anyway, so I was awfully good at hiding. My strategy was to try and meet women. I really love women. And I thought, *Gosh, women are great. I'm sure I can meet one I can become pals with and suffer through this sex thing and be okay not having that attachment I feel when I'm around a guy. For the sake of my career, I'll just pretend. I'll survive it.*

I was very creatively driven, career driven, and project driven. So I thought it was a small sacrifice. And I was fairly successful at finding these wonderful women who were my friends, and didn't seem to mind the fact that we just didn't have much in the way of sex.

What that strategy makes clear is that yes, I was convinced that if anyone did find out I was gay, it would severely limit what I could do with my life. That was the other reason to not be discovered. Number one, I didn't want to lose my family, but number two, there was a lot I wanted to do. And you can't do that from prison or from a mental institution, and that was what I was taught would happen to me.

You eventually became an apprentice at Western Stage in Salinas, California, which changed the course of your life. It was the first time you encountered openly gay people. What was it like to all of a sudden come face-to-face with people who were just like you?

It was sort of like the first time I ever went to the Botanical Gardens and was like, *Where have all these plants and flowers been my entire life?* I didn't know these things existed. I didn't know that lilies existed that blossomed in the way they did at these gardens.

I will never forget the first moment one of my mentors walked into this meeting where all the kids would be. He had all of these colorful scarves draped around his neck and they were dripping onto the floor. I thought he was pure magic. I'd never seen someone be so overtly gay. There was no terror or fear on his part, so I didn't feel any terror or fear for him or about him. I just thought he was the most beautiful creature I'd ever laid eyes on. And not in a sexual way, just in how liberated he was.

It would take a lot more than that for me to finally accept myself, but it was also the fact that all these openly gay people were so inspiring. It was very helpful that they were truly mentors and were dedicated to each of us learning what it meant to work in the theater. So I had great admiration for them. Not just the fact they were gay, but the fact they were doing so well, were kind, generous, *and gay.*

This was defying all these stereotypes I had learned about these supposedly "horned creatures," who were destined for hell and had to be fixed. I was like, *There's nothing to fix with these men.*

I will never forget one of the directors bringing in a cassette tape and playing a speech given by Harvey Milk. That was one of the first times I'd heard of an openly gay man succeeding in something that was not considered a safe, gay haven. He was succeeding in *politics*. As a kid who grew up with President Ronald Reagan and Anita Bryant as the "icons" of my political world, this was a revelation. That really expanded my sense of what was possible. That was the last time I ever contemplated ending my own life because of who I knew I loved. There were too many possibilities to happen.

It sounds dramatic and maybe a bit overblown, but that's because I was a teenager and teenagers are dramatic and overblown. And so easily inspired, as well as so easily broken down. I got really lucky that I had my life intersect with these folks at this theater company. I got lucky to learn that there was such a thing as an openly gay man who succeeded in something as difficult as politics.

That's what motivates me today: that we do not have to depend on turns of luck for young people not to take their lives. For young people to be able to be inspired by the forefathers and foremothers who came before them, who laid the groundwork for a better life. This should never have to depend on luck again, the way it did for me.

Do you think there's any connection between being queer and your ambition, drive, and work ethic?

Yes. Particularly early on. Not so much now. Yes in that the fear of rejection from those who you actually care for and love—family members, members of your community that you're close with—made me overcompensate in many ways. I felt so sure I was broken and wrong, that I felt like I had to do everything I could to portray at least this outward appearance that I was marvelous and extraordinary.

I did work very, very hard. And when I first came out it didn't go terrifically well with everybody. So then that upped my desire to achieve more; to win back love and affection.

I don't think this is unique to LGBTQ+ people. This is true for any group of people who have been told, either by society or the law, that they are "broken," that they are somehow "less than," because they're just "too different" for the world.

We have so many people that we hear day in and day out are "too different," and don't deserve the same access, the same rights, the same treatment, the same pay. And that can go two ways. It can go the way my brother went, which is down a path of self-destruction, where you manifest your destiny. You're told you're broken, you're told you're wrong, you're told you're not worthy of living well. So then you're going to drug yourself into a grave. I watched that happen.

Or it can go the way it went with me, which is to try and achieve, and overachieve, in order to prove this wrong. Neither is terrifically healthy, because you're doing it for other people.

Writer Audre Lorde talked about being a Black lesbian, and how "other" she was. I read her work when I was around nineteen, and I found it really inspiring. Because she wasn't saying, *I'm so other and it's fucked up.* It was saying, *What a gift. I am on the outside.*

And being on the outside means you can actually see the machine. You understand that the machine is not half as solid as it looks from the inside. That most of this stuff is just manmade and is changeable.

It gives you an objectivity to try and fix it. To see where it's really broken, where it's not functioning in a way that benefits people. So it's also a pretty amazing gift to be born an outsider. It gives you very fresh eyes.

I hope young people can realize that if they can push beyond the discomfort of being told "you're too other," they can find gold in that difference.

How has being queer advantaged you in your career?

It's helped to be an outsider to the norm. I felt that far more when I started my creative work in the 1990s and 2000s. At that point, gay, white men like me were still not allowed to raise our voices. We were not seeing ourselves portrayed in film and television. And certainly, our history wasn't being lifted up in a popular way. So I had this void in front of me that I knew should have been filled with our rich history. It wasn't. It was like an entire section of a library of human history was mostly empty. Not entirely, there were a few incredibly brave people who dared to record our histories, but for the most part it was underpopulated, and massively so.

Because to write our history meant risking being put in prison, being put in a mental institution. Certainly losing your job, your home, your family, all of that. So there was not much of an upside writing queer history books. Studios certainly weren't clamoring to make gay movies. There was a great void that needed to be filled. And it turned out that every time I had a conversation with a gay elder, who thankfully had survived the plague, my heart grew. I felt lighter. I felt larger. I understood what it meant to have roots for the first time.

Most queer folks aren't born into queer families. Even if you have the most wonderful, loving parents in the world, they don't know what it is that you need to know. They don't know how to water your roots. And so being queer has meant I have a *mission*. I have a *purpose*, in whatever ways I can, while my heart is still beating, to attempt to rebuild a lost history. Little stones, little chips, little bits—kind of like a mosaic. I'm providing as many little bits as I can before I drop dead.

That outsider status has helped me understand how soft the clay of the machine really is. And that it *can* be changed. It's one of the reasons why I did so many queer episodes of *Faking It*, the *Pedro* movie, putting gay stuff into *Big Love*, and then of course *Milk* when I had the opportunity to do that.

If it wasn't for my outsider status, where I understood the power of story to push on the clay to change things, I wouldn't have been crazy enough to help file the Supreme Court case against Proposition 8. Only outsiders who understand how very soft the clay really is would be "mad"—and I'm using words people in the gay movement said to me—*mad, wild, naïve enough* to file such a case. Being a queer person lets you see how soft our reality really is. And how much easier it is to change it than you might have been taught.

LORD JOHN BROWNE

Executive Chairman, L1 Energy

Lord Browne of Madingley is a champion of top-down corporate policies for queer inclusivity. In 2007, he became one of the first openly gay chief executives of a Fortune 500 company, the energy company BP.

Born in Germany in 1948, Lord Browne is the son of a British Army officer and Hungarian Jewish Auschwitz survivor. He received his bachelor of science degree in Physics from the University of Cambridge and his MBA from Stanford University.

As chief executive of BP from 1995 to 2007, Lord Browne ushered in the company's golden era of diversification and growth.

Today, Lord Browne is executive chairman of L1 Energy, fellow and president emeritus of the Royal Academy of Engineering, fellow of the Royal Society, and member of the American Academy of Arts and Sciences. He is chairman of the Queen Elizabeth Prize for Engineering and a member of numerous other corporate and philanthropic boards.

He is the author of multiple books, including *The Glass Closet: Why Coming Out Is Good for Business.*

Lord Browne was knighted in 1998 by Her Majesty The Queen, and made a life peer of the United Kingdom in 2001.

In *The Glass Closet* you write, "As my career progressed and my hours became longer, I channeled any personal frustration about my identity into my work." It's an interesting paradox, because hiding your identity is incredibly unhealthy. And yet, it is partly because you did that that you were able to reach such success.

It's a bit like eating the seed core. You can keep going, do more and more, and you're focused on your work to the exclusion of almost everything else. And then one day, you realize there's actually nothing left except for that. That's when trouble starts. You have to begin to figure out who you really are. In my case, I had convinced myself that the world would end if someone knew I was gay. As I became more well known, I went deeper into a hidden, gay life. I then made a whole series of spectacularly bad judgments as a result of that. That is typical of someone who has set to the side a very important part of their life—their identity. It works out very badly.

Also in your book, you reference a 2001 study conducted by Louise Young. Her research assumed there was a 10 percent productivity loss suffered by closeted employees trying to hide their sexual orientation. While you were CEO of BP, the company did extraordinarily well, and even quintupled in market value. Do you think you would have been able to do even more if you had been out?

I would have enjoyed it and smiled more. My last boss, before I became CEO, told me I had two modes of behavior: the sun and the moon. He said he wished there could be a bit more sun rather than moon. I was very focused on what I was doing. And I was *so* focused that I set to one side any idea of being gay. I allocated very little time to that. So it allowed for more productivity, but the consequence was that I wasn't happy at all. I could have been more productive, probably using fewer hours. I would have had a more balanced life.

How does staying in the closet limit business potential?

Business creativity is all about connectivity with other people. Ideas are not generally dreamt up by yourself. They are about interaction. And if there's a barrier towards interaction, then it reduces the chances of getting the best idea.

Can you describe the importance of straight allies in the corporate world?

Essential. Because the majority of people are straight. And in order to make something work, you need the majority looking after the minority. Not the other way around. The more you include people, the better your business result, both internally and externally. Inclusion and results go hand in hand.

ALI KRIEGER

U.S. Women's National Team & Olympic Soccer Superstar

Ali Krieger, born in 1984, was raised in northern Virginia. Her father was a professional soccer player and coach, and she has played soccer internationally. In college, she played for Penn State University, where the team was the Big Ten Conference champion for multiple years. Krieger was named the Big Ten Freshman of the Year.

Krieger played on defense in over a hundred games for the United States' women's national soccer team, representing the U.S. in multiple FIFA Women's World Cup tournaments. The team won the World Cup in 2015 and again in 2019.

Krieger suffered a major knee injury, which prevented her from playing on the 2012 Olympic Team. However, she was able to play for the United States at the 2016 Olympics.

She played for the Washington Spirit team in D.C., but left after declaring that she and her girlfriend at the time, Ashlyn Harris, also a professional soccer player, refused to tolerate the owner's homophobic hostility. They left to play for the Orlando Pride, an entirely different team environment that has even sponsored Pride Night.

Harris and Krieger married in 2019.

You and your wife, Ashlyn Harris, kept your relationship a secret for a long time for fear of losing endorsement deals. When you two did come out, did any new opportunities arise that surprised you?

We've had so many more endorsements come in now that we've been our authentic selves and come out as a couple. We were nervous of losing our jobs because we are on the same team, both with club and country. We didn't know how U.S. Soccer or Orlando City were going to react.

It felt like we were hiding, and I felt like I wasn't being my true self. Ash also felt that way. We weren't our authentic selves together. We said, *This is our life and this is our story. And we refuse to feel like it's not okay. And also, this could help so many other people, both in our sport and just in normal daily life.*

We came out as a couple and it was the best thing we've ever done. There've been so many new endorsements. So many people want to work with us, and it's not just this one-off thing. They want to be part of this movement. It's actual caring.

What has surprised me is the level of genuine love and support from these companies. They want us to be part of it because we are good at what we do, we are good human beings, and we're inspiring a lot of people. That's why they want us to be a part of it—it's not because we're together. That's what is so refreshing.

How has being queer and out advantaged you in your career?

I'm a better person at work playing the sport I love, and with my family and friends, because I am authentically myself. I feel so free. I can put everything I want into my family, my friendships, and the sport I love, just by being my authentic self.

I'm able to give everyone everything of myself. That's the biggest difference from when I was growing up. Now I feel like I am giving you everything I have, whether at home with my wife, or whether that's in a family setting, or at work. I think you can see that, and that's something that has been such an advantage to my career and personal life.

When I was trying to come back to the national team, I got cut. I wasn't getting along with the coach. After nine years of giving myself to the team, I then wasn't on it for two years. And this was right before the World Cup, so I was devastated.

But I said, *You know what? I'm going to be me, I'm going to continue to work hard, and I'm going to play well in the league.* I knew the door wasn't completely shut, so I knew if I could get my toe in that door, I would prove everyone wrong, do my job, make this team, go to the World Cup, and have this incredible experience.

There was this last camp, two months before the World Cup roster was going to be named, and I got a call from our head coach. This was after Ash and I had come out. She had actually texted both of us right after we had announced we were engaged, congratulating us. I thanked her and was respectful and professional with her, no matter what the circumstances were.

A few weeks after that and before the camp, I got a call from her inviting me to the camp. I finally felt like I wasn't restricting myself. I was putting everything into my job. I was putting everything into my training. I wasn't keeping a secret. I was fully being me, and working my ass off to get back to the team and to the World Cup. I ended up making the team, and this was a month or two before the tournament. I hadn't been on the team for two years.

I felt like that was a huge part of me proving myself because I was able to finally be me, work hard, and put everything I had into it. That was such a rewarding feeling.

What has been the biggest difference between coming out in your professional life versus your personal life?

In my personal life, Ash and I can have this life we always imagined. We have this visibility for each other and ourselves that we're giving everything to our home and building this life we've always wanted— but we never realized we could have when we were growing up.

Professionally, we're impacting so many incredible people just by being ourselves and being good at what we do. I did an appearance for the NCAA final and after the Q&A session, one family came up and it was two women and they had three kids. She said, "Thank you so much for being here. I really appreciate everything you are doing for our community. My daughter just came up to me and said, 'Wow Mom, she's just like us.'" I teared up thinking about all these kids who are growing up in same-sex families that can have the same visibility.

What advice do you have for young queer people beginning their careers?

You can only control two things in your life: your work ethic and your attitude. And just be unapologetically you. I always try to surround myself with like-minded individuals who support me and want to see me succeed. As soon as you go down the other path, and you have people around you who are constantly trying to bring you down or not push you towards success, you're not going to get very far.

I surround myself with badass women every single day, who want to see me succeed, who want to push me, and support me to be better. Those are my teammates, and that's also my wife.

DREW ELLIOTT

Global Creative Director,
MAC Cosmetics

Born in Bloomington, Indiana, Drew Elliott has grown into one of the most influential, respected, and sought-after tastemakers in fashion, television, beauty, and advertising.

While still in his senior year in New York University's Gallatin School of Individualized Study, Elliott was named director of marketing for *PAPER*, a magazine with a strong voice in the worlds of underground art, fashion, and music. He found his footing there and stayed for eighteen years, becoming the brand's chief creative officer.

Elliott left *PAPER* in 2019 to become global creative director of MAC Cosmetics, an Estée Lauder company.

In his tenure at *PAPER*, Elliott brought the underground brand to global prominence. He is most commonly recognized for his conception of Kim Kardashian West's #BreakTheInternet *PAPER* cover.

"My colloquium for New York University was comparing Michel Foucault's panopticon with reality television, as it was applied to the Osborne family."

It was a Sunday winter morning in the East Village and I was sitting with Drew Elliott on his white couch. Drew was in a black sweatpants-and-sweatshirt ensemble (an outfit only he could make chic), and he was giving me the background of his early life. Sentences like that one perfectly summarized the cultural literacy and wiring of Drew's mind.

Although I'd known him for years, I had never fully heard about how he went from growing up in Bloomington, Indiana, to becoming one of the most influential and beloved figures in fashion, entertainment, and beauty. While most people struggle to make a name for themselves in just one of these arenas, Drew entrenched himself in all three, overlapping them into one big playground.

Petite, and often carrying a can of Diet Coke, Drew is a spark that can elevate any room he's in. His apartment exuded the same authoritative energy. Large and quiet, it was decorated with an organized chaos. A massive painting had just been delivered, and it rested against the wall. A disco ball sat in the fireplace. An entire cabinet filled with adorable porcelain dogs was placed next to the couch. There was a large framed photograph of Nicki Minaj and Anna Wintour sitting next to each other at a fashion show hanging on the wall. Also on the wall was one of Drew's favorites, a painting by Robert Longo as part of his "Men in the Cities" series, depicting men and women dressed nicely for work, all in contorted positions. "That's my life. I put on a suit some days, but inside of me there's always a dancer."

I greatly appreciate Drew not just for his creative brilliance and marketing acumen, which I look to for inspiration and guidance. But because despite the success he's achieved, he's maintained his Midwestern kindness. His mentorship has been an invaluable gift, professionally and personally. His ability to connect with people in a genuine and profound way, as well as lift them up, is one of the many advantages Drew's queerness has strengthened.

You grew up in Bloomington, Indiana, but you would commute three hours, round-trip, to go to a school in Indianapolis because they had a better arts program. Why did you feel that was so important for you?

I loved going to school in Bloomington, but I was always interested in theater. Every summer, from ages ten to eighteen, I went to a performing arts training center called Stagedoor Manor. Natalie Portman, Bryce Dallas Howard, Zach Braff, Lea Michele, and Mandy Moore were all there in my years of being there.

As I moved from sixth to seventh grade, the Bloomington schools had no developed arts program at the level I wanted. My parents found a school called Park Tudor, which was based an hour and a half away, in Indianapolis. We made the decision that for seventh and eighth grade, we would drive there.

Once I got to high school, it was clear I needed to be closer. My parents rented a house across the street from my school, and my mother and I lived there Monday through Friday. Then we would go back to Bloomington on Saturday.

Toward the end of living in Bloomington, I was extremely bullied for being different. In hindsight, for being queer. That started my parents into thinking I needed a different environment. Not that I couldn't handle it, but they understood it was only going to progress. At Park Tudor, I was always celebrated for my differences.

You then moved to New York for college, where you came out when you were twenty. As you came to understand you were gay, how did that impact your vision of your future?

It was like an exercised muscle that I didn't realize was going to allow me to sprint. It was a part of me that I felt I never hid, but I had a feeling was there. There were times where I was trying to understand why I was different. I knew people who were queer, but I was not really sure that was exactly who I was.

The queer people I had met were very flamboyant and theatrical. I met them in the context of New York or California, so they felt very comfortable. Whereas, in Indiana, queer people present differently. So it was me trying to understand, *Is this me?* It wasn't until I moved to New York that I started exploring that as an option for myself.

What was that transition like, moving to New York?

I was already very familiar with New York City. My friend Natalie Portman spent a lot of time there while she was in a Broadway show. So even as a young person, I would come to New York and run around with her. I had also been a *PAPER* magazine reader since I was fifteen. I knew a vision of New York that I felt I would love.

The second I moved to NYU, I didn't have anything to do with the university, other than the courses I took. My personal education was meeting the people who I had seen in *PAPER*, who would be interested in understanding my personal trajectory. I met those people in nightclubs, theaters, and all kinds of places that weren't NYU.

What changed in your life where you then felt comfortable to come out?

My best friend from growing up, Tripp, went to NYU and we reconnected when I got there my sophomore year. Tripp was queer. He was out in New York and living the life. He pushed me to see what queer culture was like in the city.

I'll never forget the first time we went to Limelight, a popular club. I walked in and it was all these guys—it was like an Abercrombie & Fitch catalog. These men were buff, young, cool. I remember saying to him, "I thought this was a gay party."

And he said, "This *is* a gay party." It wasn't like any type of gay person I had come across. I hung out with these guys for a long time and they were in sports clothes and rugbies, and it didn't match me. Then I would meet the club kids. So I got this understanding that "queer" didn't look like anything. Tripp helped me understand what queer looked like in a completely different context.

You had a lot of success in nightlife, hosting parties at clubs. How big of a role was the queer community in your success with that?

It was the foundation I could build on.

I remember my mother came to New York to check on me and she took me to Vivienne Westwood. There was this sweater I'd dreamt of having and she bought it for me. I went to the club in this sweater and club kid Kenny Kenny said, "Is she Westwood?"

I said, "She is."

Kenny said, "Come sit with us." I was put into a banquette and welcomed there. I had educated myself on New York subculture in an almost academic way. I knew the points I wanted to hit, and the club was the place I could present them.

It made me understand marketing, events, promotion. I then brought that with me to my first job at *PAPER*, where I was the director of marketing by the time I was twenty years old.

How were you able to balance finishing NYU while working at *PAPER*?

I interned for *PAPER* when I was nineteen, and by the time I was leaving college, I was offered a job immediately. I was an assistant to the founder and coeditor, so I worked for her for three months. I was a failure as an assistant, but I was moved up quite quickly. I was young, but they knew I understood the world of *PAPER*, because it was a community I had studied and read. Also, that I was such a participant in New York culture. Not just queer culture, but *all* culture in New York.

When I was interning, I would go to NYU in the evening, then get ready and go out to the clubs until four in the morning, wake up, and then do it all over again. This was five nights a week. Going out was part of my success at the job.

How does being queer impact the way you approach your work?

I have a unique point of view that is informed by being queer. And understanding how, when you are queer, you are an underdog. And so what you really want to do is win. I'll give you a weird example: sports stars. When you watch their trajectories on ESPN in those short clips, it's always the disenfranchised, underserved person who persevered, and that gave them a leg up. You see those stories so often in sports and business, but we tell them less about queer people.

At my core, I am a businessperson who uses art as my currency, and being queer is the foundation.

There is a sense that people think you only know about queer culture, which I've had to overcome many times. You have to let them know from the beginning that you have a clear knowledge of how to solve a problem.

I have a very clear understanding of who I am as a queer person. I bring all that to bear when I think about what I am building. And, I will say, the queer community makes things pop off. It's just the way of the world. We see it so much in language and in all those things that are happening. Queer people develop a lot of things that get pulled into culture. I really do believe the concept of *subculture to mass culture* is the way a lot of things work.

I've worked for huge corporate brands my whole life. My value comes in what I have learned from queer culture and what I have learned around community, artistry, and those things that are innate to a queer community. I bring those to a mass sense.

Whether it's thinking about people of color, or a community that is less spoken to, I understand that because that has been my whole life. I have empathy for that person or group of people who understands that nothing has been built for them.

How has being queer advantaged you in your career?

It has allowed me to take risks. And I've really had to exercise confidence at every step of what I do. I'm very good at selling an idea. When you're queer, you have to help break down the things of who you are, and understand how you can best fit in. Whether that's right or wrong, that's what you do.

Being queer has always given me a confidence I wouldn't have otherwise had, because I had to overcome something to become something. That's a really important piece to who I am.

Anything you'd like to add?

Being queer has helped me distill things in a way that people will understand them. Because often, when you're queer, you are left to explain yourself. Why you are the way you are, what you believe. You're not welcomed at the base level. I always have to rethink how I'm going to present something that I strongly believe in. I've been lucky because almost all the ideas I'm most known for are things that were usually a "no" that I had to turn into a "yes."

Being queer, you realize you have to fight not just for what you believe in, but for who you are. You have to really stick to your guns and make those things happen.

BARNEY FRANK

American Politician

Barney Frank is a former Democratic congressman from Boston. Born in 1940, he was raised in a Jewish family in Bayonne, New Jersey. He graduated from Harvard University in 1962.

Frank's long career in government began when he worked for the mayor of Boston and later for a congressman. He went on to graduate from Harvard Law School, having attended while serving as a Massachusetts state representative.

In 1980, Frank won a seat in the U.S. House of Representatives. By the time he announced his retirement in 2012, Frank had won election sixteen times. He was widely considered one of the most powerful members of Congress. In a survey taken of staffers on Capitol Hill, Frank was voted the brainiest, hardest working, and funniest member.

Part of his significant legacy is Frank's cosponsorship of the Clean Water Act's amendments as well as the National Forest Protection and Restoration Act. He was at the forefront of those promoting the interests of animals, especially laws prohibiting animal fighting for sport. One of his greatest legislative accomplishments was the passage of the Dodd-Frank Wall Street Reform and Consumer Protection Act in 2017.

He lives in the Newton area outside of Boston with his husband, Jim Ready.

I was sitting in bed watching reruns of *Grey's Anatomy* when I received a phone call from a Washington, D.C., number.

"Andrew, this is Barney Frank." We had bad cell reception, but his voice was unmistakable. "I'll do your interview. I'm in New York now. Meet me tomorrow. 1 p.m. The Roosevelt Hotel."

Before he hung up, I was able to squeeze in a shaky "Thank you!"

I arrived one hour early, anxious to make sure there was no chance of being late. From all of my research, one thing was very clear: Barney Frank did not appreciate his time being wasted.

As I stood in the elevator bay, I thought back on my hours of research, trying to comprehend Barney's achievements in his decades of public service: chairman of the House Financial Services Committee; leader in the passage of the Credit Cardholders' Bill of Rights Act; pivotal in the creation of the Housing and Economic Recovery Act of 2008; in the political vanguard during the early development of the Internet; member of the Congressional Internet Caucus.

Barney and his husband, Jim, met me in the lobby. They were both dressed casually, Jim in a T-shirt and shorts and Barney clad in casual slacks with a blue Carhartt shirt.

Jim went to grab lunch, and Barney and I found space in the hotel's computer bay. Just as I had anticipated, he looked at me straight on, his expression all business. Despite Barney's matter-of-fact and rapid-fire way of speaking, I was disarmed by his quick wit and brilliant sense of humor. In one sentence he could be speaking of highly complex political and social dynamics, while also somehow squeezing in a clever joke.

Afterward, I joined Barney and Jim at the hotel bar, where the former congressman ordered an iced tea. He laughed with the bartender, recalling the prior night when a hotel guest wouldn't stop bothering Barney with questions about politics. Jim acknowledged it was a constant occurrence wherever they went.

The casualness of my entire encounter with them was something I had not expected, but also greatly admired. No formalities, no airs of grandeur. Despite his immense accomplishments, Barney was just another man sipping his iced tea with his husband at the bar.

Have you generally responded to slurs with humor or by ignoring them, instead of outwardly lashing out?

There were two very homophobic California congressmen, William Dannemeyer from Orange County and Duke Cunningham from San Diego. Two very right-wing Congressmen.

Dannemeyer was basically advocating many people died of AIDS, that it was God's plague. He did a discussion in the Congressional Record on the floor of the House about how AIDS was transmitted, and talked about how the penis is inserted into the anus. I later went out to his district, and somebody asked me about him. I said, "Well, you know he talked about how the penis is inserted into the anus. But the more interesting question is how the people of Orange County inserted an anus into the House of Representatives."

And then when Cunningham had prostate surgery and gratuitously said, "It was really unpleasant, except I suppose Barney Frank would've enjoyed it." I said I would go easy on him in responding because, given that he had just had a prostate operation, he might have suffered brain damage.

If you can be funny, it helps even more. I always responded, and I responded personally, when a member would say something in particular. I would confront them and say, "I think you're a bigot."

You came out in 1987. Did you feel your congressional colleagues treated you differently after that?

Yeah, better. It's interesting. People knew I was gay. They knew I was thinking of coming out and several of the most liberal, ultimately pro-gay members came and said to me, "Please don't come out." They thought I would be minimized; that I would become a one-issue person and they would lose my help on other issues.

I couldn't deny it. I had to explain to them how deeply personal I felt I had to do this. But when I came out, there was not much hostility and there was a great deal of "good for you" and protectiveness.

The fact is, from the day I got there, I had been a major advocate of gay rights. So for people who were terribly offended by that, I had differences with them anyway.

People were generally protective and supportive. And there was another sense that I was better at my job, because it's the most interpersonal of any government work. They said, "Look, you're happier with yourself, you're easier, you don't get angry as much. You're better at your job now."

When you came out and colleagues told you they found you nicer and easier to work with, did that surprise you?

Yes, it did. I had not realized the extent to which my anger at myself, and my unhappiness, was stunting my personality. I was not that self-aware. I didn't realize that being in the closet was having that negative effect on my personality. Some said, "We didn't want you to come out, but now we're glad you did."

When John Kerry was running for office, he asked for your opinion on how to handle the marriage equality question.

We were on the way to a Human Rights Campaign forum in the car. I said, "My advice is to tell them you're against it, but don't elaborate on why." He asked why. I said, "The people who are also against it aren't going to demand that you explain yourself." Because nobody in the history of the world has ever demanded that someone who agrees with them explain why they agree with them. "And as for gay people, any explanation you give will make them angrier."

And he said, "Well, people will think I'm only doing it for political reasons."

I said, "I hope so. I'd hope you're not personally against it. And yeah, that's what you want them to think."

He said, "Oh no, I can't do that." So, he explained—and of course that made the community a little madder.

How did that feel to tell him to oppose it?

I've always accepted reality and then gone from there.

Everything about you screams an optimistic spirit. Do you think that has helped in your political career?

My optimism was based on my observation of what was happening. Something I said after I came out was "It turns out the American people are much less homophobic than they think they're supposed to be, but unfortunately more racist than they want to admit." So, my optimism is based on my sense that the prejudice was pretty thin and not based on much.

Have you had to work harder because you're gay?

No. Probably because, in some ways, it helped me. I accepted the fact that once I became a member of the House, that was as far as I was going to go politically. So, I was much less governed by ambition, and I didn't have to worry about the next step.

Once it became clear to me that I had a safe district, I didn't have to spend much time ingratiating myself politically, because I wasn't going to run for anything else. Knowing I was at my limit as a gay man, as a member of the U.S. House, helped me in the sense that it let me focus on that job. I wasn't distracted in any way by the ambition to go further. Ironically, because of that, I did better.

Has being gay advantaged your career?

It gave me more prominence, which was very helpful. It gave me a policy area in which I could get things done and demonstrate my capacity. And then it helped me with my colleagues. By the eighties, and since then, LGBTQ+ people have been an increasingly important part of the constituency of Democrats. And I became a pathway for them to that. I've done a lot of fundraising, I've signed letters and been to events. My support has helped my colleagues. It's enhanced my influence with my colleagues, not just on gay matters, but on other issues because I was an asset to them.

At first when I came out, I said I would campaign for the other members. But it generally was within twenty miles of an ocean, because that's where the gay people were. And then by the 2000s I was campaigning for people in Iowa and Tennessee and elsewhere.

One of the things I've found myself embattled with is people on my left who are being unrealistic. And many of them have this unfortunate tendency to accuse you of not agreeing with them for base reasons. Not because you disagree with them intellectually or politically, but because *you're afraid, you're a coward*. Well, being an openly gay man, one of the few, I was insulated against that. It insulated me from attacks on my political integrity from the left. If the guy came out, how much of a coward can he be?

Aside from your professional career, how has being gay positively impacted your personal life?

It's wonderful. The dedication in my memoir, *Frank*, to Jim is, "We made 'better late than never' my favorite old-time cliché." It opened a whole new dimension to me.

RYAN O'CONNELL

Writer, Producer & Actor

Born and raised in Ventura County, California, Ryan O'Connell struggled with "coming out" about having cerebral palsy.

After attending the New School in New York City, O'Connell started blogging for *Thought Catalog* in 2011. He also contributed his witty and provocative writing to *Vice*, *BuzzFeed*, the *New York Times*, and *Medium*.

For years, he told people that his disability came from a car accident, rather than his cerebral palsy.

O'Connell's memoir, *I'm Special: And Other Lies We Tell Ourselves*, was published in 2015 after he wrapped writing season two of MTV's *Awkward*. The book details his journey to self-acceptance. With the help of actor Jim Parsons, who came on as an early producer, O'Connell's memoir was adapted into a short-form series, *Special*, which aired on Netflix in 2019. The show, which was widely acclaimed for centering on a disabled, gay character, received three Emmy nominations.

O'Connell has been honored with the Visibility Award by the Human Rights Campaign and was included on *Time*'s 2019 100 Next List.

You had an unusually positive high school experience. In your memoir, *I'm Special*, you wrote how anywhere else you would have been a "freak." But when you came out, it actually made you even more popular. How important was that positive reaction as your first entrée into being an out gay man?

I was born into a loving and supportive family. I went to a high school where jocks and cheerleaders were persona non grata; the nerds were reigning champions. And I still hated myself so much. Even with all that positive reinforcement and acceptance, I still had to contend with society, and society was still a giant asshole. Society didn't value queerness or disability.

I thank my lucky stars that my foundation was strong, because if I hated myself with all those amazing things around me, imagine what it would've been like without them. It really was me internalizing the hatred and feeling left behind by society.

Even talking to you about that, my first thought is *Why did I not like myself? Why was I so deeply ashamed about being gay?* Because that's the message I was getting from my television screen and from media. When I turned on the TV, I saw no one like me being reflected. And that told me I didn't matter. Representation trumps everything else.

When you realized you were gay, did that change your perception of your future?

Yes. I was like, *Wait, you're gonna make me gay* and *disabled? That is literally the rudest combo I've ever heard of.* I was so pissed. I was like, *Well I guess I can say goodbye to having sex or having any kind of intimacy.* Because my perception of the gay community, even at thirteen, was that it was very focused on looks and being hot and having abs.

I remember renting *Queer as Folk* from Blockbuster Video, and that show was all about living, laughing, and fucking. Everyone had really nice bodies and I was like, *This is what being gay means. It means having lots of sex, but only if you looked a certain way. Otherwise you're fucked.* And I really put myself firmly in the fucked category. I really felt being gay *and* disabled was a death sentence to my love life.

You had a really difficult time "coming out" about your disability. For a long time you told people it was because of a car accident. Why do you think it was more difficult to come out about your disability than coming out as gay?

This goes back to representation. To a point, gayness has been accepted. There are gay characters on television and people talk about coming out. It's part of the zeitgeist. Disability is not discussed. Disability has not gotten the same treatment being gay has.

It's not whether or not we accept disabled people, and it's not about abuse with disabled people, it's about neglect. People don't think about disabled people *at all.* We're not a part of the conversation. My brain metabolizes that as being *Because disabled is not chic, it's shameful.* People don't value disabled people's lives.

In terms of gayness, I feel we've come a long way in acceptance. Here we are on TV, here we are in movies, there are op-eds written about it, there's Ellen DeGeneres, there's *Will & Grace.* But where's the disabled *Will & Grace?* Where is our disabled Ellen? It hasn't been part of the culture. That told me it was because no one cares. I still feel that way to a large extent.

There have been so many amazing conversations about being transgender, nonbinary, and gender fluid. I keep waiting for that moment to happen with disability. There are a few examples of disabled people in the spotlight, killing it and getting that press, but it's not as much as I want it to be.

You wrote, "Even the proudest gay men have a certain level of self-loathing about who they are." Do you still feel that way?

I don't feel that way now. I wrote that when I was twenty-six, and now I'm fully addicted to being gay. Truly, if anything, I have heterophobia. I literally feel bad for straight people. I'm like, *Wow, that's so sad* . . . I only want to be around gay people. What I think is really interesting about gay men is that, even if it can be unfriendly at times or can feel intimidating, we all have a coming out story. Most experience feeling like the outsider or the underdog or feeling shame about who they are.

Even the best of circumstances comes with a little dollop of self-loathing, shame, and panic. And as hard and unfortunate as that is, I think it's actually a great way to bond and bridge the gap. In our trauma, we are unified. It's unfortunate, but I also think that's an incredible thing.

When did that shift happen, when you started loving your gayness?

My life changed when I was twenty-seven and I moved to Los Angeles. Before that, I was addicted to drugs and was in a really dark place in my life. Slowly, over the course of that first year of moving to LA, I got my shit together. I quit taking painkillers and I started exercising, which was creating this loving relationship toward my body, which I always thought of as a thing of failure. I always looked at my body through the lens of what it *couldn't* do, rather than what it *could* do.

And then I found a good group of gay friends. In New York, I didn't find a good group of gay friends because I wasn't in a good place myself. I was not cooked, honey. If you'd eaten me, you would have gotten salmonella poisoning.

I wanted all these things, but I was not ready for those things or for the people. I wasn't fully formed. Twenty-seven and twenty-eight were really formative years for me when I went from *Okay I want to burn everything to the ground, I hate myself, I hate my disability* to being *I think I actually might like myself?*

Once I came out about my disability, and once I started exercising and creating this healthy relationship with my body, the rest came. The right friends came, my boyfriend came. Life opened up for me in such new and exciting ways that I was ready for. I had done the work on myself.

Where do you think your drive and ambition stem from?

Being disabled has given me this Superman complex where I feel chronically underestimated by everyone around me. I always want to feel like, *You think I can't do that? I'll show you.* Ninety-nine percent of my driving force is *I'll show you.* If I hadn't been oppressed and marginalized, what would motivate me to get up every day? I really am driven by defying expectations and showing people that their perceptions are wrong. But I think it's a double-edged sword because I don't allow myself to be weak.

Has being queer added to this and given you an advantage in your career?

It's given me a really distinct point of view. I think there's a queer sensibility that is so real. There's such a specific gay language, sensibility, and sense of humor. My sexuality and my sense of humor are fully on, all the fucking time. They're so pieced together. Also, any kind of oppression is metabolized through an "LOL" lens in my brain, and I feel like being gay has given me a lot of my "LOLs." It's really shaped my point of view of the world, and my point of view has been my breadwinner. So yeah, being gay has given me my brain, which makes me all the money.

MICHAEL KORS

Fashion Designer

Born in 1959 and raised on Long Island, Michael Kors was always interested in style. He enrolled in the Fashion Institute of Technology in New York City in 1977. His tenure at the prestigious design school lasted only nine months, at which point he was offered the unique opportunity to sell his own creations at Lothar's, a New York-based store. Through this, he caught the attention of Bergdorf Goodman. Within three years, Kors's collections were stocked in all major luxury outlets in the United States, including Saks Fifth Avenue, Neiman Marcus, and Bloomingdale's.

In addition to his eponymous label, Kors was appointed the designer of the LVMH-owned French label, Celine. He stayed until 2003, leaving to focus on his own brand.

In 2004, Michael Kors himself came to the forefront of pop culture when he was cast as one of the original judges on the Emmy-nominated reality show *Project Runway*. He remained on the show until 2012.

Kors married his longtime partner, Lance LePere, in August 2011.

His company went public in 2011, and in January 2014 *Forbes* reported that Kors had reached a personal fortune in excess of $1 billion.

The summer following my sophomore year of college, I interned at Michael Kors. One day, when Michael was presenting his newest collection to editors and buyers at the NYC headquarters, I was asked to help the public relations team set up. It was frantic—everyone making sure the models were dressed perfectly, the room looked beautiful, and each guest had their correct seat.

A few minutes before it began, a senior PR woman asked me to sit in one of the front-row chairs. A top magazine editor was running a few minutes late, and she wanted to make sure they had a good seat. I sat in the chair, feeling dizzy with glee. *I was reserving a chair for an editor? Best life ever!*

I was (literally) on the edge of my seat with anticipation when Michael Kors himself walked out and began his presentation two feet from me. But the prestigious editor had not arrived. I exchanged a horrified look with the publicist. There I was, frozen in the front row at the Michael Kors fashion show, a twenty-year-old intern surrounded by fashion's elite. It was not my fault, but to get up would have disrupted everything. So I collected myself and took in the presentation. It was electric. Having been an avid *Project Runway* viewer as a kid on my couch in Cincinnati, I was mesmerized to witness Michael in action.

At the time of this debacle, I had only been out for three years, and I was still unsure how being gay would impact my professional life. But here was Michael, fully out, and he was one of the most respected, influential, and successful designers in the world.

I looked around at the others in the room. They were as transfixed as I was, hanging on his every word.

To have the full attention of Michael Kors for this project was special for me. Questions I had wanted to ask when I was his employee but never had the opportunity to finally got asked.

In 2010 you recorded a video for the "It Gets Better" campaign. You emphasized the great power of being "different," stating: "If I was like everybody else, I couldn't do what I do. I couldn't be Michael Kors." When was it that you were able to harness your difference to improve your life, and how, specifically, were you able to make that difference work positively for you?

I was lucky enough to grow up in a family that celebrated being different. I knew at a young age that I was different than other kids. Queer kids know very early that they are not part of the pack. And you can take that feeling of being *other*, of being outside the pack, and you can either let it crush you and diminish you, or you can say, "Wait a minute, I've got secret magical powers." The more we stress that to kids and young people who feel *other*, the more empowered they'll be to channel their difference into something positive for themselves and positive for the world.

Queer people know well what it is to be "otherized." When operating in the business sphere, do you still find it an advantage to be different?

I think that feeling of being *other* is often what makes you successful—because to be successful, in any field, you need to see things differently and find opportunities that most people don't see. You need to sense a good idea before it happens.

You operate a global business. Do you feel that the queer individuals who contribute to your enterprises bring unique skills or perspective not seen among others?

When it comes to business, when we think about a global world and the variety of people in it—people of different ages, backgrounds, religions, sexual identities—if you live in a box, if you think that everyone is the same, you will never have a far-reaching business.

You've spoken before about how you were bullied when younger. With years having passed and the phenomenal success you have achieved, do you still think back to those moments? What long-term effect did the bullying have on you?

For myself, by the time I was ten or eleven, I realized that a sharp retort and street smarts could protect me. Humor became my way to fight back. Humor became my shield. My guard is still up in hyper-straight, macho situations. It never goes away.

It is clear you have tremendous drive and an unparalleled work ethic. Is there a connection between those qualities and you being queer?

When it comes to being bullied, I still have that memory of feeling like I had to "try harder." I always knew I wasn't going to be the little boy who was the star of the baseball team. My competitive spirit was born out of this idea that I had to win at something, so I was going to win at being smart and successful. There's forever this kind of *I'll show them* attitude. And to be successful, you need that competitive spirit and you need to find your strength.

You were one of the original judges of *Project Runway* when it premiered in 2004. Given that many of the viewers might not have been LGBTQ+-friendly, did you feel any need to alter

your self-presentation or mannerisms? Has that ever been a consideration in your life as a public figure?

In retrospect, I think *Project Runway* was really the first time where a show had so many LGBTQ+ people who were not trying to change the way they spoke, dressed, or acted. I never thought about not being myself or toning it down or acting differently just because I was on TV. I was being my authentic self. And that might have been the first time when you had an audience of young people who saw people like them and thought, *These people are successful and they're just being themselves.* People of all ages benefit from spending time, even if it's on television, with people different than themselves.

For years you have been a significant role model for many in the queer community. How has being queer advantaged you in ways not readily apparent to those who have followed your design and business success?

Being queer showed me early on that there is a huge variety of people on this planet. Once I started designing and went into business, it was more interesting to design for people of different ages, sizes, cultures, and points of view. That mixture of clients has been a huge part of my longevity.

What advice do you have for young queer people who are beginning their careers?

I think that young queer people often gravitate towards the creative industries because they think you can be as wild as you want. But the truth is, all creative industries—from fashion to art to entertainment—have a commerce aspect and you have to be able to put your business hat on. But that doesn't mean you have to rein in how you dress or your mannerisms. Often what makes you different is also what's going to make your creativity shine through. Balancing art and commerce will give you the ability to have longevity in your career.

ARLAN HAMILTON
Founder and CEO, Backstage Capital

Arlan Hamilton grew up in Texas, encouraged by her mother that she could accomplish anything she set out to do.

Hamilton has no college degree and taught herself tech and investing by reading books and by watching YouTube venture capital videos. Hamilton was homeless and slept at the San Francisco airport while attending a finance workshop at Stanford University, surviving on food stamps.

She launched Backstage Capital at age thirty-five, in Los Angeles. The purpose was to change the landscape of entrepreneurship to greater inclusivity. She is the first Black queer woman to create her own venture capital firm. The fund has tailored its interests to underrepresented individuals such as women, people of color, and queer people.

In 2018, Hamilton was named to the list of *Fortune* magazine's 40 Under 40. In 2019, Hamilton was named by *Business Insider* as one of the most powerful LGBTQ+ people in tech. She has been on the cover of *Fast Company* and made it onto *Vanity Fair*'s New Establishment List.

Hamilton is the author of the book *It's About Damn Time: How to Turn Being Underestimated into Your Greatest Advantage.*

As you were growing up and came to understand you were queer, how did that impact your vision of your future and what that might look like?

For a few days, I thought my life was doomed. I had a very loving mother, but she was bound by her religious beliefs. I thought I would be kicked out of my home because I was "evil" and "sinning." I knew people would make fun of me, and I would always have a problem in life being "other" and "weird" to people.

Growing up in a religious environment, I thought there was something wrong—even though I had a lot of love for myself and other queer people. I had always stood up for myself and others, even at a very young age.

I base things in logic. It wasn't logical to me that a God would create someone who was doing everything else right, but also create something in that person that was innately terrible and doomed them.

I had great timing with the Internet and being able to talk to other people who were like me. I took a lot of that and actually ended up writing an essay about being gay in my eleventh grade Sociology class, which outed me. That was my coming out at school, where I outed myself. First, I was outed by my mother *to* me. She let me know that she knew.

I had a very great coming out with my mom. Some parents, if they're not totally terrible people, are mostly just scared for you. *What kind of life are you going to have? Are you going to get hurt?* Usually the family itself has 90 percent of the power in making you feel welcome and good about your entire life, based on the way they react and the way they nurture and protect you. They are the ones saying, *The world is not going to like you.*

The world is 10 percent of what you have to deal with. You can be your child's hero. Yes, they are going to have to go through some things, but they are going to care the most about what you thought about them. Parents have a pretty easy way of being a hero, which is just being comforting to their child in that moment.

Backstage Capital invests in underrepresented entrepreneurs, and you've said that following your instincts has been vital to your success. For many queer people, though, that can be difficult when they've received so many negative messages about themselves throughout their life. How can a person get to feel that self-confidence and trusting of their instincts, when for so long they have been conditioned not to?

It's more of a habit than a lesson or course. With self-esteem, you're dealing with it your whole life no matter who you are. There is always going to be someone that steps in and tells you that you can't do something or that something is out of your lane. People have different degrees to which they'll listen to that, or how loud that is in their heads, or how much that dictates what they do.

I've always felt, and I still feel, that we all deserve to be here. We're all here for a reason. We all deserve to take up the same amount of space. There's no one better or worse than the next person. If you think about it from that lens, it makes it easier to exist.

When someone doesn't get that they are worthy, I tell them there's someone who's watching them, looking to them to be an example or to be an inspiration, that they don't even realize. A lot of times, if you can do something for somebody else, that really motivates you.

Sometimes I ask people to take other people's pain into the room, or represent other people in a room. That's what I do. I can be the most confident person in the world, but I wouldn't be motivated to do all the stuff I do today if it weren't for other people, knowing others could benefit from it. That changes things really quickly.

You've also emphasized the importance of self-care. What made you realize that always helping others is of no long-term value if you're not properly taking care of yourself?

People with good intentions seem to give everybody else everything and then they have very little left for themselves. I had a panic attack once on a movie set where I was a production assistant. I had to go to the hospital because I had given everything. That's when I didn't have any wealth, but I had my time, energy, and passion—and I gave it all away.

Then there's relationships. You have all these relationships that are terrible, and then you meet someone, like my wife, and you understand what it's supposed to be like. How you're supposed to be treated. And you understand, *I was giving away too much of myself for nothing or less in return.*

A car doesn't go on zero fuel or energy. You have to refuel, and we have to refuel as people. We do that by taking care of our minds, our mental health, and our bodies. I've seen what happens when I try to do too much and when I don't fuel myself. I run out of steam and that could put me under. I've also seen what happens when I take really good care of myself, unapologetically, and without compromise. How much more I am able to do for other people is powerful and scalable. You do a lot for a little amount of time, or you can do a lot sustainably. There's no competition which one is worth more.

The people you invest in and work with are people who have been historically disadvantaged. What skills do these groups of people bring to business that others who have not been marginalized don't have?

There's a risk tolerance I have that has served me really well in venture capital. Because I've seen grown men—and it's mostly men—lose it and crumble because something, one time, doesn't go the way they thought it would. Or because they were so used to things being very stable, that anything that challenges that is truly scary to them. If something goes wrong at a company they've invested in, or the market is slow or bad. For me, that's a Tuesday.

And now the stakes are much higher. $100,000 is supposed to be wired into our fund account and I'll get a phone call that morning saying the investor had to back out. There's no recourse. I just have to figure something out.

It was that foundation of *Okay, things are really chaotic, but if I fall apart and panic, we're not going to get anywhere.* I learned that fast and I take that with me in all of what I do now. And by the same token, I can talk to founders who we've invested in and they can say, very timidly, "We're running out of money."

And I can say, "It's okay. I understand. Let's figure out if there's a way to fix this. Let's talk about it."

The fact that my team and I can have such a long view of things, and can be so patient and understanding, has already started to pay off. It's that risk tolerance, patience, and understanding that it's not the end of the world.

I've also been around so many different types of people and had to survive with those people. It wasn't like I visited them, shook their hand, and left. I had to *live*, to *thrive*, to *adapt.*

One day you might be talking to millionaires at one meeting, you might be over here talking to corporate, you might be over there talking to a group of women who have never raised a dime and are trying to understand the jargon. All of these different groups, and you can be a chameleon in all of them. Not everyone can do that. But the foundation you had, of having to adapt and figuring it out, taking all of that with you, really starts to pay off.

It's like *The Karate Kid*. You don't necessarily know what you're learning when you're learning it. But when it comes up and you say, "Wax on, wax off," and you're throwing people away, blocking punches, it's because it is *embedded*. It was embedded because this was a muscle memory of the thing learned ten years ago.

How has being queer advantaged you in your career?

I was talking about this topic with another female entrepreneur. She raised twenty-something million dollars, is gay, and is in our portfolio. We talked about some of this resilience we have. Some of this *walk into the room and own the room* that we have, comes from being gay—specifically being lesbian.

We think it started when we had to stand up for ourselves, because we knew we were going to be considered different when we came out. You have to have this resilience, almost just to get through that part. Sometimes, that transforms in a lot of people into a high level of confidence and a really beautiful understanding of themselves and other people.

I feel confident and I feel grateful. I know that people before me had to go through a hell of a lot more. Just like being Black has made me very appreciative of everything that I do and every opportunity I am afforded, because of the work before me. I don't take it for granted. I'm not going to sit out a vote because I know that people were hosed and beat up for trying to get the right for me to vote. It's the same thing that I'm not going to cower and not do anything with my life because I know too many people fought to give me the freedom to marry my wife. I'm going to live out loud all day long, and a lot of that, every day, comes from the part of me that's about the orientation I identify with. I identify first as Black, I identify as queer, and I identify as a woman, in that order. It's with me every day.

DEREK BLASBERG

Fashion Journalist

Derek Blasberg, who *New York* magazine touted as "the Truman Capote of Instagram," was born and raised in St. Louis, Missouri.

In 2000, Blasberg moved to New York City to attend New York University, where he studied Dramatic Literature and Journalism. His first entrée into the world of fashion began at Elite Model Management, writing model biographies. This led to internships at *Vogue*, *W*, and *V*.

After graduating in 2004, Blasberg landed a much sought-after gig at *Vogue*, assisting the magazine's managing editor. Throughout his career, he has lent his many talents to international editions of titles such as *Vogue*, *Vanity Fair*, *Harper's Bazaar*, *W*, *Glamour*, *WSJ Magazine*, the *New York Times*, and the *London Sunday Times*.

His *New York Times* bestselling book, *Classy: Exceptional Advice for the Extremely Modern Lady*, was published in 2010. A sequel, *Very Classy*, was released in 2012. In 2015 he published *Harper's Bazaar: Models*, a photo book. He has also held positions as *Vanity Fair*'s "Man on the Street" and as the host of the television show *CNN Style*.

As of 2018, he is the head of fashion and beauty partnerships at YouTube.

I vividly remember the first time I heard Derek Blasberg's name. I was nineteen years old and in my first-ever internship, at Hearst Magazines in New York City. I was interning in their public relations department, and Oprah Winfrey was hosting a screening of her newest film, Lee Daniels's *The Butler*, at Hearst Tower. All of the heavy-hitters were going to be there, and I was instructed to put Derek's name on the VIP list.

I was still wrapping my head around who the key players were in the fashion world, and I typed his name into Google. With a few clicks, I realized that Derek Blasberg was, quite literally, *exactly* who I wanted to be. From the Midwest, living in New York as a top editor, best friends with every celebrity and model known to mankind, and traveling around the world. My fantasy was his reality.

While I would not meet him at that specific screening, I would meet him many times after. Once, I convinced my college to hire him to come to Indianapolis to speak. (Some people on campus desperately needed his expert guidance.)

I met Derek in the Meatpacking District in New York, at his YouTube office, where he's been appointed their head of fashion and beauty partnerships. His office was minimally decorated, and I found Derek at his desktop typing away. He'd been traveling and was exhausted, but was flying out the next morning to go to Los Angeles. It was quiet inside his office, and though dressed casually, he was perfectly put together, in true Blasberg style.

His childhood and sense of ambition to make it out of the suburban environment he grew up in resonated with me. Like me, he'd discovered his deep love of style, film, and celebrities as a young boy. On his childhood bedsheets, in Sharpie, he wrote, "NEW YORK OR BUST."

We're both from the Midwest and I've always admired how fondly you've talked about your childhood. But at the same time, having come from a similar place, I can imagine not everyone was as supportive of you as your parents were. Did you have a hard time growing up?

High school's a tough place emotionally for all teenagers, and each person typically has something they're teased about. Mine was being arty and flamboyant. In hindsight, being teased for being flamboyant and artistic, and for the lack of a better word *stylish*, made me confront at an earlier age why I was different and about being gay. It inspired me to come to New York and to find other like-minded individuals.

I knew that was where I needed to head, whereas I think there are a lot of teenagers who don't really have a direction. I knew mine was to art, fashion, beauty, theater, movies, Hollywood, glitz, glamor. And that's the way in which I went.

When I was in high school, there were no out teenagers, out teachers, or out people. I went back ten years after I graduated and there was an LGBTQ+ support group. I shouldn't say it surprised me; I was thrilled to see that. But it was not the same high school I had graduated from, in that perspective.

Do you think that feeling of being different has helped you?

I know being different in a place like Missouri is what inspired me to begin my life. There are other people who grew up where I grew up, who fit into that world and that culture, and they're still there.

I have an older brother. All his friends are his best friends from college, he married his high school sweetheart, he has three kids and his life is very different than mine.

I grew up gay and I wanted to be in the world of photography, fashion, and art. I got what I wanted; he got what he wanted. I am very proud of myself to have had the wherewithal and inspiration to leave where I grew up and to chase this life. I'm extremely lucky, and proud of my parents for giving me the support system to do that, too.

And furthermore, maybe if I had grown up in LA or New York or the tri-state area, I don't know if I would've been so ambitious and if the different paths would have been so marked. Being different creates situations where you really have to question yourself. *What do you want? What are you working for? What makes you fulfilled?*

Have you had to work harder because you're gay?

I had to work harder to fit in when I was in high school. I don't have to work harder now. As someone who probably felt left out—there was no one really like me—there was a certain twinge of homophobia. So I had to learn how to make friends, be social, and get along with a lot of different types of people who weren't necessarily like me. All those life skills come in handy when you're older.

How has being gay advantaged you in your career?

Growing up gay and where I did was a perfect storm for learning very quickly—and in some cases, in the manner of tough love—how to fit in, strike out, and figure out what's important.

What advice do you have for young queer professionals?

To speak from an area of tech and engagement . . . people who perform well on YouTube, for example, are the most organic and authentic. That applies to real life, that applies to work life, and that applies to digital life. Authenticity is the single most important thing to think about with human interaction.

CHUCK JAMES

Hollywood Talent Agent

Chuck James grew up playing competitive tennis in Florida, later attending Southern Methodist University. He began his career in the mailroom at ICM and soon after became an agent trainee working for high-level motion picture agents. After a few promotions, he left ICM in 2003 to join the Gersh Agency, where he was a senior motion picture talent agent before becoming a partner there.

In 2008 James returned to ICM, where he became a founding partner at the newly renamed company (ICM Partners) solely owned by the agency partners. His clients include Regina King, Megan Fox, Karamo Brown, Josh Duhamel, Trey Songz, Meredith Vieira, and Anderson Silva.

In 2012, James was named to *Out* magazine's annual list of the 100 Most Influential People in America. He has also been named to the *Hollywood Reporter*'s annual list of the thirty-five most influential entertainment executives in the industry.

James founded ICM Partners' InQlusion Initiative. Its aim is to uplift LGBTQ+ voices internally and externally to encourage positive change in the industry.

James became a member of the Academy of Motion Pictures Arts and Sciences in 2019.

I ventured into the offices of ICM Partners, one of the premier talent agencies in the world, suddenly very conscious of my H&M suit. I sat in the waiting area among twenty-somethings nervously awaiting job interviews, their padfolios and résumés in hand, staring at the high ceilings, modern furniture, and tall windows.

A young assistant strolled out to get me and led me back into the suites. I was brought into Chuck James's office, meticulously decorated and organized. He got up from behind his desk in front of floor-to-ceiling windows and limped over, one of his legs in a cast. Even with the injury, he looked flawless.

His assistant brought in tea, poured it, and left us. Impeccably groomed, immaculately dressed, sincerely kind and genuine, Chuck spoke thoughtfully, choosing each word with care.

I became interested in speaking with Chuck after reading his poignant personal essay in a Pride issue of the *Hollywood Reporter*. "Gay people make some of the best agents," he wrote. He described the impact of his late mentor, Ed Limato, a highly influential gay agent who had taken Chuck under his wing.

With Chuck himself now in a position of high authority, he has an acute awareness for lifting up young queer talent within the company, just as Limato did with him.

You wrote a beautiful op-ed for the *Hollywood Reporter* about being gay and how that has affected your life in entertainment. You mention that both of your siblings are also gay. Even though you were able to see both of your siblings come out before you, you still struggled with your own coming to terms with being gay?

I still did this week. All the time. My mom passed away, so my dad's by himself. My siblings and I don't have any children, so the lack of grandchildren is not easy. So that's part of the struggle. It's not about not being proud of who I am or my society, community, or identity. But that had a huge impact on delaying time—not being in a relationship as a gay man—and then maybe missing the window for kids. I'm not sure my brother or sister wanted kids, but none of us having them made the family union become, if anything, altered, to say the least.

So your struggle with coming to terms with your sexuality has been more family-oriented rather than for personal or career reasons?

Yeah, it's more thoughts about a family. Once I was promoted and I was an owner, I didn't have to worry about what people were saying behind the door, of wanting or accepting a gay agent or partner. Once I was promoted and no longer junior in the company, where I felt I was under the microscope all the time, I felt more immune. In those ways, that *constantly* worried me.

Hollywood and the entertainment world don't strike me as being conservative. Is that the case?

We started an inclusion initiative here at ICM, which is amazing. We were getting feedback from some of the interns and assistants, so many asking, "Do you have an LGBTQ+ inclusion initiative?" They say it without any thought. It's not even an ask or a want; it's expected where they are going to work. I was reflecting on that the other day because there was nothing even remotely like that when I started. But also, if I had started what I started now, then, I think I would've been fired. It just wasn't around.

In this town, we're creating movie stars and fancy clothes and telling stories and everything you would think this community is about. The community is creating it all, but we're still not in enough boardrooms per se. It's not a conservative town, but it still is more conservative than ever.

Renowned talent agent Ed Limato mentored you. He was openly out, yet was able to have a thriving career. Why was he able to be both out and successful while so many others couldn't?

Because of his clients. He represented the biggest stars in the world at the time: Denzel Washington, Mel Gibson, Michelle Pfeiffer. His clients made him very powerful.

Even his style made him immune, and I think it also made him accepted. He could not have been further from the people on the boards and other management at the company. He was very flamboyant looking; not acting, but dressed incredibly well. Very fashionable, Italian, boisterous, lovely, classy, and made every client feel like they were the only one.

He was able to sign actors very easily: interesting and big movie star–type actors. I always think of someone like Mel Gibson, who I find interesting. I know there've been comments about him being homophobic, and statements he's made and certain things. And it's so interesting because when I think about him, there're two things. One, when I was working with Ed, Mel Gibson couldn't have been more kind, more accepting, more loving than anybody else on Ed's client list at the time. I also remember Ed's memorial, and when he got up, Mel was the last one to speak. Everyone was sort of hush-hush in the audience, and he had the most sincere, unbelievable tribute to Ed I've ever heard.

But how was Ed able to sign these actors? I would imagine these men would've been nervous to align themselves with an openly gay man.

Actors have always been the great part of this whole scenario, for me and everybody else. Look at Russell Crowe. He's had a gay agent his whole career. Mel Gibson and Denzel Washington were both with Ed Limato. It's a given that women love being with gay men because they feel like they are protected, they're not going to be judged or sexualized or any of that.

On the male side, there's something comforting about that. Because I think, and this is being prejudiced, gay male agents work harder than almost anyone I have ever witnessed. And I can't say why other than I think that, going back to my earlier time, you had to work twice as hard. Exactly like how women and women of color feel in this town. Working twice as hard to be able to get to the place of a straight white male.

Actors were not only accepting, but in a non-selfish way, they think they're going to get more for their money. I think they go, *This guy's gonna take care of me. He's gonna work 24/7. He doesn't have seven kids. We are his kids.* Ed made all of them feel like they were his children. He had a baby grand piano in his house and he had one photo of his Italian mother, who lived with him till the end, and one photo, each in beautiful silver frames, of Mel, Michelle, and Denzel. Those were his kids.

People always ask me, "If you were an actor, who would you sign with?" And I say, a gay male or a woman.

Did Ed assume you were gay and wanted to help you?

I think so. I think he also saw my work ethic, and maybe he knew the work ethic was because I was struggling, hiding, or wanting to work three times as hard as the other kids in the mailroom, because I was the gay one. I sort of felt like I started a little bit late: not Jewish, gay, no famous parent in the business. I didn't have anything really going for me in that respect.

This past year, as you were on your way to the Oscars, right before your client Regina King won her first Oscar, your limo passed an anti-gay protest. You have this huge achievement and yet you're still hated by so many people.

That was a big moment. I go by that corner almost every year going to the Oscars or the Emmys. This last year, hitting that corner, I was feeling so good about the circumstances of the moment. I remember I had one of my mom's pieces of jewelry on and I had this flower from my garden. Going around the corner, I'm sitting with my colleague Lorrie Bartlett, who works with Regina, too, and is African American, as well as Dar, my office neighbor who works with Regina who has Iranian ethnicity. So it's all three of us, but on this specific night, on this specific corner, the people weren't saying they hated Jews or Black people or Iran.

It was all anti-gay. *Fags are going to hell. You're a sinner.*

I was like, *I cannot believe I am two blocks from the theater, on the corner of Highland and Hollywood Boulevard, right in front of Hollywood High School.* We were in Hollywood, California, celebrating artistic achievement, and here I am going to see my client who I've represented for over twenty years, who is an African American female. The whole thing was shocking.

196

I was thinking, *If I stepped out of this car, and I walked across the street, they would accept me if they wanted a photo with Regina King. But they would never accept me walking across the street as myself.*

How has being gay positively impacted your career?

I have a sensitivity and an understanding of the artistic endeavor that we're all trying to sell and create. Create, sell, reward. It's made me a sensitive, caring person. It made me work harder to learn the business, to get ahead, and to be as confident as possible. There were times where I was overlooked, where it really wasn't even possible to be overlooked because the booking numbers and the creative eye don't lie. It was a situation where I knew something wasn't right, and I didn't want to make it all about me being gay, but I think that had a lot to do with it. So rather than quit or walk away, it made me twice as strong. I also think I had a very good connection with actresses. I was able to sign them early on and work with them and create real careers for them.

All of this has been positive. Now I look back at it and think, *I'm so glad I am gay because I don't think I would be as successful.* And when I say "successful," I don't mean that I'm an Oscar-winning agent. It's more about being successful in that I can walk away knowing I have clients who have won awards and achieved real creative recognition. I have brought in people who worked at a Home Depot and made $40 million in a movie franchise. Now it's more important to me that we can make an impact on the community, so people won't have to go through as disjointed a journey as I did.

AARON PHILIP
Model

Born in 2001 in Antigua, Aaron Philip (pronounced A-Ron) was born with quadriplegic cerebral palsy and was assigned male gender at birth. She now identifies as a gender nonconforming female.

At three years old, Philip and her family came to the United States, landing in the Bronx, New York, in search of better health care.

Philip became obsessed with fashion as she grew up and decided her dream was to become a model, despite fashion's history of not hiring models who used wheelchairs. She came into the spotlight in 2017 when her sharp-witted tweet caught the attention of Elite Model Management, one of the most prestigious modeling agencies in the world: *honestly when I get scouted/ discovered by a modeling agency it's OVER for y'all!* Philip made history as the first Black trans model with a disability to be signed to a major modeling agency. She has landed multiple campaigns, including with Dove and Sephora, the cover of *PAPER* magazine (where she was interviewed by Naomi Campbell, no less), and countless magazine editorials.

Her memoir, *This Kid Can Fly: It's About Ability (NOT Disability)*, was published in 2016.

The world of fashion is all about change: new trends, new faces, new collections. And yet, for an industry that calls for innovation and evolution, its concept of beauty has been slower to keep up.

Enter Aaron Philip. Though she considers herself just a girl from the Bronx who models, it is in her tremendously successful modeling career that she is pushing the beauty and fashion world forward.

I met Aaron at the offices of her modeling agency in New York City. I found her casually relaxing in the agency's lobby, scrolling through Instagram on her iPad. She wore dark jeans, a rust-colored sweater, and her shoulder-length, tousled hair in a style she described as "grungy glam." She had an infectious warmth. As we were led into a conference room by one of her agents, everyone in our path stopped to say hello, air kiss, or hug.

I learned quickly that Aaron didn't care for the "pioneering" title credited to her. Or rather, she didn't understand it. As she saw it, nothing about what she was doing was revolutionary. Her career was about what she always wanted to do: model. She wanted it, went for it, and got it.

Aaron took me along her gender journey, one that has been an evolution of finding her true self and navigating within the narrow confines of society's views of gender and women. As she described some of her hardest moments, I appreciated how she didn't seem to look back at them with anger or resentment. She reflected on those moments and saw how, through those difficult times, she found herself.

This is something I've come to find in many of the queer leaders I've spoken with: the skill of *introspection*. Queer people, by the very nature of realizing our queerness, are forced to think about who we are, how we present ourselves, and why we feel the way we do. It's a gift, albeit an ongoing and difficult one.

In Aaron's case, she was the beneficiary of being born at a time when the Internet was right at her fingertips (one of the many beneficiaries of Megan Smith's revolutionary work, also profiled on page 301). She had access to different people, cultures, voices, and was able to connect with them and see what resonated with her. And once she found those that clicked, she combined them with her lifelong dream of fashion. By seventeen years old, she had manifested her future and made her dreams a reality.

Can you tell me about your childhood growing up in the Bronx?

I was not bullied as a child, but I was very isolated and ostracized. People didn't want to talk to me. I didn't feel there was enough of anything for me growing up.

Sometimes we're more conscious of things before we can verbalize them. As a child who's trans, and doesn't have the words to express it, you know something's off. You know the way the world is treating you is off and you know that it's not the way it should be. I didn't even care about my body. I just wanted to be treated the way I saw the girls being treated by the boys. And I wasn't. I tried to get that in my body and in my existence as little Aaron who was socialized—but as a boy. And I found that as I got older, unknowingly, I more and more came out of that box. I started expressing feminine tendencies.

I didn't like to call myself a boy because it just was not true. I was navigating things little kids don't navigate, and that's emotional and tough, and that does a lot to your mental health. It's hard when you don't have people in your life who are aware of what you're going through, because you can't verbalize it.

When did you realize you felt different?

It was when I was twelve and started falling in love with people. I didn't have the words for it, but I wanted so much of that attention, and so much of that presence. *I love you,* and not as Aaron the boy; as Aaron the girl. Isn't it funny how love can become a language to express certain things? The feeling of falling in love with people can make you reevaluate everything you've ever been, and everything people have placed upon you. Love as a language can be so powerful.

The intersection of disability and being young and trans is also huge. I didn't yet have the power over myself to dress how I wanted, or be who I wanted to be. My father used to dress me and take me to school and he'd buy boy clothes. I had a shaved head. I wore glasses. I wore blues and greens and all those gross colors.

Identity is so crazy and it's so real. I didn't realize how real it is until I had to sit and think about it. When I was around ten, I fell in love with boys in my class. They were my best friends because they treated me kindly. And I'm just like, *I feel big, heavy, sparkling things for you.* I knew something about that was wrong. Because the love is not wrong; the fact that I was a *boy* was wrong.

What has been your process of discovering your gender?

I've had a whole gender journey. When I first came out, I was four-teen and in eighth grade. I came out as gender fluid. I went by she/her and they/them pronouns. I identified as a transgender person, but I was gender fluid. I had finally come out of the shell I'd wanted to break for so long, and I was happy as hell.

I remember fourteen-year-old me. I was geeky. I was literally an e-girl. I used to sit in my bedroom, be moody, wear baggy T-shirts, and take selfies in front of my curtains. I grew up on the Internet, so I was emulating what I saw people do on there. It was like method act-ing, but based on Internet aesthetics and Tumblr. I had to constantly express the fact that this was my identity.

People didn't think about transgender people a lot. Especially back then. People did not consider transness an option for someone. So for me to come out as trans, it blew a lot of people's heads off be-cause they just didn't think about it.

My parents were really mad at me when I first came out. I was an-gry because I felt like the world didn't catch up fast enough with me. And I knew I wasn't the only person like me. I was wondering, *Why is it taking so long for other people to understand—and let me do what I want, now that I am who I am?* And they didn't let me for a while. I remember being so angry all the time.

After eighth grade, I was hospitalized for a year and a half. I was at a facility in upstate New York. I had a surgery on my left hip that went wrong, and I was bedridden for a year. That was devastating. I lost a lot of my childhood and a lot of the ability to do things that fourteen- and fifteen-year-olds do. I was robbed, but I also developed this crazy sense of self. Because when you're bedridden for a year, all you have is you and your mind. And, luckily, I was able enough to still use my tablet, phone, and computer. So I would be with my friends on Tumblr and Instagram.

I spent a year digging into myself; doing a lot of self-discovery and internal soul-searching. Even with all the sickness, I still had my sense of self.

When did you stop using they/them pronouns?

After my hospital stay, I was reintegrated into high school, and that was a huge transition. My sophomore year was really lonely.

But I got through the year and I started my modeling career in junior year, which was insane. I give a lot of props to seventeen-year-old me. Seventeen-year-old me is my favorite version of me by far. She was crazy. I wanna be her friend. She made so much shit happen while being in high school. I don't think people honor their past selves enough. I think there's a lot to be found in the past self and who you once were, and the shit that you did a year or two ago.

Seventeen-year-old me took everything by storm because I could, and because I wanted to. I also had to do more thinking about my professional career and what I wanted people to see me as. When you go by a set of pronouns, what I found personally is that as a Black, trans person, it's harder to be socialized as someone who's feminine if you're nonbinary. Because when you think about society and the way people view Black people, there's racism, too. People see Black women as loud and angry. And then if you don't look like a Black woman and you are, they'll call you a man. They'll call you *this*, they'll call you *that*. And that's real.

I knew first and foremost I was feminine, but I was also gender nonconforming. I found that people didn't see me the way I saw myself. People used to refer to me with only they/them pronouns and disregard the fact that I'm just as much feminine as I am nonconforming. At the time, I felt people were exploiting my explicit gender nonconformingness to their advantage; to say, *Look at this person. I fuck with them because they're gender nonconforming,* and it made them look woke.

There's an order to my pronouns on purpose: *she/her, they/them.* I always thought about it as primary and secondary colors. I'm a girl first, but I'm also very gender nonconforming, and I don't conform to gender even though I am a girl. People didn't seem to respect or acknowledge that.

So when I was signed to my modeling agency in the summer of 2018, I made the decision to drop my they/them pronouns completely. I realized there are infinite ways to be a woman, and one of those is being gender nonconforming. Behavior does not dictate gender. Style does not dictate gender. Everything is subjective when it comes to gender. You can *do* anything you want and *be* anything you want.

There are so many ways to be a woman, to be celebrated as a woman, and to exist as a woman. I think one of those ways is definitely being someone who doesn't conform to what society dictates women should or should not do. I realized, *Wow, I can have my cake and eat it, too.* So, I dropped those pronouns and that was it from there. I've been like this since and living my best life.

Are you surprised that your trans identity has not limited your success?

No, actually. And that's amazing because I think fashion is finally in a place where fashion and queerness are going hand in hand. There are so many queer designers, so many queer people in fashion, that it would only make sense to extend that community to models. I have seen so much work done in the community lately to show we are here and we're doing things. Fashion is so gay, and that's the best part about fashion.

People describe you as *Aaron Philip—Black, transgender, disabled model*. How would you prefer to be described?

I see myself as Aaron Philip. No, *Aaron Philip, model*. Period. Maybe, *maybe* my pronouns. I see myself as a Black girl in a wheelchair from the Bronx and from Antigua. That's it. And the way I live my life says exactly that. Aaron Philip is a Black girl in a wheelchair from the Bronx. That's the way I see myself, so why can't other people see me that way, too?

Do you think there is any link between your motivation and work ethic and your queerness?

Definitely. I think queerness, drive, and work ethic go hand in hand. I don't know what it is about queerness itself, but queerness is so resilient. It's *so resilient*, it's *so powerful*. It's something that has so much light and energy. It's just like . . . go off!

When it comes to me, I am a queer, trans woman. Which I love. I love being a queer woman. Queer women are so important, and I think we don't see enough queer women who are trans. And especially queer teenagers. I love being a queer teenager. I wouldn't trade it for anything in the world. I'm having fun because of it. I can't imagine what it would be like to be a cis teenager. That'd be boring. I love being queer. I'm just gonna live my life as who I am. I want to live as authentically as possible, have fun, have a major career, and do all the major things I've ever wanted to do—as me. Because that's where the power lies. The way you see yourself is the way people see you. If you know you're it, you're it. Period.

How has being queer advantaged your career?

Intersectionality is how. Unfortunately, there are not a lot of Black trans women with the platform I've had. I've managed to make a really big platform as me, and I think people always talk to me about representation; what I'm representing for people. I guess people think I'm representing trans Black women, and I guess I am. It's just crazy because it should've happened so long ago and I shouldn't be a big name. It should be so many women. The world is so bigoted. Black trans women are under attack right now in society. I hate the fact that it took this long for someone like me who's a Black trans woman to get signed to an agency or do things like that. Why is history being made? These things should've happened.

Can you expound more on the intersectionality?

I am a disabled woman who's trans, signed to one of the most major modeling agencies in the world, and I'm eighteen. So, I'm young, I'm queer, I'm not cis, I'm not abled, and I have this really big thing going on for me. That's craziness to a lot of people. To me it's not crazy. To me, it's just me doing my job. And I love my job so that's why I do it.

I don't break boundaries. I'm just being me. And the craziest part is people really see me as someone who's breaking boundaries. All I've ever done was sit here, want to love fashion, be myself, love people, love life as who I am, and try to navigate life, even though it's hard. I'm just trying to live life. And somehow, by living my life and chasing my aspirations, as a person who should be chasing aspirations, I've made history.

What advice do you have for young, aspiring queer models?

Ride till you can't no more. Be loud as hell. Serve. Love yourself. Love yourself *especially*. Don't be afraid to experiment with yourself. Find people who love you. If it's not there for you up front, make it for yourself. Because that's where the power really is. Make it all for yourself or do it until you don't have to no more. Trust yourself. You have a lot more power than you think you do. The world is yours. It's your oyster. Go grab it. Don't think you have to be more mature to achieve your dreams. Revel in your youngness. You're young and that's where the power comes from. You're young, you're queer, and you're poppin'.

BETH FORD

First Out Lesbian CEO of a
Fortune 500 Corporation—Land O'Lakes

Beth Ford was born in 1963 and grew up in farm country in Sioux City, Iowa. Ford's large family—she was one of eight children—was working class and Catholic. Her mother, a registered nurse who later obtained a master's degree and became a psychotherapist, was a significant positive influence in guiding her life and providing a template for navigating her career. Her father was a truck driver and used car salesperson.

Ford worked numerous small jobs, including cleaning bathrooms, to pay for tuition at Iowa State. She later obtained her MBA at Columbia University Business School.

When she was tapped, in 2018, to lead Land O'Lakes, Ford became the first openly gay female CEO of a Fortune 500 corporation. Headquartered in Minneapolis, Minnesota, this agricultural cooperative produces butter and dairy products, along with Purina dog food.

Ford and her wife, Jill, have been married for over three decades and have three children.

How do you see your position as CEO and the visibility it holds helping bridge any gap between the queer community and the farming community?

I don't know that I look at it that way. I think there's a misconception that there aren't folks from the queer community that are also in farming. That's certainly what I see. I've had different constituencies reach out to me that are in farming from small towns, and they are pleased to have the visibility.

We are a farmer-owned cooperative, so our board consists of twenty-eight local farm retailers. They are the ones who selected me for the role of CEO. The visibility you achieve is always terrific, especially for young people and adults who are trying to understand their place. But I think it is just evidence that what really matters is performance, and connection with the mission of a particular organization. The fact that I'm gay wasn't anything that was part of the assessment they did for me in this role. That is always a confidence booster to anybody who wants to be valued based on what their capability is, their leadership, and their ambition. Being gay wasn't a hindrance. It did not stop me from achieving. That's exciting.

Throughout history and still today, queer people know well what it means to feel otherized. How has that helped you in navigating the complexities of your career?

Earlier in my career there was a feeling of that. That was in the late eighties, early nineties, and the world has certainly moved ahead. It was much more familiar for professionals like me to not be quite so out and open about their sexuality. Certainly in my thirties, I put that aside: I met my wife; we have a family. It really became part of who I was. Since my twenties, I haven't felt otherized.

There's a sensitivity you develop for the marginalized, or for those people who you recognize may not feel as included. It makes you more sensitive to reach out and to make sure that folks in your organization, folks on your team, people you meet, are included and are not feeling like "others." It makes you more empathetic and sensitive to the issues.

I tend to thrive in businesses that are people-intensive. Being gay is part of a whole mosaic of issues that made me into this.

What advice would you have for young queer professionals beginning their careers?

Your ability to have the humility to ask questions, to bring other people along on the journey with you and develop relationships, is central to career success. Just because you're part of the queer community, don't be afraid to build tight relationships with others outside the community. Really step into that because relationships are critical to career success. Careers are not a zero-sum game. When you enable others' success, it helps develop your own career.

TEDDY GOFF

Partner, Precision Strategies

Teddy Goff grew up in and around New York City, in a Jewish family. He graduated from Yale University, having studied English and Political Science.

Goff later became associate vice president at Blue State Digital, developing its global presence. He worked on projects with American Express and Microsoft, political figures, and cultural influencers including Carnegie Hall and the Metropolitan Museum of Art.

Goff moved on from there into the political area. He was named digital director for President Obama's 2012 campaign and was the leader of the digital strategy team that helped Obama win the presidency twice. As a communications and organizational expert, Goff presided over Obama for America, a campaign team of over two hundred individuals across the United States. At the time, it was the largest online political marketing campaign in history.

Since 2013, Goff has run Precision Strategies, headquartered in New York City. He also advised Hillary Clinton's 2016 presidential campaign.

Goff has been profiled in *Bloomberg Businessweek*, *Rolling Stone*, *New York* magazine, and many other publications. He has been named to *Time's* 30 People Under 30 list.

I met Teddy Goff at the headquarters of his company, Precision Strategies. The office was minimal, quiet, comfortable, and decorated with a downplayed, carefree aesthetic. The staff were casually dressed, huddled around one another's laptops, deep in conversation.

Teddy and I had met once before, a year prior, and I was excited to reconnect. He greeted me in a T-shirt and jeans. Just like the rest of the space, his office was minimalistic. A painting was propped against the wall, waiting to be hung.

Teddy carried himself with the same quiet reserve as when we'd first met. While we had discussed his career and the world of digital media previously, I was keen to figure out what his queer advantage was, and how, if at all, it had helped him rise to the top.

What was your coming out process?

I came out when I was around twenty-three. I'm privileged to have grown up in a progressive environment in New York City. I got an almost uniformly positive reaction. I was very surprised. Most of my friends from college were straight men. I was afraid it would cause them to rethink their whole friendship with me or think the whole thing had been predicated on false premises. And it was almost the opposite, to the extent that they wished they could have been more supportive.

Before you came out, was it something you were self-conscious about?

Beyond worried. It was such a paralyzing fear that I concocted a persona, some of which I still exhibit. A persona that is very unrecognizable as "gay," according to whatever kind of cultural tropes you associate with what gay people are. I was terrified of the idea of coming out and being gay. So to protect myself against that fear, I made myself totally unrecognizable as gay. Nobody knew. In terms of my mannerisms, I made myself so nondescript, "straight acting," that it came as a total shock to everybody. Or so they claim.

Was that something that enveloped you? Or did it become so natural you didn't think about it?

It was almost deeper. I created barriers between myself and people. I was very careful not to get too close to people and not to make men, gay or straight, think I liked them. So it became almost a kind of inhibitor on free and joyful humanness in general.

Did being gay, and the insecurity about it, create a sense of desire in you to outshine people?

I have thought about this a ton. I definitely had a mom who expected I could be president, a billionaire, or whatever I wanted to be. She had no intention of doing this—she's a lovely, non-homophobic person—but I think that was actually a contributor to my staying in the closet for so long. Because, whatever my perception was as a teenager, I felt room to be a star—president, CEO, whatever—and being gay didn't fit into that.

I come from this liberal family on the Upper West Side of Manhattan. Why was it so hard for me when, meanwhile, I have friends now who come from Tennessee and Alabama who came out at fourteen? I definitely think this sense that I had to make something with my life was a big part of that. The first gay CEO of a Fortune 500 company was Tim Cook, who didn't come out until 2014. Certainly at the time there were no real role models.

It was more of an intangible feeling, like what it *means* to be successful. It was more of an image for me of what success looked like—of what being a good, enviable role model–type person could be.

If you believe you're going to be president or if you believe in a big career, your models for that are straight. Once I came out then yes, I absolutely felt I owed it to the community, and to younger people, to make good on those years of paralysis and go be successful. To be someone who could be a good role model for young queer people, or just a good model for straight people looking at the gay community.

I remember I had worked with Obama 2008, and came out right after that election. I didn't go into the administration, but then I went back to Obama 2012 as an openly gay man. There were a lot of people who I either hadn't talked to, or had barely seen for the intervening two-and-a-half years from the election to when the re-election started, for whom I was in a new leadership position. And now a newly gay man. I absolutely took pride in one, doing a good job, but two, being one of the gay members of leadership and being someone who the younger gay staff could see was respected and could go into the campaign manager's office and be a person in full. Not shy, not insecure, not ashamed of who he was.

There were two-hundred-something people on my team and a huge number of them were LGBTQ+. I remember wanting to do right by them and feel they could be proud to have a gay boss, who was the kind of professional they might want to be when they wound up in that job later on.

I always think about how many gay people I know from the South, or from rural communities, or from other countries. They're the only one of the kids in their family who is gay and, in my opinion not coincidentally, also the only one who went to a good school, made it to

New York or Los Angeles, or has a really good job. That's a super-interesting phenomenon. It's not exactly my personal story, but I definitely think that's a thing that drives many people to get themselves out of where they are if they want to survive. And be able to meet other people and have a social life.

Has your perception of being gay changed?

One hundred percent. I now think it's the biggest blessing. I feel bad for my straight friends. For example, they have to deal with the expectation of marriage and kids by a certain age. To some degree, they probably have to continue to adhere to those expectations I've held myself to—of being a professional of a certain kind. Achieving a certain kind of success as externally defined, rather than internally defined. Which, when you come out, you unshackle yourself from.

Straight men are wonderful, but a lot of them keep each other at arm's length. They don't get too close, aren't that friendly, feel they've got to be a certain idea of what it means to be "macho" and a "man." And a man is solid and not that nice. If they have an emotion, it's anger and no other emotions besides that.

Being gay has helped me understand that, no, being friendly is great. You *should* be friendly to everybody, you *should* make relationships with people: straight men, women, nonbinary people, whomever. It's helped me understand how to not be judgmental. It's helped me understand how to try to make my own way in life and not to find success according to money or a title, but according to fulfillment.

Empirically speaking, when I look at straight men in the world, so many of them seem boxed in by toxic masculinity and this idea of being strong, tough, and not vulnerable. And that's bullshit. Being gay helps you get out of that toxic masculine vortex and start thinking, *What are my values? What kind of person do I want to be?* For most,

215

that helps us be friendlier, more open, more positive, more inclined to be supportive of people, and less inclined to judge.

Being gay has shaped who I am in a huge way and made me a more positive and optimistic person; someone who can deal with people better, who can be more mature, and more self-confident. I am also a white guy though. I am a beneficiary of that privilege, too, and it behooves me not to put this all on homosexuality as if I get to claim minority status and not recognize the rest of my privilege.

What was it like to come back to the 2012 Obama campaign as a newly out gay man?

At that time, I perceived being gay through a filter of damage avoidance and risk mitigation. I wasn't able to think, *What are the great things that are going to come out of being gay? What wonderful, beautiful consequences will there be?* I thought if I could just make sure nobody's opinion of me changed, and that nobody thought I was lying, or nobody thought I was some gay who no longer fit into their image of what a confident leader of a team, or strategist, could be, that was good.

When the campaign started, I was twenty-six. I was by far the youngest member of senior staff. I had one of the biggest teams by head count. So I already felt extremely vulnerable and nervous. There were forty- and fifty-year-olds on my team and I had to make them respect me and listen to me. If you've ever worked for a weak boss, who nobody gives a shit what they have to say, that's not good for anybody. I wasn't trying to lead with an iron fist, but to have the respect of the team and to be able to lead the team in a proper way.

I do believe there is homophobia that people feel which they don't express. Do I think there are tons of people who would never use a slur or even vote the wrong way or oppose policies who, deep in their hearts feel a little—I'm talking mainly about men here—belittled or a little emasculated having to report to a gay man? Probably.

The team was roughly 50 percent male, of whom they were roughly 80 percent straight. Would they be able to see me as someone they could respect, look up to, listen to, take direction from? A leader like any other and not just their gay boss? That forced me to work twice as hard.

DAN LEVY

Actor, Writer, Producer & Director

A Toronto, Ontario, native, Dan Levy has catapulted up the ranks of Hollywood elite. As a writer, director, and producer, he is one of the creators and stars of the Emmy-nominated TV series *Schitt's Creek*.

The son of actor and comedian Eugene Levy, who captured hearts through his performances in films such as *Best in Show* and the *American Pie* franchise, Levy grew up in Canada and attended York University and Ryerson University, where he studied film production. He began his own career in entertainment as a cohost at MTV.

In 2013, Levy formed Not A Real Company Productions alongside his father, which resulted in the creation of *Schitt's Creek*. Levy signed a three-year deal with ABC Studios in 2019 to produce and develop scripted content.

Growing up, as you came to understand you were gay, how did that impact your vision of your future?

As a person who wanted to act, being gay in the late nineties–early 2000s was a really scary time. Mainly because it was a career-ender. It was a time where people couldn't see past your sexuality and see what you were capable of, beyond who they decided you were defined as. It was scary to know that I wanted to get into entertainment, but also knowing that being myself in that world was not necessarily going to be met with open arms.

When I got a job as a television host, I was out of the closet to my friends and family but was not explicitly out on television. I didn't want to be put in a box or defined by it. Being gay is such an important part of my life, but it is not the only part of my life.

At that time, you were only seen as one thing. It's quite amazing how far we've come in terms of acceptance, celebration, lifting people up, and having a community of queer people who are out and proud in the media. And publicly support one another. It's been a big shift, but it was scary in those early days because it was a completely different landscape, as a gay person, to be out in the media.

When did you feel comfortable in your professional life to start talking about being gay, outside of just family and friends?

I would always take a stand politically when I was hosting the show, and it wasn't until halfway through my time at MTV when I gave up. I gave up trying to tiptoe around something I didn't want to ever tiptoe around. The common thread with people who have to hide parts of who they are is that it gets to a point where it's so sad. And as someone who has always been so inspired by the queer people who have come out, I started to feel like I wasn't doing myself or my community any good by choosing to leave out such a definitive part of who I was.

I don't think there was ever a public proclamation of "I'm gay." I struggle generally with feelings of inadequacy—particularly back then. So part of it was I didn't feel people cared enough, and I didn't think I was important enough in the media to make a proclamation about myself. I felt like there would just be three people around a water cooler saying, "Way to go, buddy."

But it was important to advocate for things publicly on television. It was important to take a stance and stand up for things when you had a platform that reached so many people. As an outward-facing person in the media, I became more and more comfortable. And the more comfortable I became in my own skin as an out gay man, the more passionate and vocal I became.

I mandated myself with the responsibility of saying, *I have a platform that's even bigger than it was before. There has to be something that I'm saying about my own experience that has to work its way into whatever I'm creating artistically.* And then came *Schitt's Creek.*

Do you find there to be a difference when writing a lovable queer character versus a lovable straight character?

Not at all. The minute you start writing people differently because of who they are is the minute we run into problems. The success of *Schitt's Creek* was because we didn't write anybody differently than anybody else.

Growing up, a lot of the queer characters I would come in contact with in TV or movies were caricatures or characters that were written with a specific purpose—to offer the tragedy or be part of a lesson to be learned. It was important for me in writing the show that we treated every character equally, and dealt with their lives with the same ease we would anybody else. We're not going to treat the queer characters any differently than we would the straight characters, because people see that. People see when you are writing characters with precious gloves on. We don't need that. What we need are honest depictions of our lives.

How has being queer advantaged you in your career?

It's made me a stronger person and it's made me a person who has stood more firmly in my own beliefs and my own sense of self. It's not necessarily been easy, but I do feel like walking into a room confident in who you are, and what you bring to the table, is an advantage.

Unfortunately, for so many of us, it comes at a cost in terms of what we had to go through to get there. There are so many people still living in communities who don't have that luxury, or who have grown up with families who have not given them that kind of space to learn and grow. It's still a privilege to get to this place of confidence where you truly can walk down the street owning your space. There are a lot of people who don't have that freedom, or who have not been given the kind of encouragement or support to get there.

It's also being grateful. Knowing that everything you do, every success you have, being grateful for the opportunity, and knowing there are a lot of people who don't have that kind of advantage. In a way, the work I'm doing, and the work I hope to do, is to continue to tell stories that provide more spaces for other people to find that footing, and to feel encouraged and supported.

What advice do you have for young queer people beginning their careers?

Be confident. It's the hardest thing you can possibly do. I struggle with it every day. I'm not an inherently confident person—in fact, I'm quite the opposite. I am the first person to overanalyze whether I deserve to be here. But the reality is, especially in entertainment, there's so much money on the line that if you don't show up really owning your space and feeling confident in your idea and in your vision, someone behind you *will* do that. And that's where people are going to invest their money.

KIM CULMONE

Global Head of Design, Barbie and Fashion Dolls, Mattel

Originally from New Orleans, Louisiana, Kim Culmone holds Design degrees from Louisiana State University and the Fashion Institute of Design & Merchandising in Los Angeles.

Culmone began her career at Mattel, Inc., in 1999 as a designer for Barbie. In 2019 she was appointed senior vice president and global head of design for Barbie and fashion dolls at Mattel. In this role, she oversees all creative direction for the Barbie brand.

Throughout her tenure at Barbie, Culmone has pushed to innovate the brand to ensure the doll reflects modern society. She was the subject of the 2015 Hulu documentary *Tiny Shoulders: Rethinking Barbie*, which showed her leading the design of the most diverse doll line in Barbie's history, including three new body types. The reinvention generated over five billion media impressions, led to a *Time* cover, was named one of the Top 25 Inventions of 2016 by the magazine, and received the Barbie brand's first-ever "Doll of the Year Award." Under Culmone's stewardship, Barbie is the most diverse and inclusive doll line on the market.

Further pushing diversity and inclusivity efforts across the doll portfolio, Culmone oversaw design of Creatable World, the first gender-inclusive doll line to challenge traditional views around who a doll is for. The line, inviting all kids to play, sparked cultural conversation heard around the world and was named one of *Time*'s 2019 Best Inventions.

My favorite activity as a young boy was playing with my sister's Barbie dolls. The hair, the outfits, the accessories, the glamor—even now, as an adult, I think back fondly to the hours (and hours and hours and hours) I would spend with them. My Barbies became princesses, they were mothers, even superheroes destroying the villainous G.I. Joe. It is of real significance (and of great poignancy to me) that the person now in charge of this hugely popular toy, my favorite toy, is queer.

Kim Culmone has spent the past two decades at the helm of Barbie. Her creative vision stewards the next generation of kids around the world.

During her tenure at Barbie, Kim has not just maintained the doll's premium brand but has also boldly expanded our notion of who Barbie is. Since 1959, when Barbie was first introduced, she has been more than the feminine model—she has been the feminine *ideal*: tiny waist, big breasts, long legs.

In 2015, however, as portrayed in *Tiny Shoulders*, Culmone relentlessly diversified Barbie's public image. This important film not only highlighted Culmone's talents as a creative visionary but showcased the powerful way she advanced the cause of diverse acceptance in the world. Unthinkable during my long days with the doll, today's Barbie has more inclusive body types, different skin tones, and various hair textures. Barbie now, for the first time, reflects the customer base of the kids who hold her. Kim grew up in the South and now lives in West Hollywood. Her Southern warmth combined with California energy is palpable, and her love of the brand she has so carefully shaped is endearing.

It is reassuring to know our beloved Barbie is in the best of hands.

Growing up in New Orleans, you came out when you were sixteen. What type of reaction were you met with?

I was an only child and my mother accidentally found a letter in my room that I had written, and there was information in it about my girlfriend. I was actually at my girlfriend's house and she called me and said, "We need to talk."

I didn't have the intention of coming out. It was definitely something that was confidential to my girlfriend, my friends, and me at this point. I was going to an all-girls Catholic high school, and I was in school with the girl I was dating. I'm not going to sugarcoat it; it was very challenging.

That was not in my mom's story of who she was or who I was going to be. Now that I can step back and have empathy, she was amazing. She went through her hard times, but the primary concern within her frame of reference was she didn't want me to struggle in life.

But she was a single mom. And the miracle of the universe was that she worked with her best friend, Linda. Linda said to her, "What's wrong, Cathy?"

She said, "Kim's gay."

Linda's reaction was "So what? Two of my kids are gay." These two women were best friends, and Linda hadn't shared that knowledge with her. And now my mom was presented with someone she was very close to as her own role model of behavior as a parent of someone who was queer.

I'm always so grateful to Linda for helping guide my mom through what was a difficult time for her. It was a different time in the world. It's difficult for many parents if they haven't gone into their parenting with the concept that their kid might be queer.

When you understood your sexuality at sixteen, did that change your perception of what your future could look like?

It didn't. I was very politically active as a kid. I was going to marches, rallies, events for women's rights and for choice. I was a rebel kid.

I do think there was some part of me internally that was looking to recreate a heteronormative life. We didn't go to prom. My girlfriend's dad gave us his credit card and we went to a gay restaurant in the French Quarter.

But I now love seeing in queer teenagers this mentality of *We're gonna show up and we're going to have these experiences. We're gonna do it our way.* I love that there's a demand for access.

I didn't realize how much I was trying to fit in, versus me figuring out exactly who I was and how I wanted to live my life. I didn't have a concept of it limiting me. But I might have been trying to make myself fit a picture of what an acceptable adult was, versus me really digging deep and saying, *This is who I am and you're welcome, world.*

You were the first person in your family to go to college, and you went to Louisiana State University and then the Fashion Institute of Design & Merchandising in Los Angeles. What was it like as a young queer woman, going to school in the South and then being in LA?

Being a young gay woman and going to school in the South was fascinating. My girlfriend and I moved in together in an apartment off campus for freshman year. The funny thing is I think we got away with stuff I wouldn't have been able to if I had been straight. There's no way my mom would've let me move in with a boyfriend at eighteen years old. But because our parents were wrapping their heads around what this was, they let us move in together.

When you were interviewing for your first jobs, did they know you were queer?

I never hid anything. I've been working at Mattel on Barbie for nearly twenty years. I remember this feeling of *I can't wait until I get to the point when I can just tell them.* It's very difficult to operate in our workplaces *not* out. Because you're not bringing your whole, authentic self to the workplace. And you constantly feel like you're halfway holding your breath.

I can remember when I would shift managers, and it maybe was someone from outside our core organization, and I'd have to get to that reveal point again. I felt it wasn't really relevant information, but it certainly made life a lot easier. And I love the way I feel now, because rather than it being an announcement, I simply talk about my life in a normal way.

As I've gotten older and as the world has shifted, it feels so much more comfortable knowing it doesn't have to be a moment of announcement. I'm not caretaking of the people around me to make sure *they're* okay with who *I* am. It's actually a conscious shift for me.

If I could say something to kids coming up and coming out, it's that, *Don't project any anxiety you have onto the receiver of your information. Just be who you are as much as they are being who they are. Don't take such a sense of responsibility for other people's feelings or reactions to who you are.* And I always felt that way. As if I had to pick a time that was comfortable for *them* to let *them* know.

As society is evolving and kids are becoming aware of their sexual orientations and gender identities at a much younger age, how does that impact your work with Barbie?

There is no doubt in my mind that my lens of how I filter information has been impacted by the fact that I'm gay. Everyone has that. The way I see the world is through having been otherized at times in my life.

While I'm telling you my background and it wasn't super-challenging, it doesn't mean I didn't suffer. Would we have wanted to go to the prom with everybody else? Totally. Would I have preferred not to have to fight for marriage equality? Absolutely. And would I have preferred not to live and come up during the time of the AIDS crisis? For sure.

It has built up in me a burning passion for inclusion. I see things differently. Other people in my position, through their lens and with no ill intensions, may look at a product line and thinks it looks "diverse enough." Because of my lived experience, I know what it feels like to not be seen. So I have empathy and compassion for those who may also feel that way. That informs my work, it informs how I hire, and it allows me to see things a little bit differently than other people.

In 2017, Barbie posted a photo to her Instagram account wearing a "Love Wins" shirt. Do you see a future where Barbie could be marketed as having a wife or a girlfriend?

The thing about Barbie is that she's a blank canvas for storytelling for kids. While there is a narrative around a blonde, blue-eyed, Caucasian character who sometimes has a boyfriend named Ken, that is not the true nature of the Barbie brand.

If a kid is playing out a story, and he or she has two dolls that are female who fall in love, that's their story. The part of the brand I love the most is that open-endedness. And when you watch kids play, their doctors have fairy wings, they send puppies to the moon, and in a span of five minutes, the characters will change.

It goes back to how kids play and what they see in doll play, versus what adults see. Adults are looking for definition and literalness. Kids see nothing but possibility and open-endedness through their magical kid lens.

Have you felt the need to work harder because you're gay?

No. I've felt insecure at times, wondering if I will be liked. *Is my queerness going to be a barrier to natural relationship-building with people who are influential in my business and company?* I worried about it, but I'm now sitting in the most powerful creative position for one of the world's biggest toy brands. Clearly it hasn't been an issue.

How has being queer advantaged you in your career?

In today's business world, we are building purposeful, intentional, authentic brands, at the demand of our consumer base. Growing up the way I did, and feeling isolated and not represented, benefits me. I have a fire in my belly about fighting for and making sure lots of different kinds of folks are included in the work we do.

ADAM ELI

International LGBTQ+
Activist & Leader of Voices 4

Adam Eli Werner was born in New York in 1990. He grew up in a Jewish family focused on activism.

Eli has relied on his religious values to promote his secular work. He is the founder and driving force of Voices 4, an activist group working to create positive change for the LGBTQ+ community around the world in a nonviolent way.

Eli has been organizing protests since he was in high school. He learned techniques of protest from ACT UP, and figured out the power of social media. He has been involved in numerous marches and protests, including after the Pulse nightclub shootings. He harnessed queer power through platforms such as Instagram to create highly publicized rallies, meetings, and marches.

In 2019, Eli was asked by Gucci to help create their zine, called *Chime*, a source for information on fashion, art, and issues of interest pertaining to queer people.

I met Adam Eli at the Marlton Hotel in Greenwich Village on a sunny summer afternoon. He arrived with gusto—and gifts.

The born-and-bred New Yorker has a signature look: tight, curly hair, a pink kippah, pink mascara, and often a Barbra Streisand shirt.

Adam brought me my very own pink kippah, as well as a newly printed edition of *Chime*.

This was the first time Adam and I had met, though I had been aware of him for years, his digital presence powerful and wide. A latter-day Larry Kramer, Adam has used his social media savvy to galvanize people around the world to rise up and speak out—in particular about Jewish, queer, and gender-related issues.

We huddled in a corner booth, splitting a burger and fries. Adam's book, *The New Queer Conscience*, was going to be announced the following Monday, and we excitedly swapped our first-time publishing experiences.

In truth, I had been nervous to meet Adam. Though we had dozens of mutual friends and he genuinely didn't seem to have a mean bone his body, I could never quite muster up the courage to introduce myself.

My reasoning? Adam Eli is *brilliant*. He is a walking encyclopedia of queer history, current events, and Judaism, and is able to speak intellectually and passionately about it all. In transparency, I felt like a fraud.

I love being queer, have spent time educating myself on the history, and I actively work to keep up with what's going on around the world. But I worried I would quickly be sniffed out as the imposter I felt I was if I ever actually engaged in a conversation with him.

I did not tell this to Adam, but it became evident I didn't have to. The wealth of knowledge was something he certainly owned, but wielded with kindness and as a resource for others—not as a weapon of belittlement. If I didn't know about something he referred to, I didn't pretend, and he kindly and happily informed me.

It was touching to see him post on Instagram a few days later about how people who have questions or who may not know about a certain issue should just *ask*. His openness to share his thoughts and insights was something I hadn't experienced before from many activists. Rather than holding himself on a pedestal, condemning people for not knowing, he acted as an equalizer.

Thank you, Adam, for proving me wrong.

When you began to understand you were queer, how did that impact your vision of your future?

Growing up, my parents went to an Orthodox synagogue and I went to a conservative Jewish school. I also had a very severe learning disability where I couldn't read until I was in the fourth grade.

I caught up with the rest of my class at eleven years old, but by then they had already moved on to learning Hebrew. By twelve, I started going through puberty.

I knew I had a really privileged life. I knew my parents loved me and I knew being gay was okay. I wasn't tortured, in my mind, thinking I was sinning, like the adults around me were implying. I also pretty much knew my family was going to accept me when I came out. And I knew I was lucky for that. Everyone has struggles, and I felt the defining arc in my story was that I was gay and Jewish. And because of my Judaism, I felt I couldn't come out.

I went to an Orthodox high school and I got Ds in all of my Hebrew subjects. I was like, *I do not consent to being here and I will not engage with this.* I wouldn't wear my kippah, I would not put on my tefillin. I would break the rules as openly, and flagrantly, as often as I could.

The night before my freshman year of college, I made a silent prayer. I told myself, *Adam Eli, you are no longer Jewish. You are washing yourself and your person of this. You will not go to synagogue, you will not go to Hillel. You will not make Jewish friends. You will not talk about Judaism, and it will not be a part of your life with the exception of when it intersects with family.*

And then I went away to college, where I told people I was not Jewish. When people asked me if I was, I would lie and say I was Greek.

That's how I lived for about six years. And then about three years after I had graduated from college, something in me shifted. I started becoming interested in the intersection of being queer and Jewish, and I came back.

People always ask me, "How did you come to terms with your queer and Jewish identity?" The answer is, I was really open about it and I talked about it a lot—particularly online. I was really confused and upset about these two intersecting identities; they didn't make any sense to me. I just kept talking about it and I started to use fashion to express my queer Jewishness. I started to wear my hair really curly as a Jew 'fro, which was very flamboyant and styled. I also started wearing Barbra Streisand shirts and other shirts that indicated my queer Jewishness. The reason I did that was because I was lost and I needed a community. And at the time, I was trying to build for myself a presence and establish a voice. And when I talked about being queer and Jewish, it wasn't saying, *This is the greatest thing ever.* I talked about my struggles with it. And people connected with that almost more than anything else that I was saying, which I found interesting and frightening. I didn't understand why.

I came out in 2009, when I was eighteen. So it was Ellen DeGeneres, President Obama, gay marriage, #ItGetsBetter, and Lady Gaga.

The biggest shift in my life was after the June 2016 Pulse nightclub shooting in Orlando happened. It was the first time in my life I had ever seen a direct attack on my community. I was beside myself, completely shocked, and I didn't know what to do. So, I broadcast my emotions online. I was a real estate agent in NYC at the time, showing apartments, and I posted nine times that day, exactly what I was feeling, exactly what was going on. My big message was to reach out to your queer friends. Because I was posting so much, people kept asking me what to do. This was before I had any type of following. I said, *If you're upset about what's going on and you don't want to be alone, meet me at Two Boots pizza and, all together, we'll walk to Stonewall.* Thirty people showed up, which is a lot for an hour's notice and with a small following. And I realized, *Oh, it looks like social media can be used for direct action. Who knew?*

Then I sat in on the first Gays Against Guns meetings, silent, because everyone there was much older. On the night before our first action, they said we needed someone to do the social media. I raised my hand. I did the social media for that protest, and overnight I became the social media manager.

The rest of my generation freaked out when Trump was elected, and wanted to become activists. I just happened to have had that freak-out four months before. My voice cut through the masses because I had practice using social media to directly organize people.

After a year of responding to Trump, I heard about the purge taking place in Chechnya. And, as I'm doing this activism, I'm feeling more like myself than I ever have. My platform is growing *immensely,* people are connecting with my activism and also when I talk about my Judaism.

I wrote an article about why being queer and being Jewish is great—or I say "the chicest thing ever"—because it allows me to have empathy from both sides. Because both of my peoples were oppressed. Therefore, I have an inherent knowledge and obligation of showing up for other people. Especially with the intersection of Trump.

So when I heard about Chechnya, this sort of metal plate just banged off in my head. Because, if you read that original Masha Gessen article from the *New Yorker*, it sounds like the Holocaust. They're rounding people up, interrogating them through their cell phones, holding them in places, torturing them for information, and killing them. I'm thinking, "never again" is *now*. This is what I trained for my whole life in Hebrew school.

I decided to march from Stonewall to Trump Tower. Out of that march came this group called Voices 4. And Voices 4 is the coolest thing I've ever done. As we're speaking now, Voices 4 protests are taking place in Berlin and London for Intersex Awareness Day.

I used the building blocks I learned in Judaism to build what became the foundation of everything I am today, everything that I'm passionate about, and everything I'm known for. I took those tools, I *queered* them, and the world responded.

What were those building blocks?

The mission of my life is to make queer people feel more connected to each other, and the idea that queer people anywhere are responsible for queer people everywhere. I took a quote from the Talmud that says, *All the people of Israel are responsible for each other*, and I took that and made it gay.

It also became really clear to me that my great-grandparents left Russia because of the pogroms, which was government-sanctioned violence against Jewish people. Then my mother was really active in the Soviet Jewry movement, getting the Jews behind the Iron Curtain out. And then forty years later, here I was fighting for the same exact thing.

We used a tactic my mother used for the Soviet Jewry, where you would "adopt" a Refusenik.* You would write letters to your public officials on their behalf. Every Friday you would say a prayer, have bake sales to send money back, and at your bar mitzvah you would be paired with someone in their town, and you would have a bar mitzvah for them because they couldn't be bar mitzvahed.

There was this gay Uzbek journalist named Ali Feruz who was imprisoned in Russia, and was going to be sent back to Uzbekistan, where he surely would have been killed. So we did the same thing. We "adopted" him, but we did so on Instagram and made it gay-themed. I got all of these queer Instagram artists to draw his picture, we had a big protest, and we smuggled pages of his diary out of jail. We got them to the U.S. and then auctioned them off at gay bars, and had drag show fundraisers.

---

*Soviet Jews who were denied permission to emigrate, primarily to Israel, by the authorities of the Soviet Union.

Within the DNA of being Jewish is showing up for other Jewish people, simply because they're Jewish. And it is my life mission to have queer people feel the same way. People really resonate with that message.

I used to pray, and wish so hard, that I wasn't Jewish. I didn't really even wish I wasn't gay. And now my superpower, the success I've had, and the authentic version of myself, is rooted in that intersection.

When did that shift happen, where you went from resenting your Judaism and queerness to fully embracing it?

I literally woke up one morning and realized I had no gay Jewish friends, and I wanted that. I made the decision that the best way for me to do that was to throw a party. I called it the Gay Jewish House Party. At the time, I was living with three gay male models in this disgusting apartment. I made a flyer showing a picture of my chest hair with the Jewish star necklace and incorporated Barbra Streisand imagery. I posted it on my Instagram. I also posted it on Grindr and invited strangers over. And then the model boys and I cut out gay porn and covered the entire bathroom in it. I threw this house party and it was a big success. From that moment on, there was no going back.

You were filled with so much anger. Why do you think you were able to take that anger and turn it into fuel to create positive change?

This is a great question, but I didn't do that. I am not interested in taking traditional Jewish spaces and making them more queer-friendly. That requires a lot of patience, which I do not have. I am also too angry to deal with it. My goal, and what I want to do, is bring

Jewish principles, people, sensibilities, ethos, and frankly, logistical tactics, to the queer movement.

So my anger did not inspire me to go back to those places to help them change, which might be why I still have some of that anger. What motivated me was that I feel in my bones and in my blood the screams of my ancestors—gay and Jewish—dying in the Holocaust. That is part of my day-to-day life. It's part of my function.

I was taught very early as a Jew to know my history. And so I did the same thing when I first came out and I learned a lot of queer history. So the anger came from the *history*, not my frustration.

Do you think you can attribute any of your ambition and drive to being queer?

One thousand percent. When you grow up in a world that constantly tells you that you are *not enough* or that *you're wrong*, you often have a lot to prove. And even though I know that to not be true, I still feel like I have a lot to prove. And the issue I'm facing now is what happens when you want to show the world how great you are, and then when you do, and it still doesn't feel good. Or it doesn't have the satisfaction you thought it would. What do you do now? That's where I'm at today.

How has queerness benefited your personal life?

Whenever I find myself in a new situation, I always look for a queer person. That gives me a point of connection. Queerness is a trait like no other in that it is ever-present and literally non-erasable. There have been existences of queerness and gender fluidity through every culture and through every time.

Whenever I travel, the first thing I do is I ask for people to set me up with queer friends. I go to the queer neighborhood, and I walk into places and spaces where people look like me and talk like me. And even if I can't speak the language, I can talk to someone in a gay bar about a Lady Gaga song with dancing hands.

What advice do you have for young queer people beginning their careers?

What I learned the hard way is that the truth is more interesting than the lie, the truth is more human than the lie, and it's more relatable than the lie. I know it sounds corny, but I genuinely believe that life only works, and success only works, if you're being authentically yourself. Because when I wasn't, it just didn't happen for me. But when I talk about the issues that are really hurting me, like my Judaism was, that's when people responded. So in my experience, the only way to achieve success is by sticking to what is authentically true to you.

Anything you want to add?

I genuinely and wholeheartedly believe that being queer is a superpower, and the best thing that's ever happened to me. It's one of the things I like most about myself, and if someone could give me a button to change, I would run away so fast. I would not give it up for anything in the world. I didn't always feel that way, and now with my whole heart I do.

My friend and I were at a family dinner, and there was another girl there who had just come out and her family wasn't very supportive. She turned to my friend and said, "Are we being too gay at the table?"

My friend responded, "There's no such thing as being too gay."

At the time I still really wasn't comfortable with it, and I just sort of made the executive decision to fake it until I made it. I decided in that moment there was no such thing as being too gay and I'm obsessed with being gay. I decided to act like that until I believed it, and then I really believed it, and then it became my life.

MARGARET CHO

Comedian, Actress & Writer

Margaret Cho was born to Korean immigrants in 1968 and raised in San Francisco. She began writing her own comedy at the age of fourteen and by sixteen was performing professionally.

Cho won a competition and got to open for Jerry Seinfeld. She moved to Los Angeles in the early nineties, and within two years performed over three hundred shows.

ABC gave Cho her own sitcom, *All-American Girl*, in 1994, which she starred in and executive produced. The show was ahead of its time, and controversy and conflict ensued over the portrayals of Asian American characters and lack of direction. The series was canceled after one season. The trauma Cho experienced filming the show, as well as the rocky ending, resulted in her developing an eating disorder as well as an alcohol and drug addiction.

In 1999, after getting sober, Cho launched her successful Off Broadway one-woman show, *I'm the One That I Want*. She released her autobiography of the same name that year as well.

Throughout her extensive career, Cho has dabbled in everything from television to film, comedy to fashion, and burlesque.

She earned a 2010 Grammy nomination for Best Comedy Album for *Cho Dependent* and in 2012 was nominated for an Emmy for her guest role on *30 Rock*.

Let's start with your childhood. You grew up in the Castro District in San Francisco, your parents owned a gay bookstore, and you lived in an extremely mixed neighborhood: racially diverse, drag queens, hippies. And yet, despite all of that, you were *still* bullied for being different. Even with all of that difference around you, why do you think you were still deemed "other"?

I was surrounded by very diverse adults, but kids still had their own ideas about if somebody was different. I definitely identified as queer early, whether or not I had the words to express it. There was so much gayness around me that was being modeled by all of the people who worked for my parents at the bookstore that my queerness was always on show—and that was alarming to other kids. I think children are naturally fearful of anybody who is different—especially ones who don't follow gender norms.

I found a lot of comfort in hanging out with people who were older than me. People who were gay, who were tattooed, who were getting pierced. They were riding motorcycles to work and I was getting on the back and feeling free amongst people who were very, very different. I felt safe there.

Do you think having such a strong sense of humor was helpful as a child when dealing with kids who were teasing you?

Humor is a great tool and ultimately a coping mechanism. It's something we use in order to get over things and to help ourselves through loneliness. I was always constantly amused because I was just making myself laugh, and that was really a comfort. So humor is about coping. It's also a good defense mechanism when you need to get out of a situation. My humor developed from my sense of isolation.

You started doing comedy because you wanted to feel safe. Why comedy? What was it that drove you to pursue that as a career?

Comedians like Joan Rivers were really important in my development. Seeing her on television meant so much because she had so much power. She had friends in the audience. That was a very early signal to me that if you do comedy, you'll have friends.

And then there were people who were very unusual in comedy who inspired me, like Paula Poundstone. I was seeing people who really made a difference, who broke out of this idea of being othered, and then they were onstage, which is a different way of being othered. It's sort of like, *Yes, we're different, but we're being celebrated, and celebrating this difference, and these oddities.*

What has been the biggest difference between coming out in your professional versus your personal life?

I came out in the nineties as a professional, which was good because I don't know if I can necessarily hide my queerness. Also, within the queer community, I'm still othered because of being bisexual. There's this weird value system that we have about gayness, and bisexuality is a little bit of the other in a community of others. Sometimes people think that if you're bisexual, there's a part of your sexuality that you're holding back. When people are coming out, and they are uncomfortable about it, sometimes they will say they are bisexual because that somehow lessens the blow.

You've done so much throughout your career. Can you attribute any of that drive and work ethic to being queer?

Yeah, that's true. You have to be so much more focused and so much better than straight people to be considered. If you look at all of the queer artists out there, there's such exceptional talent that is born out of this drive to be counted as equal. And because of that, drive really sets us apart. All of the things that make you different also drive you to be treated equally.

What advice do you have for young people beginning their careers?

Get out there and do it. Do what you want to do. Your life is your own and it doesn't have to be beholden to anybody's expectations or ideas of what you should be. Claim your life as your own and that's the most political thing you can do.

Queerness has really been a great thing in my life, and I encourage anybody to embrace their own queerness. It's really special.

BILLY BEAN

Major League Baseball Player &
Ambassador for Inclusion

Billy Bean was born in Santa Ana, California, in 1964. He was a multi-sport star and graduated valedictorian of his class. Bean received a baseball scholarship to play for Loyola Marymount University. He was offered a signing bonus by the New York Yankees but turned it down to finish his college career, and his team made it to the 1986 College World Series.

From 1987 to 1995, Bean played for the Detroit Tigers, Los Angeles Dodgers, and San Diego Padres. He retired at the conclusion of the 1995 season.

Bean was only the second Major League Baseball player to come out as gay, during a 1999 interview with Diane Sawyer on *20/20*. His story found nationwide media coverage, including on the Sunday cover of the *New York Times* and on CNN.

His bestselling book, *Going the Other Way: An Intimate Memoir of Life In and Out of Major League Baseball*, discusses the complexities he faced in dealing with his queerness in a macho arena.

Bean is a board member of the Gay and Lesbian Athletics Foundation. In 2014, he was named ambassador for inclusion for MLB, a job he holds to this day.

As a young boy, I loved twirling around my house in my older sister's dresses. I envied her sparkly skirts, sequined shoes, and over-the-top dance costumes. The more glitter, the better.

Needless to say I never imagined I'd be stepping foot into the NYC headquarters for Major League Baseball. I was there to speak with Billy Bean, the retired major league player who now holds the position of ambassador for inclusion.

I was curious to meet Billy and understand what it was like to be a professional player in America's favorite pastime, secretly hiding his gayness. We sat in a small conference room, and I couldn't help but chuckle at the irony of me, the only one of my friends to care less about baseball, now sitting in the MLB offices.

He's a strongly built man, and Billy's voice and vigor faltered only slightly when recounting his darker days of being in the closet and hiding his true self. His tenacity, though, was readily apparent when speaking of his current role at MLB, spreading awareness for inclusion within the sport he has loved his whole life. His efforts, once focused on keeping himself hidden, are now solely focused on making sure that nobody else in the sport has to.

The strides Billy has made felt only more poignant as we finished our conversation and he led me back to the elevator bay. Navigating through the cubicles, I was moved to see an employee's desk proudly—and prominently—displaying an MLB flag, emblazoned in rainbow.

Growing up in California, it seems like you had the childhood every boy dreams of. You were quarterback of the football team, on the varsity basketball team, and your high school's valedictorian. Is it safe to say you weren't bullied?

I was definitely never bullied in a way that a lot of LGBTQ+ youth are. I am the oldest of five boys, so I was tough with my brothers. Having success in sports leads to feeling self-confidence.

I didn't understand my sexual orientation until my mid-twenties, in part because of the conservative way I was raised. Everything I thought I would want was exactly what I grew up around.

I didn't grow up with my biological father. My most vivid memories come to this: *What did my coaches think of me?* I felt if I wasn't the best player on every team I was on, I was the worst player. I put that pressure on myself.

There's a void for any child that doesn't grow up in an environment where you're 100 percent sure love is unconditional, that no one will ever abandon you. I was driven to feel needed or important to people. When I started playing Little League, I put the two together.

Why do you think it took you until your twenties to understand your sexuality?

To try to explore something while I was a Major League Baseball player, before the Internet, I was wandering aimlessly. It was a very sad, dark time. That's probably why I completely fell for my first partner. The chance to have not only someone I was attracted to but also able to talk to, made me feel like I had value. All my references to the gay community were at First Presbyterian Church in Santa Ana, and they were all negative. I didn't understand why I would put everything I had achieved and worked so hard to accomplish at risk.

The only news about being gay was that men were dying of AIDS because we were bad and were all going to hell. I wasn't in a position to pursue more information. I was just navigating around where I had to be with baseball. I have so many friends who were crystal clear how they had to navigate it when they were eight or nine. I don't know why that wasn't the case for me.

When you made it into the major leagues, what was your relationship like with your teammates?

The first decision I made was that I should live at least twenty-five miles away from the stadium. I just picked a number in my head because I thought it was too far for people to drive. I knew I had to create distance.

We had a very young group of guys. Not everyone was married yet. But if you are a player and you don't have that sort of visible interest, the questions will pop up immediately. Same if you're on a high school football team. The mindset of *If all the boxes are checked, then we're good and I don't really care what's going on.*

The thing that was even more complicated was that my brother was going to San Diego State. I was living in Del Mar, and my parents lived in San Clemente, which was about twenty-five miles north. My family was going to all of my games and I was trying to hide my partner.

One of the more difficult memories of that time was my brother wanted to live with me. I had a nice place, he was a college kid, and my parents couldn't afford for him to live at college. I told him no because I had a man living with me (though he didn't know that), and he was very upset with me. I think he felt that now I was in the big leagues, he wasn't good enough for me anymore. I would have loved to have him live with me. It should have been the happiest time in my life and it was awful.

What was driving you to succeed?

I think there was something about the need to prove that someone like me could do it. I regret I wasn't able to sit in the company of a few other people like me, who had overcome that period of their lives, and could help me get fired up. To say, *Get your ass back out there and do it.* That is what I needed. I was associating the negativity, the stereotypes, and all the bad things that were the only part mainstream television used to tell us about LGBTQ+.

Maybe that's internalized homophobia where if I'm not better, then everyone's going to think of me as just this one thing and then I'm worthless. That is my challenge. I see people who overcome obstacles in all different kinds of life. I think it's just about how isolated I was, and that part is hard to reconcile. Because I did have the talent to play and I could've been a much better player than I was.

It's that competitiveness that drives me today. I think of the old adage, *If I had known then what I know now.* It would certainly be fun to go back and try to give it another shot and see what I was capable of.

In your current role at MLB, you have made huge efforts to spread awareness about inclusion. How have you gone about that?

At the beginning, there was really no definition for how we were supposed to go about that. Because of the relationships I had created as a player, people still respected me. There was a willingness to listen to this part of my story.

Accepting comments about an LGBTQ+ kid could absolutely save their life. A picture of Aaron Judge with his arm around a little kid, getting a scholarship on the field, or the plaque the Yankees just put up for Stonewall. Do you know how many millions of people are going to learn about Stonewall? It's profound and humbling.

How has being queer helped you in your career?

It is every part of my fiber and I don't hide it. I'm my best self. It allows me to have a layer of sensitivity and compassion that some people don't have. I don't look at it as a curse anymore. I look at it as a gift because I honor it, and I love my partner, and I've had great romances.

Being gay drives me every day. I would love to leave a legacy to this sport that is respected and loved. The world moves fast. Not everybody is sitting around saying thank you, hugging you, and patting you on the back. You have to have an internal furnace.

JONATHAN MURRAY

Originator of Reality Television

Born in 1955 in Mississippi, Jonathan Murray grew up in Syracuse, New York, and received his bachelor's degree in Journalism at the University of Missouri in 1977.

Murray began his career in local television, spending six years in news, documentaries, station management, and programming. In 1987, he partnered with Mary-Ellis Bunim to form Bunim-Murray Productions. (Bunim passed away from cancer early in 2004.)

In 1991, Murray and Bunim pitched *The Real World*, an unprecedented idea for an unscripted drama series, to MTV executives over breakfast. By lunchtime, MTV had purchased the show.

Murray is widely credited with inventing the modern reality television genre. Bunim-Murray has created and executive produced some of the industry's most innovative unscripted television programs: *The Real World*, *Keeping Up with the Kardashians*, *The Simple Life*, *Road Rules*, *Making the Band*, and *Project Runway* as well as Emmy Award–winning *Born This Way* and *Citizen Rose*.

A resident of Los Angeles, Murray was inducted into the Television Academy Hall of Fame in 2012.

Growing up, how did you come to terms with your sexuality?

I grew up in a time when there really wasn't a lot of consciousness of gay people. If you were gay, you didn't necessarily put that word next to who you were. If there was any media representation of gay people, it was usually someone who was extremely effeminate, tragic, or suicidal. I didn't feel like any of those things. I knew I had an attraction to men at a young age, but I didn't know what to call it.

By the time I was in high school, I had an understanding I was different from some of the other guys, but I really put off dealing with it and focused on school and activities. It wasn't until I was out of college and in my second job when I finally went to a gay bar.

I got a job in Green Bay, Wisconsin. Green Bay was a small market with lots of people like me who weren't from there. It was their first job; they knew they wouldn't be in Green Bay forever because they were aiming for New York, Los Angeles, or Chicago. It was a great group of people, but it was very heterosexual. I would go to parties and people would be hooking up. There didn't seem to be much of a sense of anyone being gay. I just focused on my work.

I was only in Green Bay for about nine months and then I was offered a job in Atlanta, Georgia. Atlanta has a great gay scene, and it was there that I first went out to gay bars and nudged my way into that world.

What changed where you felt comfortable to do that?

Most of us have a longing to find someone we love; to find that one person in your life. I was cognizant enough of who I was that I wasn't going out and dating women to cover up.

When I was around twenty-three years old, I was in Atlanta and I decided it was time to take those steps of exploring my sexuality.

The first gay bar I went to was on Cheshire Bridge Road. I went because they were having a performance of a play called *Boy Meets Boy*. I said, "Great, I'm going to see a play." I grew up in a family that went to a lot of theater, so that was my reason for going there—I'll sort of "check it out."

After the play I stayed around and enjoyed the music. I didn't meet anybody but it was a good first time in a gay bar. I definitely went back the next week.

From that point, did you start coming out to people?

No. I had some hookups, and not long after that I moved to a job in Rochester, New York, to help reinvigorate a newsroom producing the six o'clock news. It was there where I met a gay community and started to have a lot of gay friends. And, granted, it was a time where it generally wasn't discussed in the newsroom. I wasn't out, but I was out in the community and I had gradually started telling a few friends that I worked with. People may have assumed it, but they respected my privacy.

You've gone on to build a massively successful production company, Bunim-Murray. How do you approach not just being a leader and boss, but a *gay* leader and boss?

When I met Mary-Ellis Bunim, I was working in New York and I had these ideas for TV shows. I would come up with them on the subway, on the way to the office, and eventually I sold a couple to Hollywood. My agent had put me together with Mary-Ellis to develop one of the ideas. We developed it, sold it, and from the very beginning I was out to Mary-Ellis. She had worked in daytime soaps, where a lot of people are gay, and we were instantly very close in both our professional and personal friendship.

When we formed the company, that was the first time I was out from the beginning, both personally and professionally. It was very much known I was out, and I actually had a serious boyfriend, Harvey, who became my life partner. We've been together for twenty-seven years. He would be at events, and when we had a son, Dyllan, we had a baby shower at the office. For a lot of people that was the first time they had seen two gay men having a child. Bunim-Murray became a place where gay people felt very safe about being open about who they are. Their lives and loves were celebrated equally to straight people.

Did your queerness permeate into your work?

From those earlier projects Mary-Ellis and I were developing, we often put gay, lesbian, or bisexual characters in them. As we started focusing on reality shows, we very much thought about that. For instance with *The Real World*, it was all filmed from the idea of seven diverse people. From the beginning when we first talked to MTV about it, we talked about wanting to have people who were gay, lesbian, or bisexual in the show.

At that time, in the early 1990s, people didn't think about transgender as much. But in pitches I was very comfortable referring to myself as gay if it made sense to sell an idea. And as I developed friendships with people in the industry, they all knew I was gay. In Hollywood I never felt I couldn't be who I was, which was great.

Has being queer advantaged you in your career?

Growing up gay at the time I did required me to be very observant of human behavior. I needed to fit into the world that was straight.

I became super-observant of people, almost like a sociologist. That ability to observe people tied into my fascination with real people and real situations.

Part of my success in reality TV, and part of the reason *The Real World* exists, is because I was fascinated by human behavior. I'm not sure I would have been as fascinated had I been straight. Because growing up straight in America in the sixties, seventies, and early eighties, you didn't have to question yourself. You fit. I'm not sure you were as observant about other people.

We often joke in casting that the hardest thing to find is a really interesting straight guy. Because they've had it relatively easy. They've always fit in. They've never had to question themselves. It's interesting right now how straight white men are at an unusual point where they have to question themselves, because they're being called on their privilege.

When we formed Bunim-Murray in 1987, I was out. But it wasn't until 1992 that *The Real World* went on the air. Mary-Ellis and I had almost five years of making pilots, developing ideas, and really not having a lot of success. We finally got *The Real World* on the air, and it came back for a second season, and then the third season had Pedro in San Francisco.* I had lost people to AIDS and, in going to San Francisco, said we have to include someone with HIV.

I had a sensitivity to that world that maybe not all the people did who we were working with. So I was able to use my experience to make sure we handled that story well and to make sure that story was part of our show.

---

*Pedro Pablo Zamora was one of the first openly gay men with AIDS to be portrayed at such a visible level. He appeared on *The Real World: San Francisco*.

JAMES LONGMAN

Journalist

James Longman was born in 1986 in West London. When he was ten, his father, who had schizophrenia, killed himself by setting fire to his apartment and jumping out of a window. Longman suffers from depression himself and has spent much of his time researching genetic links in mental health.

Longman received a bachelor's degree in Arabic from the School of Oriental and African Studies at the University of London, and a master's in Comparative Politics from the London School of Economics and Political Science.

He began his career in journalism in Syria, where he reported for British newspapers. Longman was hired by the BBC in 2012 for his specialty with Syria and was based in Beirut for five years.

In 2017, ABC hired Longman to serve as a foreign correspondent based at their London bureau.

I reached James Longman on New Year's Eve. It was 5 p.m. in London and he was still at the office. A last-minute assignment had just come in and he was worried he wouldn't be able to make it home by midnight.

Longman first came on my radar in 2019. Scrolling through Instagram one night before bed, I came across a video of a journalist reporting on the gay purge taking place in Chechnya, where the government has been rounding up, harassing, torturing, and arresting gay men.

In the video, Longman interviews General Apti Alaudinov, head of the Chechen police, one of the leading men in the diabolical atrocities. They are riding in a car together, and then Alaudinov leads Longman into one of the prison cells where suspected gay people were kept. The frame cuts to them standing together in the cell, where Longman asks the general, "What if I told you I was gay?"

The response is shocking. Alaudinov seems to not care—at all. Longman explains how frightened he was to tell him he was gay, and actually takes Alaudinov's hand and places it on his chest, for him to feel his heart racing. The head of police bursts into laughter and wraps his arm around Longman in an embrace, still chuckling. "Come here as a guest and leave as a guest. It's your life, live how you like. But don't teach us how to live. That's all!" he says. He goes on to explain that for Chechens, being gay is a terrible disgrace.

The strange reaction left me baffled. My cynical-leaning mind told me that Alaudinov deserved an Academy Award for his whitewashing performance. Had the camera crews not been there, what would have actually transpired?

Growing up in West London and coming to understand you were gay, how did that impact your vision of your future?

I've gone through different stages of my acceptance of being gay. The first one was when I was around nine and was *I think I like guys but I'm going to pretend I don't and just get on with my life.*

And then a couple of years went by, and when I was about thirteen, I thought to myself, *I know I'm gay now, so I'll probably just marry a woman and kind of be gay on the side and not tell anyone.* And then I got to eighteen and I thought, *I won't marry a woman, but I probably won't be with a man. I'll just be single forever and I'll be like a monk and abstain.*

When I got to around twenty-three, I was like, *I might actually now be gay and tell people.* Before then, I thought if I kept it a secret, then it wouldn't impact my life. But when I came out, there was a problem in the sense that I was raised Catholic. I wasn't particularly religious, but there was a cultural thing about it. I went to an all-boys boarding school where the term gay was—and still is—used as an insult. It would be hard to find a more homophobic environment than an all-boys boarding school in England in the 1990s. I spent ten years trying to shake off my own problems before I could experience anyone else's problems with it.

What circumstances changed in your life where you felt ready to come out?

My coming out was quite close to a period where I went into a bad depression. Coming out was part of what got me out of the depression. Before coming out, almost every single interaction I had was a lie. Everything felt wrong and I couldn't be myself.

It was also me growing up and realizing that keeping this a secret would be mental. There was also the factor of me meeting more gay people and having less of a problem with them. I had a lot of inbuilt homophobia. You're like a homophobic homosexual for years before you actually realize all your preconceptions are rubbish. In the construct we live in, we are all brought up as homophobes. It takes a long time to get rid of that and realize it's all crap.

You've said that when you were young, you virtually had no one to look up to in the public who was gay. Were there any queer role models in your personal life?

My father died when I was ten, so my mother spent a lot of time looking for men who could be role models for me. One of them was an old family friend who became very close with us. He's gay and he still is such a positive influence in my life. He's been with his partner for thirty years and has been the most amazing role model. I'm not sure if it was even conscious, which is really the best way, isn't it? There was a man who just happened to be gay, who was very successful.

I thought, *You're great. Why wouldn't I want to be gay if you're gay?* He came into my life when I was fourteen, and I told him when I was nineteen. I sat down with him on the terrace of his apartment in Paris and said, "I've got something to tell you. I'm gay."

He said, "I know. You don't have to come out to me. I knew you were gay when I met you." And I remember it was July 14, Bastille Day in Paris, so there were fireworks that night. So I had this coming out party with fireworks.

Do you think there's any relationship between your work ethic and that of being queer?

When you're gay and you have to fight, it's the same thing as being from any other minority. You have to fight for your place—in your own heart, in your own mind. It's not necessarily about fighting for your place in society. It's accepting *yourself* in a society where you have been conditioned not to accept yourself and not to believe in yourself. Being gay has helped me be more resilient, get through things, and try harder.

I have knowledge of what it's like to feel less than and what it's like to be a minority. That's certainly helped me in my job when it comes to the people I talk to. Most of my job is talking to the dispossessed, those who've been put upon, those who've been attacked, those who feel disenfranchised and disempowered, and trying to give them a voice. Those experiences of coming out have given me an insight into what it feels like to not be accepted and to have to fight against broader societal norms. That has helped me in my work.

BETH BROOKE-MARCINIAK
Global Business & Political Leader

Born in 1959, Beth Brooke-Marciniak played basketball at Purdue University, where she was the first woman to be awarded a basketball scholarship. In 1981, she graduated with degrees in Industrial Management and Computer Science.

Brooke-Marciniak served in the Clinton administration, working for the Department of Treasury. For sixteen years, she was the global vice chair for public policy at Ernst & Young. Her work took her to over 150 nations. Additionally, she worked in diversity and inclusiveness at EY, as the global sponsor. She served on the United States delegation to the 53rd and 54th United Nations Commission on the Status of Women. She continues to serve as pathways envoy for the U.S. State Department.

Brooke-Marciniak has served on multiple boards, including the Women's Advisory Board of the World Economic Forum, and the Aspen Institute. She is also cochair of the International Council on Women's Business Leadership, founded by Hillary Clinton. She is the recipient of numerous awards, including the Theodore Roosevelt Award, the top individual honor bestowed by the NCAA, and has been inducted into the Indiana Basketball Hall of Fame. Brooke-Marciniak has been named ten times to the *Forbes* World's 100 Most Powerful Women list.

Beth Brooke-Marciniak was on a plane, glass of red wine in hand, when she began reviewing a script. At the time, she was the global vice chair of public policy at Ernst & Young, and the script was from their LGBTQ+ organization. They were producing a video for The Trevor Project, a nonprofit organization focused on suicide prevention for queer teens. They wanted Beth to close the video as a straight ally, representing the senior executives.

The following day, Beth filmed the video. Except she didn't use the script originally handed to her. On the plane, she wrote a new one, noting how she, herself, was gay. A month later at The Trevor Project gala, the video was shown and she was finally out, at fifty-two years old.

When I connected with Beth, she was no longer at EY but was still a reigning force in global politics and business. She was a perfect example of someone who felt that not just her personal life, but her career, exploded when she came out.

After beginning your career in Indianapolis, you transferred to Washington, D.C. And, despite having been married to a man for thirteen years, you realized then that you were gay. You've described how you have always felt different your whole life, but what was that process of self-discovery like?

That period of feeling different certainly was there for most of those early days. But in Indianapolis, the social pressure to conform was really palpable—the pressure early on to be married, to be part of that social network. Everyone in the office had married young. You grow up very insular in Indiana.

When I got transferred to Washington, I was still married. I was only supposed to be there for two years, and then I would go back. My husband didn't come with me. So I moved to Washington, got an apartment in Dupont Circle, and I just exploded—personally and professionally.

Suddenly, it was like the world had opened and I was having an absolute ball with incredibly talented people. After a year, it became clear I wasn't going to get transferred back. The firm wanted me to stay in Washington, and I didn't want to go back anyway. I hadn't even been going back to visit my husband. I quit going back because my life in D.C. was blossoming.

There were nine units on the floor of the condo I bought. Eight of the units were gay guys, and the woman I had begun seeing moved in with me. Our doors were never locked. We were in each other's condos every night. I was myself and I was as happy as I've ever been in my life. I felt like I was home. That was the process of discovery. I thank my lucky stars for those guys and getting to experience the gay lifestyle through them, being comfortable, and being accepted. The floor of that condo was safe, and I was really happy.

After you came out in your personal life, it took another two decades for you to come out professionally. And by the time you came out in your professional life, you were the most senior out female business executive in the world. What had changed in your life where you felt comfortable enough to do that?

I had never debated whether to come out or not to come out. My private life was my private life and I'm an extraordinary introvert.

I was head over heels with the woman I was living with through that initial period of self-discovery. About a year into our relationship, she said she couldn't do it anymore. At the time, I was working in the Clinton administration, at the Treasury Department, and she was working somewhere else. She said something in a meeting about what the government was going to do and her boss said, "You must know that through pillow talk."

She came home that night and said, "I can't do this anymore." It *crushed* me. We continued to live together for four more years, with her bringing home guys to prove she was straight. There wasn't any thought in my mind about coming out back then.

Three months after I had moved to D.C. and bought the condo, Andy Jacobs, the Democratic congressman from Indianapolis, decided he wasn't going to run for office again. And I so *desperately* wanted to run for office in Indiana. And yet, I had just discovered who I was, in Washington, and I knew deep down I couldn't go back. I couldn't out myself. This was 1994, 1995, and Indiana would never have elected a gay congresswoman. I came to the reality that I couldn't actualize my dream of running for office in Indiana because I'd now come to grips with the fact that I was gay. I was driven deeply into the closet, and that's where I stayed for twenty years.

Twenty years later, the LGBTQ+ group at EY asked me to be the straight ally closer on a video they were doing for The Trevor Project. They sent me the script and I was reviewing it as I sat on a plane. And in that private moment of going, *That's not what I would say to a gay teenager who's thinking of killing themselves*, I decided to come out. I rewrote the script, and the message I gave was about being different, and having people recognize that they are valuable *because* they are different.

You said, "You're valuable because of your difference, not in spite of your difference." How have you seen the value of difference?

I left EY and I went into the Clinton administration during their first two years. We thought we could change the world. The administration was filled with women, people of color, people from Arkansas, people from the East, people from the West. It was catalytic—explosive problem solving and innovation. It was so energetic.

And when I returned to EY at the end of my stint with the Clintons, it was just like *Wow*. It was this stark contrast of how different it looked. It took me leaving, and experiencing something different, to come back and say, "Wow." I experienced the power of difference. Thankfully, I was different at EY on so many dimensions: woman, Democrat, introvert, gay (even though closeted).

I also had the great fortune of working for a boss who was incredibly innovative and inclusive. I thrived under him. He *valued* my difference. He valued all of our difference. We were always innovating, entrepreneurial, trying new things. I saw the power of when leaders were inclusive and when I was surrounded by people with different views.

Once you did come out, did you notice any shift in the work you were producing?

I felt it immediately. Life went from black-and-white to life in full color. It was instantaneous.

You've said before that by coming out, you unleashed your full potential. What did that look like for you?

What I realized was that your teams cannot trust you, nor will they, if they can't engage with you. And engage with you in all ways—not just work-related, but part of your personal life, too. You hold back your own, different perspective. I wasn't fully unleashing my different perspective because I was holding back. That's why I say, "You're not authentic until you're totally authentic."

Leaders who are totally authentic are far better leaders. They get more out of their people, they get more out of themselves, and I clearly experienced that. I was far better in the last decade of my career than I was in the first two or three.

BOY GEORGE
Musician & Writer

Boy George was born in 1961. He grew up in Woolwich, England, with five siblings.

Influenced by David Bowie and Iggy Pop, Boy George went on to cultivate his own distinctive androgynous look.

Boy George became the lead singer for the rock group Culture Club, which thrived during the 1980s. They recorded international hits such as "Time (Clock of the Heart)," "Do You Really Want to Hurt Me," "Church of the Poison Mind," "The War Song," and especially "Karma Chameleon," which ranked number one over much of the world. The band at one time had three songs in the Top 10 hits in the United States simultaneously.

Boy George has appeared on numerous television shows and has written two autobiographies, *Take It Like a Man* and also *Straight*. Both books were bestsellers. He has also published the *Karma Cookbook*, which focuses on macrobiotic diets.

In 2010, a dramatized documentary about Boy George was released by the BBC, titled *Worried About the Boy.*

Boy George has been honored for his outstanding music by the prestigious British Academy of Songwriters, Composers, and Authors. He continues to produce, as a songwriter, singer, and fashion designer.

In 1972, two months before your twelfth birthday, you went to see David Bowie perform. In his song "Five Years," he sang, *"A cop knelt and kissed the feet of a priest / And a queer threw up at the sight of that."* That was the first time you had heard the word "queer" used in a way that was not derogatory.

Bowie was such a big introduction for so many queer people, in terms of the energy he brought. He never stopped pushing the envelope. Even though there is some argument about whether he was queer, what he did at that point in history was massive for me as a queer kid who had only ever heard horrible things about myself—at school, at home, wherever I went. The word "queer" wasn't a nice word. It was an infected word. "You don't want to be one of *those*." But in my case, it was just too obvious.

I don't remember analyzing that lyric greatly as a kid. But what I did know about David Bowie was that, in my understanding of what he represented, he *understood* me.

You once said, "I thought there was no one else like me in the world. Later on, that was to make me feel special. As a child, it just made me lonely." At what point in your life did that *loneliness* change into *specialness*?

That's only happened recently. The secret in life is to grow into the person you are supposed to be. The world reshapes who you actually are, just based on the circumstances you find yourself in. If you add any kind of gayness or otherness to that, then it becomes something you're constantly negotiating through, in almost every aspect of your existence. The world is definitely getting better and we see more gay people, but we still only see a degree of what we are.

How can young queer people learn to embrace their special-ness earlier on in life?

You have to make peace with whatever you are. The sooner you do that, the better your life is going to be. Sometimes people find out who they are much later on, but usually they know from quite an early age what's going on inside of them. With some people, it's stronger so they cannot fight it. With other people it's more of a casual feeling.

My life is filled with all sorts of people and my sexuality does spark a lot of what I do, but it isn't the most important thing about my life. When you're younger, perhaps you have more of an axe to grind. When you get older, you go, *Well, this isn't necessarily what I planned it to be.* People went through far worse things than I experienced as a young kid. There are so many people that are part of this incredible daisy chain that's allowed us all to be who we want. It's important to acknowledge that.

I love your reference of a daisy chain. We're all influencing each other. Do you think that influence is even stronger within the queer community? People being influenced and then in-fluencing others? You've referenced before how maybe with-out you there wouldn't be an Adam Lambert. Without Bowie,

there might not have been you. Without Quentin Crisp, there might not have been Bowie.

I think what each of these people do is give the other *permission*. Or giving each other permission to go *further*. When you're a performer, you want to add something of yourself to it. I was obsessed with Bowie and all of those glam rockers. But I also wanted to add *me* to it. I was like this cultural sponge.

Queens normally do have their foot on the pulse and their eye on the prize. They've got a keen eye, because they've been taught to be aware of what's going on around them. Culturally, your radar is *huge* as a gay person.

How has being queer advantaged you in your career?

It's definitely made me stand out. That's essential. People know who I am because of the way I look or the life I've led. My sexuality used to be something I was terrified of. *People can't find out because it'll be the worst thing that's ever happened.* And then it happens, and no one cares.

Saying, "Yup, I'm gay," to yourself. You don't need to do it to other people. You need to do it to yourself. You need to say to yourself, "This is who I am, this is what I am, and I love myself." Eventually, once you have the strength, then you tell everyone else.

I think we have to be careful not to define ourselves by just one aspect of who we are. I've joked before that if someone asked me if I had the choice to be gay again, would I? I say, "Yes. Of course I would be." I might have done a lot of things differently, but I've never, ever, wanted to be straight. It's why I'm here. It's important to understand that sexuality is this *huge, huge* cosmic thing.

Do you think there's any connection between your ambition and drive and being queer and having to prove yourself?

As I've gotten older, I've realized that the person I'm trying to prove something to is myself—not other people. When I was younger, it felt like a much more outward need to express that. It was like, *What's the reaction I'm going to get?* I'm not saying I don't still love to get a reaction, because I do. But it's not the important issue for me. What excites me now more than anything is the creative process—building an idea, art, music.

My queerness has given me a really interesting perspective: not judging a book by its cover, not falling for the obvious opinion. Open-mindedness and tolerance is a two-way street. You can't say to someone, "Give me the right to do what I want, and you can't." You've got to put up with people.

We have a lot of work to do to show our own cultural diversity as a community. To accept that there are other people and that our particular brand of queer isn't the only one, or the most important one.

What advice do you have for young queer professionals beginning their careers?

Don't feel pressured to make it the center of your work. Your work doesn't have to just be that. But it also doesn't need to deny it.

DOMINIQUE JACKSON

Actress & Trans Activist

Dominique Jackson is a Tobago-nian American actress and author. Born in Tobago in 1975, Jackson was raised as a boy by her mother and grandmother, fraught with confusion and sexual abuse. She details her difficult upbringing in her memoir, *The Transsexual from Tobago*. Jackson describes her childhood on the island, and the confusion and rejection she felt growing up. And how, despite resistance from her blood family and everyone around her, she still intrinsically had her sense of self and who she wanted to become.

After arriving in the United States at the age of eighteen, Jackson began transitioning into the woman she knew she was.

In 2018, Ryan Murphy's show *Pose*, about the ballroom subculture of New York City in the 1980s, premiered. Jackson's character, Elektra Abundance, was an instant fan favorite, and the show, groundbreaking in its casting of over fifty transgender actors, received critical attention and has gone on to multiple seasons.

Jackson has been cast in other projects, such as *American Gods*, and is a passionate advocate for transgender rights and visibility. In 2019, the Human Rights Campaign honored her with the National Visibility Award.

Throughout my career, I have been fortunate to work and collaborate with brilliant artists and entertainers. In 2018, I received an email about an opportunity to style an emerging actress from the new hit show *Pose*.

Dominique Jackson's character, Elektra Abundance, is the statuesque and authoritative mother figure of the community. She brings the complex character to life with a fiery ferocity, masterfully showing the audience intensity, sensitivity, passion, and pain.

While it seems that many queer people tend to have a deeper, more robust understanding of themselves, I've come to see Dominique exhibit this trait at a level unlike many others. She knows exactly who she is, in every regard.

I texted Dominique about sitting down with me for this book. Her response? "Andrew my love, you are family. Of course."

Those eight words, I have come to understand, perfectly represent who Dominique is. She loves, cherishes, and embraces people she feels close with—her *chosen* family. It's a passionate and deep kinship I was not previously used to, but have felt richly with her.

It is the knowledge she has of herself, as well as the fact that she was willing—and determined—to make what she wanted happen, that I admire so greatly. While others were rejecting her and her dreams, she did not wait for someone to save her and hand her the golden key. She saved herself.

As we sat on a large, comfy couch in her apartment, she described the haunting story of how, in 1993, while living in Baltimore and on a date, she was approached by two transgender women. They told her that the man she was about to go into a restaurant with was HIV-positive and had been infecting transgender women around Baltimore. From there, she was introduced to the world of ballroom culture, which eventually led her to New York.

The chilling story has stayed with me, shifting into perspective the hardest moments of my life, forcing me to understand the immense pain and hardships Dominique has endured. And yet, despite those moments of darkness that would bring most people to their knees, she has risen above.

Throughout writing this book and speaking with all of these inspiring leaders, I've learned so much about myself and how truly incredible my queerness has been in shaping my life and career, for the better.

We sometimes think about queerness as something that's an obstacle, instead of a gift. And it's because society tells us that who we are is not a gift. But *what* we are is actually understanding *who* we are. We understand our personalities, our depth, our truth—and much more than others who just confine themselves to society. Therefore, we are fighting against something that should be *actuality*. With that, we always think we are wrong when we're not. Because we're actually bringing life, we're bringing truth. This is who I am, this is my personality, this is me, this is my life. And my life is not what dictates your life. My life should just be a contribution or an embellishment to yours.

You left home at eighteen because your family wouldn't accept you.

I didn't have a choice. I realized I was standing in a situation where my little brother was looking at me at eight years old going, "What are you?"

And my sister saying, "You're going to kill us."

My mother going, "I don't understand this."

And so I felt, *Okay, you have to run to find yourself.* I had to leave. Of course they didn't comprehend it, they did not understand. And it hurt me for a while, but I had to persevere.

It was hurtful to feel like I had shamed my mother, and that's what everyone else made her feel like. They didn't think, *This kid is going out there on their own and being themself.* All they thought was *That is so shameful.* But my mother made it through all that.

How can a young queer person learn to trust their instincts when, for so many, they're told not to?

Many of the times when people are telling you that you should not trust your instincts, it's because they are fearful of what you can become. For me, I am all instinct. Everything I have right now—*everything*—is all instinct. I don't like to call it instinct; I call it the inner voice. It's that inner voice that has said to me, even when I felt like I would never make it, *No.* It's been that inner voice that says, *Go. Keep going. Keep doing what you're doing.* It has always guided me. I knew where I wanted to go, and so I did the things I needed to do to get where I needed to be.

From an early age, you had a clear idea of who you wanted to be. You felt in your heart you had the power to go as far as you wanted in life. With so many negative family and societal messages coming at you, what was the source of your self-empowerment?

The source of my self-empowerment was the power of saying *I did it.* That was it for me. It wasn't about having to prove myself to anyone, it was that *I did it.* When people told me I couldn't do something or I couldn't be someone, I took that as *You're not saying I can't do it, you're just challenging me. You're just a challenge to my growth.* I always looked at these things as challenges in my growth.

When was the first time you felt like you could be completely authentic?

I could never be 100 percent authentic Dominique until a few weeks ago. I just felt *I have had it,* done with everything, this is me. This is who I am, and this is what I want to work towards. Before, everything I was doing was for someone else. Working for something else that benefited someone else that made someone else feel like I look like something. A few weeks ago I said, *No, I'm the one in charge. Throughout my life it was always about someone else. Not anymore.*

Do you think the journey you've gone through with identity has helped you that much more in your work as an actress?

Of course. If it were not for my struggles, I could not relate to the characters I play. Everything I have been through has created everything that I am.

Have you felt the need to work harder because you are queer?

Hell yeah! It's helped me in the sense of making me more determined. It's made me realize how hard it is for my brothers and sisters who are saying to themselves, *I woke up this morning and I can get to a certain place.* And then they get shut down. When I get shut down, that makes me want to work even harder.

What advice do you have for young queer people beginning their careers?

The toughest times, when you feel like you are shit, that you're nothing, that no one loves you, no one cares for you, no one will help you—those are the times where you work the hardest. Those are the times where you look at yourself and say, *I have to get up and go into the office in the morning. And if I go into the office, then I'm going to get what I want. And if I don't get it right there, then I come back with the knowledge of knowing what I could go back to.*

I would say to any young person, *Don't be afraid to fail. Don't be afraid to look stupid. Don't be afraid to be embarrassed.* Because sometimes when you're embarrassed, it's because you're learning. Don't be afraid to learn. Don't be afraid to grow. Don't be afraid to feel like you don't know shit, because it's in those moments where you feel like you don't know shit, that's when you learn everything.

TOM DALEY

Olympic Champion Diver

In 1994, Tom Daley was born in Plymouth, England. He started diving competitively at a young age.

Daley was bullied at school, and all the more so as his diving reputation grew. The media picked up on this, as well as his diving prowess, complicating Daley's life. He became a public face of the National Society for the Prevention of Cruelty to Children.

Daley went on to compete in countless tournaments all over the world. He qualified for the 2008 Olympics in Beijing, 2012 Olympics in London, and 2016 Olympics in Rio, where he took bronze. He was named the Sports Personality of the Year by the BBC. Twice thereafter he won the same award.

Daley has been honored with many other awards, including Athlete of the Year and Breakthrough of the Year, and he was named by the *Sunday Times* as one of the 100 Makers of the 21st Century.

Daley has been married to Hollywood creative Dustin Lance Black (see page 136) since 2017. They live primarily in London and are the parents of a son, Robert Ray Black-Daley.

You came out publicly in a video in December 2013. Though it was a tough decision, what positive reactions did you receive that surprised you—professionally, from sponsors, or personally?

It was one of the scariest things to have to do. I was so terrified to press send on that YouTube video. I wanted to get people off my back, continuously asking questions about my love life. I knew I had found love. And I wanted people to know that. Doing a YouTube video was the way I communicated with my fans and was the only way I could say exactly what I wanted to say without getting my words twisted.

Do you feel top heterosexual athletes treat you as an equal?

I haven't felt any differential treatment towards me as an athlete. But I feel like I am one of the lucky ones. The differential treatment usually comes from some of the fans of the sport in particular. Within sport, we are only as good as we are on the field of play. Our love life isn't a factor in what we do as sport. In diving, I am judged for how I do my dives. Not who I love. When fans of sports that are less accepting of LGBTQ+ people can see them as human beings playing the sport they love, I think we will see a lot more sports people come out.

Do you think the world's perception of what a queer man looks like is changing? Specifically, a queer man competing at the highest level in the world.

There are so many ways a queer person can be, look, and feel. Just like a straight person. The whole perception of what is "right" is forever changing. *What is a family supposed to look like? What are you supposed to look like? How are you supposed to be?* I don't think the question should be about how people perceive queer men, but how people in general can be perceived. We are all beautiful and extremely different creatures. We have to be free to explore who we are, without judgment from the world.

How has being queer positively impacted your career?

Growing up as a queer person is very challenging. You are always told that you are different and you are less than. That automatically puts you on the back foot and you have to work even harder to prove yourself. Those challenges and obstacles are what have shaped me as an athlete and learning not to care about other people's opinions and what nasty things other people can say. The best thing to do is concentrate on you and loving who you are.

It's clear you have tremendous ambition and a great work ethic. Do you think any of those qualities are related to growing up queer?

When you are always seen as an outsider, you have to work even harder. That also comes from myself growing up and feeling like I needed to prove myself by being good at something to make up for feeling like I was letting everyone down with my sexuality.

PARIS BARCLAY
Television & Film Director

Paris Barclay was born in Chicago Heights, Illinois, in 1956, the son of a glass blower and tile maker. He received a scholarship to a preparatory boarding school in Indiana and was one of the first African Americans to attend. From there, he studied at Harvard University, graduating in 1979.

Barclay then worked at an advertising agency. He was tasked with directing a public service announcement for the American Foundation for AIDS Research, starring Elizabeth Taylor.

He later cofounded his own company, directing music videos for artists such as Bob Dylan, Janet Jackson, and LL Cool J.

After gaining momentum with music videos, Barclay began his career as one of television's most acclaimed directors. He has been responsible for directing episodes for series including *The West Wing*, *Grey's Anatomy*, *Glee*, *Station 19*, *Sons of Anarchy*, *E.R.*, *Scandal*, *Empire*, *Lost*, *Law & Order*, *House*, and *The Good Wife*, among many more. He has twice won an Emmy.

From 2013 to 2017, Barclay served two terms as the president of the Directors Guild of America, the first African American and openly gay person to hold the position. For the past three years, he has been listed by *Variety* as one of the 500 Most Influential Business Leaders in Hollywood.

Since 2008, Barclay has been married to business executive Christopher Mason Barclay, and they have two children.

You've mentioned before that once you came out in the 1990s, you felt more comfortable with the kinds of projects you did. What do you mean by that?

I was working on a project in which it became known I was gay. A member of the crew accused me of inappropriate behavior, which was not true. In the course of investigating the accusation, I had to be open about the fact that I was gay and that I had a boyfriend at the time. The producers of the project I was working on stopped speaking to me. We were in the middle of production, and they wouldn't deal directly with me at all. That became a big problem. And it suddenly dawned on me that this could really be used against me if I was in the closet. People discover it, and then they reveal their true selves. That could be more damaging than anything.

That's when I took the route of saying, *I'm going to be open about this. I'm going to be out. People who are homophobic, or have a problem working with homosexual people, I don't want them to choose me. I will just not have that work.* Because there's a whole world out there of people who either don't care, or really are interested in you *because* you're gay. It allows people to come to you, and for you to go to people who are like-minded. By being open about it in the industry, I probably lost some jobs. But I'm so glad I lost them, because they probably would have been environments I wouldn't have wanted to work in otherwise. And I certainly gained some jobs, because I have been on the radar of people like Ryan Murphy, who knew I was out there and gay. And then I got selected for projects like *Glee*, which really changed the world.

Within a very short time, I realized the self-selection of identifying as openly gay was much more beneficial to my career than the closeted approach I had thought would be strategically essential.

When you did come out, did you notice a shift in the projects you were working on?

I saw a change in *myself*, which was more fundamental. There's nothing you're covering anymore. I found my ability to direct more fluidly and authentically was greatly increased. I was *empowered* by not being in the closet. I could actually be who I really was, and be comfortable about it. I could share my life and the stories of what has now become my family. I was more comfortable in the director's chair. All of the strategies, and all of my strengths, became amplified by not having the metal bars of constantly disguising myself.

In many ways, my life has been a performance. I'm so often in an environment that's completely foreign. I went from being a poor, African American kid who goes to an elite prep school with mostly white students. And then I go to Harvard, which is really an international collection of misfits. But again, I'm a different misfit among them. In advertising, I was a gay man working in a very straight world, and I had to manipulate my way through that. Once I'm just a gay man and I'm open about it, then the manipulation, the consciousness, the carefulness, everything falls away. And there's so much energy that goes into that, which I now can reserve for the creative things I want to do, for the stories I want to tell, and for the style I want to direct in.

You are one of the most successful and respected directors in Hollywood. As a queer Black man, how do you see your stature compared to your straight white counterparts?

I'm tougher to peg. I wonder if the experience I've had, as a bisexual kid who eventually identified as gay, and has lived in so many different worlds, has been the genesis of my unique skillset that allows me to go to so many different worlds in television. To do something like *Marvel's Agents of S.H.I.E.L.D.* and then *Glee*. Or *Sons of Anarchy* and then *In Treatment*. Part of that flexibility and part of the sensibility I've learned from living in so many different worlds, and exhausting myself by exercising so many different poses, has allowed me to actually become a much more versatile artist. It might be that the special sauce I have actually comes from my unique experience living so many different lives at the same time.

Do you think there's a connection between your drive, ambition, and resilience and being queer?

Certainly when it comes to ambition. After I was essentially outed, I definitely felt the need to show that I could do this as a gay man in a way that'd never been done before. And even though I didn't write that on a piece of paper and attach it to the wall, I knew in my subconscious mind that this was *not* going to set me back. In fact, it was going to do the opposite. It was going to drive me *forward* to make sure I did something that was different.

As my career has grown, and as I've gotten to choose projects, I've decided more to choose shows and to work with people who have a like-minded ambition to change the world with the television they're doing. The drive has delivered what I've always hoped for, which was a voice that could speak to the underserved and represent them well.

And use the media to show people that yes, it *is* possible. Love *can* transcend all sorts of boundaries you may have put up in your mind.

I'm very happy right now to be a gay man in this particular time. It's a voice that is being listened to, it is a voice that has a lot of power, and it's a voice that, when collected with others, can be a positive instrument of change.

SUE YOUCEF NABI

Beauty Mogul

Sue Youcef Nabi was born in 1968 and raised in Algeria as Youcef, a boy.

In 1993, Nabi stepped into the offices of L'Oréal as a man in a suit. Over the course of ten years, Nabi transitioned into her most authentic and powerful self, Sue.

An agronomic and environmental engineer by training, with an advanced master's in Marketing Management, Nabi went on to become one of the most successful figures in the global beauty business. In 2004, she was named CEO of L'Oréal, and then in 2009 was appointed CEO of Lancôme. She resigned in 2013 and launched Orveda in 2017, her own gender-neutral skincare line.

A longtime champion for diversity in beauty, Nabi led unprecedented L'Oréal marketing campaigns featuring Jane Fonda at the age of sixty-eight, brunettes such as Penélope Cruz and Eva Longoria, Asian celebrities including Chinese actress Gong Li, and leading men from both the television and film industries. She also oversaw the launch of numerous key products, most notably the perfume La Vie Est Belle, advertised by Julia Roberts.

You began working at L'Oréal in 1993 as a man. Over a decade, you worked on your transformation and personal journey. What was the reception you received from your colleagues and superiors?

Just like in painting, I did what I call impressionism. I built the image of who I am by small touches. It was a touch here, a touch there. You start to use a little bit more makeup and then you start to wear different kinds of things—more colors, something more feminine. You start to play with gender symbols. This happened over time.

At the same time, in parallel, I was really focusing on giving my best doing something I loved, which is to create anything that has to do with beauty and skincare. I focused on doing the best and I was very quickly spotted in the company.

I was getting amazing results in terms of the products I was launching and the brands I was managing. It was a mix of becoming the person I wanted to be, and at the same time becoming a super-successful manager. Both merged, and therefore I didn't see any negative reaction. After eleven years, sometime around 2004, I started to ask people to call me Sue.

Human beings hate sudden changes. This is our nature. We like comfort, we like to be surrounded by the things we are used to. Sudden changes are difficult to capture. I didn't conceptualize this at the time, it's something I can only explain now. But at the time, I had the intuition to add signs here and there to recreate the new me.

I was promoted—as Sue—to head of Lancôme in 2009. It was a natural evolution.

How did transitioning affect your work life?

It was very important to me that things happened in a positive way. I strongly believe we have a vital energy. And this vital energy can be broken into a thousand pieces if people are against you. You spend so much energy just trying to fight those who do not validate you. For me, the way it happened was fabulous. One thousand percent of my new energy was focused on making everything I do at work successful.

Being successful at work validates you. That's why I always say to people, "Find a passion and become the best in your work." It helped me a lot to do it this way, and it saved all my energy to create fabulous things and also create myself.

At the end of the day, I launched successful projects and I re-launched myself like a project. Sue was also a creation of mine.

You have stated that you have "always had to pay extra attention to people's emotions." Especially facial expressions—"as a way of assessing how they're responding to me. I understood the palette of behaviors I had in front of me and knew how to respond and get the best out of them." How has this helped you in business?

I was the CEO of L'Oréal and Lancôme and people were asking me who I thought should be the next CEO of this big beauty company. I always said (kind of jokingly), "I think it should be somebody who is half man and half woman in their qualities." I think that when you have both qualities—*queer qualities*—it gives you an amazing palette of management, of doing business, and in marketing. This has nothing to do with what you look like. It's your brain and your heart.

If you use as much of the palette as possible, what we classically call feminine and masculine qualities, there cannot be a better manager or businessperson than you. Because you are understanding so many things in terms of how humans think, how they act, how emotions are important, how rationale sometimes goes against emotions, and how you can make the two merge together.

Is this something you've noticed in other queer people throughout your career?

At the beginning, very few people wanted to show who they really were. When I became CEO of L'Oréal and Lancôme, many people wanted to work in the brands I was leading because they thought they would be freer to express 100 percent of their palette of skills.

I remember one guy who was queer. He and I, together, created La Vie Est Belle, which is one of the bestselling fragrances in the world today. I can say two queer people, using 100 percent of their qualities, created it. The guy on my team felt comfortable expressing this because I was his boss, and not someone he would maybe feel less open with when expressing his vision. And together we created something fabulous about the notion of happiness.

The fragrance is represented by Julia Roberts, and the story behind it is that the best way to happiness is the one you write for yourself. There isn't a standard one. The best way is yours. And this, I think, can only come from queer minds.

Throughout your career, you have been a major advocate for promoting the idea of human beauty being diverse. Your own brand, Orveda, is a gender-neutral skincare product. How are you broadcasting your gender-neutral marketing messages to the masses?

The future of skincare is genderless. It's impossible to continue to do high-end skincare that's gendered. I usually say efficiency has no gender. A good molecule that's in a formula will not make a difference between a male and female skin. The only thing that's important is that the product you put on your face contains enough concentrated actives to do the job.

When Nicholas Vu and I cofounded the company, we decided we would reinvent everything, from A to Z, of what we thought was supposed to be in high-end skincare. Usually it is very feminine, very scented, with less actives and a nice texture, easily applied to the skin, heavy packaging. It's also telling you that aging is not something that is good—that you should not age. That's why it's called anti-aging.

Nicholas and I thought this was all wrong. We are creating a generation of people who are putting on face creams that do not work. We are building a generation of people who are using products that are not sustainable in the long term for the environment, because of all the plastic and everything that's inside. We are creating a generation of people who think a nice texture will do the job.

On top of that, I said that telling people that "this was for men" or "this was for women" was the biggest myth of skincare. The only difference in skin between male and female is that usually male skin is a little bit thicker and oilier.

The tagline of the brand itself is almost queer. It says, "Works with your skin, not against it." It works with a society that surrounds you, not against it. It's an inclusive tagline because we want to put everyone in the same boat.

The marketing is also quite simple. The men who buy Orveda say they love it because it's all about efficiency. The main claim is not going to be about age. Because a lot of men don't care about aging. In fact, a lot of men feel good when they age. But they all say they want the same thing: *to look our best. We want to look healthy. We want our face to be the mirror of the health that's inside.* That's the reason we position this line as a glow activator. Every product in the Orveda skincare line is all about glow. The choice of glow as the main claim is, in a way, a political choice. It says that you can be a man, a woman, young, old, you can be somebody who has not decided which gender they are, but all of us want to look our best. We don't want to make people feel guilty about age. The moment you say age is wrong, you are discriminating against people. Even in the way we wrote our claims, we tried to make them a kind of manifesto towards society.

You mentioned bridging the masculine and the feminine. How does that help you when it comes to the complex business decisions you face on a daily basis?

The beauty industry has been a masculine industry for decades. You couldn't find a lot of women or people who were openly queer.

Because of social media, and because of the power of all these people who express themselves, we moved from a model that was top-down to a bottom-up model. And the bottom-up model, by definition, is a model that needs to take into account all the different genders and any kind of skin you can find on earth. If you have a bottom-up model, it needs to be taken care of.

For me, when this change happened, the industry started to become a little more inclusive. I say "a little" because there are resistances. At the end of the day, it's a huge business. The amounts of money are huge. A lot of people are moving from the oil industry into the beauty industry. These people come from the "old world" and they are tough.

So, at the same time, you have more women, but you also have more "old world" people doing business in this industry. It's a daily fight. The natural evolution that will happen in the coming years is to have an industry that reflects all tastes. There are ways of doing business that are more masculine, ways of doing business that are more feminine, and we're doing more queer ways of business, which is a totally new and interesting category for me.

Do you notice this dual masculine and feminine approach helps with your ability to deal with people in business?

When I was promoted to general manager for L'Oréal France in 2004, I was the head of the second biggest L'Oréal in the world. Half of the company was female, half men. It was people in sales, logistics, marketing, finance.

The fact that I had been using both qualities . . . I didn't act like the managers I had when I was younger. They were all about fighting and *We're going to beat the one in front of us*. I didn't say the same words. I used my own, which were a mix of ambition and inclusivity. I gave them the same energy to fight for their company and their brand.

These masculine-meets-feminine qualities help you put a much larger number of people on your side. And it helps you really make sure no one feels excluded, whether it's a man, woman, queer person. It was a very, very strong tool for me as a manager.

What advice do you have for young queer people beginning their careers?

A lot of people think time is an enemy. I always thought time was my best ally. Good things take time and even creating the new person I am today took time.

Look for respect. Respect is stronger than love because respect lasts forever. Respect has nothing to do with who you are inside. It has to do with what you do. Love is something you should reserve for those who are your closest people. For the others, don't look for their love. If you look for the love of everyone, you will be very disappointed. Look for respect. Ask people to respect you and act in a way that makes people respect you.

Don't try to please everyone. Pleasing everyone is pleasing no one. We are taught at a very young age at school and by our parents that you have to be a person everyone loves. No. You have to make a choice. You have to decide who you are. When you create your own company, you create it because you want to fill this precise gap—not all the gaps in the market. Don't look to the left, to the right, or behind you. Just run with your story and passion.

How much do you think your ambition, resilience, and drive are connected to being queer?

Queer people develop these qualities when we are very young. I remember I was a young boy living in North Africa, in Algeria, and feeling different from the others. I was listening to different music, wearing different clothes. There were two options at the time: try to enter into something more seamless and hide my queerness, or express it strongly. I chose the second option.

I'm not saying everyone should do the same thing, but I chose to be 100 percent of who I am. And it worked. I don't know why. Maybe there was a lot of chance. But it worked.

At a very early stage of my life, my queerness was valorized by my friends at school, by my teachers, and by a lot of people around me. Of course I met some people who tried to express negative emotions, but usually what I said to these people was *Don't judge me on who I am, judge me on what I do.* The only things that are important are your acts. What you are deep inside you is just a matter of yourself.

Are you a good person or are you not a good person? This helped me to navigate in the world.

I think 99 percent of my resilience, drive, and ability to be passionate were built by my queer identity.

MARK TAKANO

United States Representative

Mark Takano was born in 1960 to Japanese American parents. His grandparents and his parents had been interned in World War II relocation camps.

Takano graduated as valedictorian from his high school and went on to Harvard University. He later received a master's in Fine Arts from the University of California, Riverside.

For over two decades, Takano taught British Literature in secondary schools. He also served on the Board of Trustees for the Riverside Community College.

Takano ran multiple times for Congress. His political opponents attacked him for being homosexual. He was first elected to the House of Representatives in 2013, from the Riverside area, in Southern California.

Representative Takano serves on various committees and subcommittees, including the Committee on Education and the Workforce; the Committee on Science, Space, and Technology; and the

Committee on Veterans' Affairs, on the last of which he serves as vice ranking member. Representative Takano also is a member of the Congressional Arts Caucus, the Congressional Asian Pacific American Caucus, the United States Congressional International Conservation Caucus, and the U.S.-Japan Caucus.

What was your coming out process?

I had an inkling at a very early age—as early as four or five years old—that people of the same sex were more exciting to me.

I first came out when I was eighteen, and I wrote my mom and dad a letter. Their response was "Don't decide quite yet." For a long time I thought it was something you could decide. I struggled with the idea that your sexual orientation could be a choice. It took me until my thirties to come to the conclusion that it wasn't a choice. It was after losing my second attempt to run for Congress that I said, *This is ridiculous. I can't continue to live in this netherworld.*

During your first two political runs for office, were you out?

I told my family and friends during my first run in 1992 that I was gay and I wasn't going to change. I also told them it could become an issue and I wouldn't run if they were upset about it becoming an issue. But I didn't, on day one of that first campaign for Congress, say that I was out.

I was outed in my second run in 1994. After I was outed, I was reelected to my local office. Pretty much everybody assumed I was gay, and I was reelected several times after 1995.

When you later successfully ran for Congress, do you think being gay was neutral or an overall advantage for you?

By 2012, it had become an advantage. And I would say that now in Democratic politics, it's an advantage. Being out—especially being out and also someone who is a person of color—telegraphs to a lot of the people who want to support me that I share their experience of being somebody who knows what it's like to be vulnerable.

It's become an advantage because it rallies people around me. It rallies people who feel like they're marginalized in some way; that I'm someone who will be their champion. And I've tried to behave through my votes, my actions, and my words, that I am a champion for people who feel marginalized.

It's clear you have a tremendous drive and work ethic. Do you think any of that is linked to being gay?

I began to conceptualize my life in terms of seeing that being gay was like a card nature had dealt me. That it wasn't good or bad. Some people could look at being gay in a lottery of life as a low card. But I think the important thing to remember is "gay" is just *one* of the things you have to deal with in life. What leverages all the other cards in the hand is how clever or thoughtful you are about how you play your hand.

Have you ever felt the need to work harder because you were gay?

I felt the need to work harder and smarter. In my experience, coming out is something that never stops happening. Because even after I've been elected with 65 percent of the vote—I keep getting reelected by bigger margins in my district—I get introduced as the "first openly gay representative from California." That still kind of feels like post-traumatic stress of being outed earlier in my life in a very public way. And then when people cheer—that this is a point of pride to them that they elected me—it comes to me as a remarkable thing.

I'm the chairman of the Veterans' Affairs Committee, and I spoke at the Student Veterans of America National Conference. At some point during the speech, I was talking about how the Veterans Administration needed to adapt to the ever more diverse veterans' population. I talked about how 20 percent of the people in military service are women, and more and more are racial minorities. It was before a military crowd, and I wasn't sure I could bring up LGBTQ+, but I did. I said, "We need to make sure that, ever since the overturning of Don't Ask Don't Tell in 2010, you have to know there's probably a lot more people who joined the military who are queer."

And then the audience shouted, "Yeah!"

And I go, "Oh, well this must be a good time to tell everybody I'm the first openly gay person of color elected to Congress."

And then the whole convention erupted into a big round of cheering. They were applauding. These were younger, college-aged veterans. It was another moment where I had to come out again. It still takes nerve to make a place for myself in the world.

When you were outed, is it safe to say that made you angry?

It was more being scared. My fear was that I was going to be left to fight my battle alone. I understood the world was unfair. I didn't come from a place of anger. I came from a place of anxiety. As it turned out, what got me through that moment was that I wasn't alone.

My phone started to ring from people on the sidelines who thought I was too young to be challenging someone for office. They said, "We stand with you." For a moment I felt fearful, but then I was struck. I was struck by how people who weren't gay—people who understood what was happening, who didn't like to see unfairness happen or some injustice happen—began to express empathy and help me.

I would lose that election. I almost won in 1992 but I lost big in 1994. I don't think it was related to being gay. I joked that being openly Democrat was a bigger problem for me than being openly gay.

Has being queer advantaged you in your career?

Yes. I wouldn't want to change anything. I think having the thought that *I wish I were not gay*, or *I wish I were different*, is a form of irresponsibility. If you find yourself saying that, you are denying or refusing to accept the place from which you can create yourself. "I wish I weren't" is a complaint. It's understandable, but you're still not responsible in the sense that you're not responding to what you've been given. And so you get to the place where you go, *Not only do I accept it, not only do I deal with it, but I've come to view it as a gift I've been given, too.*

MEGAN SMITH

Former U.S. Chief Technology Officer

Megan Smith served as the third chief technology officer of the United States from 2014 to 2017, appointed by President Barack Obama, and was the first female to hold the position. Recruiting top tech talent around the world, Smith helped the president and his team utilize the power of technology, innovation, and data.

Smith grew up in Buffalo, New York, and Fort Erie, Ontario. In 1986 and 1988, she received her bachelor's and master's degrees in Mechanical Engineering from MIT (where she now serves on the board).

Following MIT, she worked with a variety of start-up companies, including Apple and General Magic. She was later tapped by Planet Out, an early Internet-based site serving the LGBTQ+ population. There, she was chief operating officer, and later appointed chief executive officer.

In 2003, Smith joined Google as senior vice president of new business development. She managed early-stage partnerships across Google's engineering and product teams, led the acquisitions of Google Earth, Maps, and Picasa, and later served on Google X's leadership team.

Smith is the cofounder and CEO of shift7, a tech company that tackles systemic economic, social, and environmental challenges.

As you came to understand you were queer, how did that impact your vision of your future?

I didn't figure out I was gay until college. I grew up in the late 1970s, early 1980s. During my formative elementary and middle school years, so much was going on around Vietnam protests, Nixon resigning, the women's movement, the LGBTQ+ moment, the civil rights movement, the Native American movement, and the environmental movement.

I was a high-achieving kid. I was interested in a million things and focused on a range, from community impact to STEM. As a kid, we had a mandatory science fair that was a key influence on me. Our teachers didn't assume that only some children did STEM—they made all of us do it. If you assume all kids can do anything, they can.

My friend Tom Rielly, who founded Planet Out, where I eventually became CEO, contributed a piece to a book called *Queer in America* by Michelangelo Signorile. It was about the power structures, with media in Hollywood and New York, and government in D.C. Tom added a component called "the silicon solution." There is a pattern that sometimes LGBTQ+ kids either overachieve or underachieve, as a way to deal with being gay. The silicon solution was talking about some of the kids who were super overachieving and going towards tech. Even though the industry skews towards white and Asian men, it was more openly accepting of queer people very early on, and the gay ones also got accelerated.

You were eventually brought in to run Planet Out in 1998, which was one of the first social networking sites for LGBTQ+ people. What results did you see?

The gay community was online. It was the best medium for us because you were able to confidentially explore all kinds of content as well as find community. We had members from every part of the world—even from Vatican City.

The Internet is one of the most underreported parts of the LGBTQ+ civil rights movement. We had people coming out on the site in high school, all the way to people in their eighties and up. All of a sudden, you could come and find empathy, and other folks to talk to, realize you weren't alone, have conversations, and get the confidence you needed.

I remember when I was in the White House, President Obama made Stonewall into a national monument. We were there for the event, and one of the speakers was saying that when they weren't at Stonewall Bar, the Internet allowed them to be their whole selves and have this sense of empowerment. And then when people came to try to destroy that, it gave them the power to fight back.

All over the world, people who wondered if they were gay, or had questions, or knew they were gay and were hiding, could find people and practice being gay and see what it was about. The Internet was the perfect medium.

It's so important to see ourselves and know we are not alone, and the Internet was the scaled way for that transitional change. We built this amazing forum, and from that, a million people were online with us. In the early days of the web, that was a lot of people, proportionately. We were part of the mix. Jeff Bezos, who was a huge supporter, was at the opening of our offices. LGBTQ+ people, because of Planet Out, were in the mix at the beginning of the Internet. Completely equally accepted, venture-backed, and there were a bunch of players working together to do this work.

As a queer person and as a woman, you are part of two groups that have historically been put to the side. Are there a certain set of skills that groups of people who have been marginalized bring to business and innovation that others, who haven't experienced that, might not have?

I definitely think that's true. In our company, shift7, we focus a lot on this concept of *collectiveness*, and the different techniques and methods to drive that. You can really solve things if you open up the team, the approaches, and look around. One of my methods is called "scout and scale." Someone in the world has already fixed the thing you're trying to fix. Who is it? How do you find them? How do you help them, or several of them, move faster? Also, building community as a practice and connecting people across that.

From research, we know that the more diverse the team, the better the product will be from both a revenue and quality perspective. There is an advantage to having differences, knowing difference matters, pulling people together across differences, and expecting talent from anyone.

Being queer is one of the differences, of an infinite number of human differences, that put people into experiences where they wake up to the challenge of difference. And then if they are lucky, they are able to transform their confidence into the benefit of difference. The queer advantage is in the collection of advantages everyone on the planet has.

BLAIR IMANI

Activist

Blair Imani, born in 1993, has dedicated herself to advocating for the rights of marginalized people around the world. A Los Angeles native, Imani is a queer Muslim historian, activist, public speaker, and author.

In 2014, while attending Louisiana State University, Imani founded Equality for HER, a nonprofit organization that provides resources and a forum for women and nonbinary people to feel empowered.

Imani's two books, *Modern HERstory: Stories of Women and Nonbinary People Rewriting History* and *Making Our Way Home: The Great Migration and the Black American Dream*, center on women and girls, global Black communities, and the LGBTQ+ community.

Imani is a frequent speaker at universities such as Harvard and Yale, and has been a contributor on MSNBC and FOX News.

Can you walk me through growing up in Los Angeles as a young queer woman?

I figured out I wasn't straight, but I didn't have the vocabulary to identify what it meant to be queer or what queer was. For me, that was figuring out that I had a crush on this brother and sister. I didn't really know what to do with that because I hadn't seen that type of representation where a girl likes a girl, but the girl also likes the boy. I spent so much time trying to convince myself that the reason why I thought they were attractive was because they looked very similar and clearly that was just my type. And it wasn't that. It was very much that I liked different qualities about them and gender wasn't my concern.

And then I started to think about, *Why do people pair up this way?* But instead of asking these questions, which my parents would have been very happy to discuss, I put it away and tried to fit into this box that society was feeding me. I didn't see Disney princesses hooking up with other Disney princesses, so I didn't think that was a possibility for me. I eventually ended up coming out when I was fourteen. I was going to this all-girls school and I was like, *Everyone's hot! What am I gonna do?*

So I sat my mom down very dramatically and said, "Mom, I'm a lesbian."

And she was like, "Okay, but I think you're bisexual." I didn't know what that was. We went on the GLAAD website and we looked up bisexuality and what that means, and that made a lot of sense to me. That's how I've identified since.

What was your reaction to understanding your queerness?

I had this very good yet skewed way of growing up, where people were informing me that it was going to be hard as a woman and as a

Black person. And for whatever reason, I was skeptical. I was interested in history, and I was very aware of the fact that people have the ability to go beyond what is told to them or what they're able to do. In 2010, right after Obama became elected, it was a time when people were capitalizing off of difference. And so I felt encouraged by being somebody who didn't fit into the mainstream.

While you were going to school in Louisiana, you founded an organization called Equality for HER. How did that get started?

Before I started Equality for HER, I worked with a couple student organizations. What I found was that queer students were very interested in respectability. One organization felt so committed to people's harsh and difficult experiences that it became a cycle of grief. And that is very important, but it felt like anytime you would see one of our members thriving and doing well, that was snuffed out. I felt like we couldn't continue to have that existence. And maybe it was because people hadn't been able to imagine what it would look like to be thriving and queer in school. I wanted to create that space.

I also wanted there to be space that accounted for the racism. Just because a white man in the South is gay, it doesn't mean he's not racist or not problematic. I constantly felt like I was being marginalized as a Black woman while being in queer spaces. But then when I went to Black spaces, those were not intersectional either. And so I created Equality for HER because I was frustrated and I wanted to have space. The ironic thing was that there was so much on-campus politics that the reaction was *How dare you? We already have one gay organization on campus.*

My reaction was *Yeah, you have one gay organization for a school of thirty thousand people. There's a lot of need.* I wasn't even able to register as a student organization. But it was such a blessing because then

I started working nationally and internationally on different issues. It pushed me beyond that realm.

If there was such opposition to the formation of the group, how did you still bring Equality for HER to life?

It was through this argument/pep talk I was having with my mom. I was trying to complain to her, but she won't ever let you complain. She'll say, "What are you doing to fix it?" I was getting ready to go back to school, and I ended up sitting on the floor in my room with my laptop, creating a website.

The name HER, meaning *health, education,* and *rights,* had come from this counteraction we picked for anti-choice groups that came on campus. This was an event I had organized with friends to be pro-choice and pro–bodily autonomy. So I already had the branding, I had an idea of what I wanted it to be, and I moved forward. And then it was getting my friends to be like, "*Hey will you be the secretary?*" "*Will you do this?*" "*Will you help me file this paperwork?*" I was so frustrated with other groups that I had poured my time, energy, and resources into, that didn't care about my views.

I realized that, in my pursuit of trying to work with and care for the community, I was being used because I did graphic design and web development well. So I said, *Well I've done this shit for these organizations that don't care, so I'm gonna do it for myself and for a mission I care about.*

In 2015, you converted from Christianity to Islam. Has there been more hostility toward you?

There are a lot of Islamic countries that are extremely harmful and antagonistic to queer people, where they can't even be out. But in the same way, there are states like Louisiana, where you can be denied housing because you're gay. So it's something that is a problem but it's not specific to Islam. When I was converting, I never felt I couldn't be Muslim because I'm gay.

If you look at Muslim countries outside of the context of colonization, a lot of Jewish and Christian people would go to Islamic countries to feel accepted. Because Islam, at its core (and it's still very much part of its core), is about modesty and this idea of what happens in your home happens in your home; leave it there.

Do you think there is any link between your drive for success and that of being queer?

Anytime you go through a marginalized experience, there's a drive to attain what the privileged people have. Not necessarily to duplicate it or to duplicate harmful systems, but to say, *I absolutely deserve the things I need and want to be successful in life.*

In college, I was also a counselor for queer students who were coming out. There was one white girl who had a charmed life and she was complaining to me. She was going through this thing of "If I were straight my life would be perfect." Because she was in a sorority, she was on the softball team, she was there on scholarship, she had men who were interested in her. She was living this Southern belle dream—and then she was gay.

I told her, "Well, your sisters in your sorority have never in their life been told they don't fit in. And one day they're not going to fit in. They're going to have a divorce, or they're not gonna be able to have kids or something's gonna go 'wrong' in their perfect, ideal life. And they will be completely shattered by it because they've been lulled into this idea that they don't have to figure out who they are for themselves. Everything they are is defined by an outside system."

I was talking to her, saying how being queer is a blessing. When you have the opportunity, whether it comes because we want it or because of society, to determine who you are against a machine or system that says who you can't be, we get self-actualization and self-agency.

Those things are crucial to being a whole person. I really lament people who don't have the opportunity to discover themselves. There is an inherent human need to have things that are fundamentally provided to us, whether we believe that's by our creator or by the universe. And when someone tries to take that away from us, there's a drive within us to say, No. *This belongs to me and I'm gonna achieve it for myself.*

ANNISE PARKER

First Openly Lesbian Mayor of a Major U.S. City

Annise Parker was born in Houston, Texas, in 1956, and she continues to live there today with her wife and children.

Parker attended schools in Houston, although her family moved to Germany when she was fifteen. Parker later attended Rice University on a National Merit Scholarship.

Parker spent the first part of her career working as a software analyst for the oil and gas industry. She was president of the Houston LGBT Caucus in the late 1980s, served on Houston's City Council, and later was elected to the position of city controller. She later ran for mayor and was elected, serving from 2010 until 2016.

When Parker began her term, she was the first openly gay individual to serve as mayor of a major U.S. city. In 2010, *Time* magazine named her one of the 100 Most Influential People in the World.

Parker contributes to the Policy and Global Affairs Committee of the National Academy of Sciences and serves on a number of boards. She is now the CEO of the Gay and Lesbian Victory Fund and Leadership Institute. Their mission is to help elect LGBTQ+ candidates to public office, with communications and fundraising efforts.

What was your coming out process?

When I went to my freshman orientation for college in 1974, I decided I wanted to be openly gay to the broadest extent possible. I made the announcement in my freshman orientation group. I was shy and an introvert, and was disconnected from the social life of my residence hall. But the outgrowth of being the only public lesbian in the dorm meant my roommate and I ended up with a triple room without a roommate. And I ended up as the only junior to get a single room because no one would enter the room lottery with me. Apparently, I was notorious.

I was playing a powderpuff football game and my girlfriend's mother was in the stands. She was sitting behind some guys and one of them said, "That one over there, she's a lesbian and that's her girlfriend." He pointed her out, and it was this woman's daughter. That's how she discovered that.

I was ignored and somewhat ostracized. Maybe it was because of who I was, and I wasn't trying to get into anybody's social circle.

In 1976, I got together with other lesbian undergrads and we formed a student support group. The year after I graduated in 1979, we formed a Rice University LGBTQ+ student support organization. We built our own network. It might have been a lot harder for a guy at the time than it was for me.

In terms of your career and your rise in politics, what has been a bigger obstacle: being a woman or being gay?

Being a woman has been a bigger obstacle. There's still a definite glass ceiling for women. Women candidates are treated differently; we're held to a higher standard. I was very out in college and a public leader of the LGBTQ+ movement in my early work life in Houston. That was just part of my public persona. In some ways, there's a reverse negative that if you're open and honest about the fact that you're a lesbian, you're probably going to be open and honest about other things.

What do you think is the biggest difference between being a successful lesbian and a successful gay man, relative to acquiring power and building your career?

Most of our folks, who have wanted to achieve business success, have done it from the closet. When I first ran for office, every time I saw my name in print, it was *Annise Parker, gay activist, running for city council*. The "L word" wasn't used as much. I lost two races before I was able to navigate that successfully. Too many of our community members have achieved success by compartmentalizing their lives, or by being in the closet. Is it easier for a man to achieve success and power than a woman? Absolutely. In a political context or in a business context, can it sometimes be easier for a lesbian than for a gay man? Yes. That's just as much about notions of masculinity and the good ol' boy system as anything else.

When newspapers referred to you as "Annise Parker, gay activist," did that anger you?

It didn't anger me. It was the truth. I was probably the most visible lesbian activist in Houston at that time. So it was a fact and it wasn't something I was trying to hide.

I realized that if every voter saw me as the "gay candidate," then I wasn't going to get elected. They had to see what I had to offer; they had to listen to my plans for the city. And so I was very strategic the third time I ran. I created a portfolio of the media coverage from my first two races and went around to both of the newspapers we had in Houston. I said, "Here's what my opponents do for a living, and here's how you refer to them. But you refer to me as a gay activist. I work for an oil company. You're talking about my sexual orientation." I made the case that they were treating me differently. I didn't care if they wanted to talk about me being lesbian and they are straight. But don't talk about me being a lesbian and they are a businessperson. They changed the coverage when I ran the third time. They would figure out a way to work it into the story, but it allowed me more space to introduce myself to the public.

When you consider your own tremendous drive and motivation, do you think there's any link to being gay?

I certainly came to the realization, very young in high school, that the world was not going to be kind to me, or particularly welcoming, as someone who is queer. And that I had an opportunity, and perhaps a responsibility, to try to change that. Everyone in my family were active community volunteers. They were engaged in the political process. The message I drank down with my mother's milk was that I was going to have to be able to support myself in the world, and I needed to educate myself and build a career. And I quickly saw that in order to fulfill myself, there were things that had to change.

That I had to be engaged in that process of making change for the LGBTQ+ community.

What has been the biggest difference for you between coming out in your personal life versus coming out in your professional life?

I've tried to make it as integrated as possible. For the years I was working in the oil industry, I thought I could split my life. I could be oil company employee by day, activist by night. And it wasn't that people in my office didn't know about it, because they would see me on the evening news. But we didn't talk about it. I didn't put a picture of my girlfriend on my desk. I had my personal life where I was an activist, and when I came to work, that's what I focused on.

I wasn't in the closet, but I wasn't fully integrated. And when I became a public figure, it forced me to fully integrate everything about my life. The personal is political. And everything I did as a public official, I was judged as a woman, as a council member, as a community activist, as a lesbian.

DAVID FURNISH

Entertainment Producer
& Philanthropist

Born in Toronto in 1962, David Furnish was raised with his two brothers. He attended the University of Western Ontario and studied business. Upon graduation, Furnish began working in Toronto for the internationally renowned advertising agency Ogilvy & Mather. Quickly advancing through the corporate hierarchy, he became the youngest account director ever appointed to its board of directors. He eventually transferred to work in the London office.

Furnish has written widely for publications including *GQ, Tatler*, and *Interview. Queerty* named him to the Pride 50 in 2019, celebrating those who have had a significant impact on advancing equality for the LGBTQ+ community.

In 1997, Furnish was the creative force and the director behind the popular documentary *Elton John: Tantrums & Tiaras*. He later formed his own production company, Rocket Pictures, and produced *Women Talking Dirty, It's a Boy Girl Thing*, and *Gnomeo & Juliet*, and was a producer of the Tony Award–winning musical *Billy Elliot*. His 2019 biographical movie about the life of Elton John,

Rocketman, received numerous awards, including Best Original Song ("I'm Gonna Love Me Again") at the Golden Globes and the Academy Awards, Best Song at the Critics' Choice Awards, and a nomination for Outstanding British Film at the British Academy Film Awards.

He is involved in philanthropic projects, including the Elton John AIDS Foundation, of which he is chairman of the board of directors.

Furnish and Sir Elton John are married and are the parents of two sons, Zachary and Elijah.

The David Furnish name holds weight. This became apparent as I stepped into the West Hollywood SoHo House the morning of our interview: "Hi, I'm here for a 10:30 a.m. breakfast with David Furn—" Before I could finish saying his last name, the receptionist swiftly directed me upstairs. The two maître d's who followed were just as welcoming and quick, ushering me to a beautiful corner of the restaurant with glass walls looking out over Hollywood. The couch was positioned to offer a perfect view of everyone entering and leaving.

As I waited for David, I stared out onto the streets of Los Angeles, watching people begin their day. I thought of everyone who had ventured here to chase their dreams. I was about to meet one of the few who had taken his loftiest goals and made them reality.

David wore a navy cardigan with a bold red stripe, buttoned over a perfectly ironed white shirt. Everything about his presentation was pristine. I had expected no less from a man who had been named one of *GQ*'s 50 Best Dressed Men in Britain. He was warm and gracious, his smile effusive.

I had long been interested in Furnish. Despite being married to one of the most famous and beloved figures in the world, he steadfastly maintained a thriving and dynamic career of his own. Accolades—spanning advertising, film, business, and philanthropy—have proved him a leading mind and talent. Just after our meeting, my seat would be taken by the manager of one of Hollywood's most in-demand actors, to chat about potential projects.

As we discussed the queer advantage and how David had seen it impact his career, we landed on the theme of *environment*. He noted the uncompromising power that a nurturing, supportive, and psychologically toxic-free environment could have on someone, and how that allowed the queer advantage to flourish.

At Ogilvy & Mather Furnish had been immediately accepted by his colleagues and superiors when he came out. Through that acceptance, he rose to become the youngest person on the company's board, no doubt a testament to the high-value work he produced and the respect he earned from his colleagues for being a team player.

I tell him about my own experience, where I at one point worked in a corrosive psychological environment. It led me to minimize myself, resulting in the diminishment of my creativity and passion. Mental and emotional energy that should have been spent delivering great work for my team was consumed by my feeling out of place and unwelcome. Subsequently, my work suffered. My time there was short-lived, and the impact I had hoped to have, and knew I could deliver, never happened.

Furnish nurtured his fire, and advocated strongly for others to find their own safe havens of work where they, too, could soar. When he brought the power of his identity to the boardrooms, he was able to bring out the best in himself and feed his creative abilities.

Growing up in Toronto, as you were coming to understand you were gay, how did that impact your vision of your future?

I wanted to be an actor. I was instinctively drawn to people in the arts. In high school, there were four of us in my tribe. Three of us turned out to be gay and the fourth person was Eric McCormack, who was straight, but went on to play Will, a gay character, on *Will & Grace*.

I went to university to study business, because it was the 1980s, and that was considered a "responsible" thing to do. Get a degree, get a profession. My instinct was to go for the best in everything. I sought and applied to the number one business school in Canada, the Richard Ivey School of Business at the University of Western Ontario. I was accepted and worked twice as hard.

When there's an element in your life that is uncontrollable, you grab onto what you can control, what you can shape, and what you can mold. I doubled down on those heavily. My instinct is to try to have as much foundation and security in my life as possible.

You were interested in acting, yet you went to business school. Is that because you didn't think you could have a successful acting career as a gay man?

I instinctively went for what was safe and where I felt my strengths lay. My strengths were marketing, a passion for creativity in the outside world, and a sensitivity for that. Those were areas where I felt I had a real affinity.

I put all of my focus and energy on getting into the best school and succeeding. I never had a plan B.

When you came out to your mother, she said, "I love you and I support you. But all I see is a life of unhappiness, isolation, prejudice, illness, and loneliness." What effect did that have on you?

It created a psychological void in me that I continue to fight with and struggle with to this day. The entire rule of parenting is to create the most sound and stable environment and foundation for your children to flourish. No one was a greater champion of me than my mother, and she would have accepted me under any circumstances. She didn't say she didn't believe in me or she didn't love me. She said, "I'm worried how the world is going to treat you, and I want you to have as fair and even a chance to succeed and be happy in life." It's the old principle of, if you're a good person, if you work hard, if you do your best and you give back, you will find a balance and a pathway in life that is fulfilling and rewarding in all aspects of your life. To suddenly have that rug ripped from underneath you was pretty devastating.

My mother didn't know anybody gay. David Geffen was in the closet, there was no Tim Cook. I couldn't say, "Look at David Furnish. He's in a long-term relationship. He's doing well in business. He has a family. He has kids."

It pushed me back into the closet. I had started going to gay clubs and was starting to build a circle of gay friends. I slammed the door firmly shut, which is the most unhealthy thing in the world to do. If you deny the essence of who you are, if you deny your most authentic self, you cannot be your best. You cannot do your best. It's like walking through life and navigating a series of trapdoors.

I used to go into meetings, when I worked in business, and I wasn't out. And I would think, *If they suspect or know I'm gay, they're going to think I'm* less than, *rather than* more than—*or even just equal. It's going to be used against me. It's going to be used to judge me. It's going to be used to discriminate against me.* Therefore, my de facto response to all of that was *I'm going to be better than everyone else. I'm going to work harder than everyone else. I'm not going to fly by the seat of my pants. I'm going to be as prepared, as informed, as buttoned-down as I possibly can be when I'm going to be judged. I have to shine.*

That's a weird way to be motivated, and I'm sure a lot of people wouldn't think it's terribly healthy. My uncle used to say, "The greatest gift you can give to the world is the best impression." Walk into every situation on time, with good manners. When you think that trapdoor is going to open underneath you at any moment and swallow you up, you do everything you can to make a good impression at all times.

So that was my protection and it worked. I worked hard at my job. I did well at my job. I was never out at work until I was with Elton, and then I came out with my relationship and sexuality at the same time.

Before you moved to London, you were at the Toronto offices of the advertising firm Ogilvy & Mather. You said you were living a "double life." How did that affect your work performance?

Living a double life inherently inserts paranoia into your essence of being. Nobody performs their best under those circumstances. It's not a psychologically or emotionally healthy way to live your life. You second-guess when you overcompensate.

The one lesson I've learned at the ripe old age of fifty-seven, and I apply it to my business dealings every day, is *gut* and *instinct* are your greatest advantages in business when you're a decision maker and when you have responsibility for leading. I'm now in recovery—I'm six years sober. When you're in recovery, you throw your shit off. You make your amends, you resign yourself to your character defects, you hand everything over to the universe. Everything in life is out of your hands. Your instinctive and intuitive capabilities flourish in that environment. The way it applies to an addict carrying baggage, I think the same thing applies to an LGBTQ+ person who's carrying baggage. It's an inhibitor. It's like something strapped to your back that slows you down.

As my career path advanced, I was instinctively drawn to go to London.

You talk about the importance of instincts and listening to your gut. Yet, for so many queer people, they are told *not* to do that—by society, by parents, by friends. How can queer people learn to trust their instincts, when for many, they are told from a young age not to?

The unhealthiest thing in the world you can do is to deny who you are. Everything in life is run through a filter. Yet, the best essence of someone is the unfiltered essence. It impinges the natural connection we all feel—and should feel—which brings out and allows the best of people to flow freely.

It's like when we did *Billy Elliot*. The story is about a straight boy in a mining community who wants to be a ballerina. He reads a letter from his dead mother, who says, "In everything you do, always be yourself." I put that into my own sons' upbringing every day. All I want them to do is to find their passion in life and what really makes them happy. I've had the great fortune of meeting some of the most extraordinary people in the world, who are all doing extraordinary things. What made them successful isn't twenty-eight university degrees or coming from a rich, privileged background. What made those people successful is that they knew who they were, they knew what they wanted out of life, they knew what their interests and passions were about, they followed that path, and then they worked really hard.

You asked to be transferred to the London office, where you quickly rose through the ranks. Is that where you felt comfortable enough to come out?

I started dating Elton at the end of October 1993, just after my thirty-first birthday. On my annual Christmas visit home, I told my family. I didn't want a tabloid journalist knocking on their door and hearing it from them. I treaded very carefully in the early days of my relationship with Elton. I knew that once it was public, it would be in my biography for the rest of my life. I didn't have a problem with that, but I wanted to make sure he was the right person. Gut instinct, following my heart, he was the right person.

I, probably foolishly, still tried to keep it under wraps at work. And then somebody in the agency saw me getting out of the car with Elton, going into a film screening in London. That was on a Friday and then there was a wedding the next day for someone in the agency, so half the company was there. It spread like wildfire.

Elton had been sending me big bouquets of flowers to my office. And it was a huge, open-concept office. There weren't any walls. I would come from the reception area carrying these big bundles of long-stemmed roses and people would ask who they were from. I would say, "Oh, an admirer." But when I was seen with Elton, everything connected for them.

I remember going into work that Monday, thinking I would just keep my head down, and keep doing what I was doing. That's when I was called into the managing director's office. He said, "There's a big rumor going on about you and I want to ask you if it's true." I've always been someone to give an honest answer if asked an honest question, so I said it was true.

He responded saying, "You have the full support of the organization. You do wonderful work for us. This doesn't matter to us one single bit, and if your clients have a problem with it then I will take it up with them personally and deal with them directly." That's because of the foundation I had put in place with the work I had done. I earned that. It's essential that anybody who does well in their job deserve the care and support of their employer.

I felt a little angry with myself, in the same way I did with my family as well. I had put such a wall and gulf up between them and me, in that aspect of my life. I didn't give everybody the credit I probably should have.

I'll never know whether people's open-hearted acceptance was because Elton was such a well-loved, famous, public figure or whether I would have gotten the same response if I was with a different guy from a similar profession. I think I would have. I had people's admiration and respect because I was a hardworking, nice person, and a team player.

But I remember walking into that office of around two hundred desks that Monday morning, and it went silent. It was like a movie. You could hear the fax machines whirring and phones ringing, not being answered. People just watched me as I walked across. Thankfully, I received a tremendously supportive response and that enabled me to get on with my life and then, as a result, flourish.

You certainly flourished. You became the youngest member on the board of Ogilvy & Mather.

Yes, and that was *after* I had come out. That was because of the business achievements I had made. Just before I met Elton, I won the biggest face-to-face new business pitch that the agency had won in ten years.

After that, I stayed with them for a year and a half. For the first six months Elton and I were together, he was not touring. After those six months he went back on the road with his big Billy Joel tour. I wanted to see him, so I would fly in on weekends and go back and forth. But it became exhausting to run a business in a department with a big group of people and do my job properly.

I made the decision that I needed to support my relationship and reinvent myself professionally. The agency was really angry. They did not want me to go. The chairman of the agency didn't speak to me for a while. He said, "I wouldn't have put you on the board if I knew you were leaving." Not because I was gay, but because they *believed* in me, and they had plans for me to go to New York and work through the company. But again, my gut and heart said this was *the* relationship. Up until that point, I hadn't been in a happy, successful relationship. Part of which, I think, was because I wasn't living my true, authentic self.

Living a fulfilling double life is an oxymoron. It's not possible. I don't think you can bring 100 percent of you—grounded, focused, contented you—to a private relationship if you are not 100 percent your authentic self in the workplace. Trapdoor syndrome follows you through your life in everything you do.

After leaving Ogilvy & Mather, you shifted careers. You studied at the British Film Institute, you started writing, optioning scripts, and started your own production company. What were those initial years like, transitioning to a new career and establishing yourself?

I was very insecure. The foundation of everything I'd done for nearly twelve years, in advertising and in my education, that led me to that point, was suddenly not there for me anymore. And until I was 100 percent out and in a committed relationship, I exclusively defined myself by what I was doing professionally.

There is no defined structure in the film industry. There's a million and one different ways to get into it. I went from a situation where my entire life was about structure, to having no structure. It was really hard.

One of the things I'm most grateful for in my relationship with Elton is that he's never, ever demanded I be with him at the expense of my career and pursuing my professional ambitions. While he's been on the road, and away for a period of time, and I've been unable to be with him—which is a lot—because of work, he's never said, "Why don't you just pack it all in and come join me on the road? We're fine financially." He's always known it's been an intrinsic part of my identity and continues to this day.

How has being gay advantaged you in your career?

Being gay *and out* in my career has given me complete freedom to trust my instincts, to be 100 percent true to myself, and to go into any professional situation and have all of my focus be just on that. Not going into a meeting and thinking, *Is what I'm wearing or saying inadvertently revealing something about myself?*

You cannot succeed and flourish in a toxic, unsupportive environment. As much as I was succeeding professionally in advertising, I was very unhappy and lonely personally. Some people might say, "Oh, that's irrelevant to my job. All that matters is I walk through the door and I do well." I did that and I wasn't happy in myself.

To me, the queer advantage is only an advantage when you are open and accepted by all. That's the magic of the formula. Then the true you just flows out. There's all kinds of examples of women who work twice as hard because they have to, and people who have been marginalized for their religious beliefs who've worked twice as hard. These people have pulled themselves together into communities and propped each other up, encouraged each other, and supported each other. That's when you get an over-and-above advantage, of getting another level of community support that isn't necessarily available to everybody. All human beings need support, and all human beings thrive in supported environments.

OUR LADY J

Musician & Writer

Our Lady J was born in 1985 and raised in the rural, mostly Amish Pennsylvania city of Edensville, population around two hundred.

It wasn't until 2000, when she moved to New York City, where she first met trans women, that she began to see herself.

Our Lady J's career began in New York, where she created music in both the pop and classical worlds for artists and institutions including Sia, the American Ballet Theatre, and the Mark Morris Dance Group. She later transitioned to Los Angeles, writing and producing for the Golden Globe- and Emmy-nominated series *Transparent* and *Pose*.

A glass ceiling breaker, Our Lady J was the first openly transgender writer to be hired in a television writers' room and the first openly transgender woman to perform at Carnegie Hall. She received two Peabody Awards for her work on *Transparent* and

Pose, and has been nominated for three Writers Guild of America Awards, an NAACP Image Award, and a Primetime Emmy Award.

You grew up in a small town of two hundred people, in a very religious community in Pennsylvania. Was religion a source of comfort or pain for you?

Both. It was very complicated, how we were taught to rely on religion for all of our psychological and emotional needs. There were these rigid rules that felt psychologically torturous, so it felt like a trap.

Religion rooted me in living a life that has a sense of purpose, and I'm still a very spiritual person today because of it. But I'm also able to see the trappings of organized religion, and how it's used to control and manipulate people. It took a lot of time to detangle from that.

What was the process of detangling?

In my community, any sort of questioning was not allowed. That seemed to be the number one rule. Even allowing myself to question was a journey in itself. That journey really began with pop culture. We were taught that Madonna was evil and bad. I remember them talking about Madonna in church, and yet I was so dazzled by her, and everything she represented against the church.

I started paying attention to people who were living a life of rebellion. And it was hard to get ahold of that material because I wasn't allowed to listen to secular music in my household. Madonna was banned. But I had cousins who weren't as involved in the church, so I would get pop culture through them. Through that, I learned there was something to be found with having a free mind. So step one was freeing my mind and allowing myself the ability to explore.

And this was all while you were living on your farm in Pennsylvania?

Yes. It started at a young age. Music really helped as well. I started playing piano when I was four. Most of it was church-based at first, and I started performing at church when I was nine. By the time I was twelve, I was playing multiple times every week in church. It began as worship music, but I studied classical musicians.

The week I turned sixteen, I went away to Interlochen Arts Academy in Michigan. That was a game changer for me, because I was surrounded by all sorts of culture outside of the little village I had grown up in. But in order to go there, the deal I made with my parents was that I would become a music minister. I crossed my fingers and knew I wasn't going to become one.

But the exploration of classical music transported me to another time and place that allowed more freedom in thinking. That also led me to pop culture; this idea that there was another way of living out there. Noticing that music sounded different than the music I was surrounded with, or this language sounded different, or this fashion looked different. Having those glimpses into the outside world helped expand my mind.

Growing up, was there any mention whatsoever of queer people?

There was no representation of queer people, but it was spoken about. In the eyes of our church, LGBTQ+ people were going to hell. They didn't even say LGBTQ+ at that point—it was all referred to as "gay" in the early eighties. The AIDS crisis was ramping up and it was something society could no longer ignore. And rather than the church spreading a message of empathy and care, it was all fire and brimstone.

As you started coming to the realization you were queer, how did that impact your vision of your future?

I began shutting down. I got very depressed and I started discovering ways of coping and disassociating from my body. Food was one way, and luckily music was another, healthy way of coping. I poured myself into music. As a kid I would practice seven hours a day. It wasn't because I had this great love of music—although I did love music—but because it was an *escape*. I was running. I wanted to occupy my mind with something besides the thoughts that who I was, was an abomination.

Did you ever imagine you could have a happy future while living authentically?

There were moments. Every day was an up and down, and an emotional roller coaster. My identity would start to blossom, and then that would be shut down. Then it would come up again, and then be shut down all over again. I was constantly trying to control and stop my growth.

When you finally arrived at Interlochen, that must have been complete culture shock. Were you relieved to be around people who had similar beliefs and interests?

It wasn't an immediate relief. I was terrified to be around people who were living authentically, when I was told that those people were the ones to watch out for. Those were the people going to hell. It was not an easy acclimation at all. It was torturous. Luckily though, it was an environment that was loving and affirming. People were really patient with my coming out process.

When I look at society today, I think that's something we need to work on as a community—embracing those who are tiptoeing their way into authenticity. A lot of cancel culture has the potential to keep people from coming out. In my own experience, I was terrified entering my authenticity. It's very fragile when you're crossing cultures, and so that's why I try to encourage empathy and patience in all of my writing and work.

You later moved to New York City in 2000.

Yeah, and I had about twenty jobs. My first stop was usually Marymount Manhattan College at 8:30 a.m., as a rehearsal pianist, then ballet at 10 a.m. And then I would go to American Ballet Theatre, and then over to the Actors Studio and vocal coach. Then, I would play rehearsals for a downtown show. I was *always* working and hustling.

On my first trip to New York in 1999, I showed up with a stack of résumés. I knocked on the stage door of every Broadway show and asked for the conductor. I gave each of them my résumé and I got a lot of work that way.

By the time I moved to New York, I already had jobs lined up. Even though I was working seventy hours a week sometimes, it was fun.

During this time, how were you presenting your gender?

If we had the vocabulary back then, I would have identified as nonbinary. I most definitely was rebelling against any sort of male identity,
but I was still going by male pronouns. The concept of they/them
was foreign to me at the time. I felt most comfortable being gender
fluid. I was gender creative, and it wasn't until I allowed myself that
freedom—to be a little more binary on the feminine spectrum—that
I started leaning towards the feminine binary.

The more comfortable I got, the more difficult it became to explain to people what I was doing, because at the time it was looked
down upon in every profession. Once you tipped the scale, people
got distracted and questioned. It seemed there was a certain amount
you were allowed to do. So I saved that part of my life for outside my
classical jobs.

When you started presenting more feminine, did you lose work?

The way freelancing goes is that you just don't get called back. It's
not that you get fired, it's that you don't get put on the schedule.
But there were enough whispers and glances that I knew what was
happening. At the end of a recording session when I was presenting
more female, people would start talking over me. When I tipped the
scale towards masculine, they listened to what I was saying. There
were little social cues of me not being taken seriously anymore, and I
realized losing work was a reflection of that.

I started performing shows where I talked about identity, because
I realized I had to educate some folks. I really enjoyed downtown performance art because there was so much potential for talking about

identity. I put together shows where I was singing and playing the piano. My songs were politically motivated and they were also about identity, and everything I was going through with transitioning. In between the songs, I would have little bits and stories I would tell that became a mix of comedy and heartfelt monologues. When I started performing those shows, I took up the stage name Our Lady J.

Did you notice a shift in your career when you began performing as Our Lady J?

My career just went in a different direction. Performing in nightlife is much different than showing up at eight in the morning at the ballet. And even though I loved, and still love, ballet, this seemed like a much more exciting avenue for me to express things I had been wanting to express for a long time.

You've spoken openly about how you've felt that the music industry was not welcoming to you. How does it feel to see artists like Kim Petras and Shea Diamond having such thriving careers now?

When I moved to Los Angeles in 2010, one of the first things I heard in a meeting about my music was "You're super-talented, your music is really beautiful, but nobody wants to hear a trans person sing sad songs. So learn to dance, lose some weight, and be Lady Gaga." It was infuriating, but in those meetings I stood up for myself and I turned down work in order to keep my authenticity. I left music behind for a period of time. I had to educate people on a one-to-one basis, but I hope that has led to some sort of shift in perspective from those folks. I know it did, actually.

I'm so happy seeing Kim and Shea thrive. It's really inspiring to see the change happen in one lifetime. And, in a way, it's allowed me to grow as a person as well, and to stay more open to what the future holds. To see this much change in such a short period of time is incredible.

Do you find yourself dreaming and envisioning things for your career that you wouldn't have allowed yourself to do in the past?

Absolutely. I'm forty-one right now and I'm working on brand-new music. The music industry says once you pass twenty-six or twenty-nine, you're done. I'm like, *Fuck it.* If I can fight gender discrimination and trans misogyny, I can fight ageism, too. I can go on as long as I fucking want. I can do what I want with my career. It's inspiring.

Do you think there's a relationship between growing up queer and having such a tremendous drive and work ethic?

I think there's a relationship between trauma and work ethic. Unchecked trauma can result in any sort of ruminating thought. When you learn to steer that rumination in a direction that is positive, then we call that work ethic. It wasn't going in that direction for me. I nearly killed myself with drugs and alcohol in my early twenties, and I had to get sober and learn how to deal with trauma in a healthy way.

A lot of queer folks have that same trauma I have. We either learn to steer it or we don't. The mistake a lot of people try to make is to try and suppress it. For me, it's never about suppressing my demons. It's about putting a harness on them and telling them which direction to go. And when I say go to work, then it makes me better at my job. I've learned to steer my energy.

How has being queer been an advantage in your career and life?

It definitely got me out of the village I grew up in. If I really look at how things began, all of that practicing piano came from this place of fear of my identity and the need to find beauty within that. Maybe if I wasn't queer, I wouldn't have had that same drive and I would still be in that town. I'm grateful for how it's changed my life.

Afterword

MEETING AND LEARNING FROM these brilliant and inspiring people for *The Queer Advantage* energized me. It was incredibly humbling and rewarding to have the rare opportunity to explore their minds and hearts. Operating from different personal algorithms, some are changing the world noisily, some quietly. They have charted courses for themselves, some back when there was no tangible hope, when being queer was considered not only detrimental, but a disability.

A paradox of the human condition is that all people are essentially the same, and yet each of us is unique. Taking that Venn diagram and applying it to the lives of LGBTQ+ people, we see with deepening clarity the truth of this mind-bending contradiction. The stories you have read here dramatize the similarity of experience, while also showing how each person has approached the fundamental dynamic of the queer advantage in their individual way.

I initially believed there was one basic element to the queer advantage. My thinking was limited to the often-noted paradigm of taking the pain of being dismissed, reviled, or simply otherized and channeling it into sustained and laser-focused energy. While that hypothesis certainly turned out to be correct, it was limited in scope, failing to embrace more complex and wide-reaching dynamics. The means toward leaving behind a diminished life and claiming a fruitful, self-actualized one are many. Just as there is no one queer experience, there is no one queer advantage.

The queer advantage is not linear. There is no singular, binding path for how this power can be applied to serve all of us within the global queer community. Each of us, inspired by the strategies and tactics set forth by the trailblazers featured here, must sift through their robust stories to decide what resonates most.

Any pain or suffering we may have endured, at the hands of others or even ourselves, does not need to define our entire lives. Instead of burying ourselves, the put-downs and self-anguish can become the perfect soil from which we grow—fertile and rich.

Our difference, our *queerness*, does not define us. It is a part of us, but it is not our whole identity. The extraordinary people in *The Queer Advantage* seem to be saying that there is tremendous potency if we acknowledge and embrace our specialness as we reach for our unforeseen potential.

Queer people know well life's jagged course. The individuals here have revealed to us their idiosyncratic responses in learning how to first adapt, and then to thrive, in a world where being deemed less than is often our lot. Each found a way to live Friedrich Nietzsche's words: *Become who you are.*

Having learned from the world's most accomplished, I invite you to now claim *your* queer advantage.

Resources

Below are a select few organizations and resources for anyone seeking extra information or hoping to get involved.

Ali Forney Center

www.aliforneycenter.org

Protecting LGBTQ+ youths from homelessness and emboldening them with the tools needed to live independently.

American Civil Liberties Union (ACLU)

www.aclu.org

Defending and preserving the individual rights and liberties that the Constitution and the laws of the United States guarantee everyone in this country.

Born This Way Foundation

www.bornthisway.foundation

Founded by Lady Gaga and her mother Cynthia Germanotta, the Born This Way Foundation supports young people's emotional and mental wellness in pursuit of a kinder world.

Gay, Lesbian & Straight Education Network (GLSEN)

www.glsen.org

Advising on, advocating for, and researching policies designed to protect LGBTQ+ students as well as students of other marginalized identities.

GLAAD

www.glaad.org

Countering discrimination against LGBTQ+ people in the media and promoting understanding, acceptance, and equality.

Human Rights Campaign (HRC)

www.hrc.org

Providing information and resources to educate the public and foster public policy to end discrimination against LGBTQ+ people in the United States and abroad.

It Gets Better Project

www.itgetsbetter.org

Providing hope and support, through a range of media and social platforms, for LGBTQ+ people that life does get better.

Lambda Legal

www.lambdalegal.org

Legal organization dedicated to achieving full recognition of the civil rights of LGBTQ+ people and everyone living with HIV, through impact litigation, education, and public policy work.

National Center for Lesbian Rights (NCLR)

www.nclrights.org

Legal organization advancing the civil and human rights of LGBTQ+ people and their families through litigation, legislation, policy, and public education.

National Center for Transgender Equality (NCTE)

www.transequality.org

Advocating to change policies and society to increase understanding and acceptance of transgender people.

National LGBT Chamber of Commerce (NGLCC)

www.nglcc.org

Advocacy organization expanding economic opportunities for the LGBTQ+ business community.

Out & Equal

www.outandequal.org

Working to end employment discrimination for LGBTQ+ employees.

Parents, Families and Friends of Lesbians and Gays (PFLAG)

www.pflag.org

Uniting parents, families, and allies with LGBTQ+ people.

TransAthlete.com

www.transathlete.com

Founded by Chris Mosier (page 40), a resource for students, athletes, coaches, and administrators to find information about trans inclusion in athletics at various levels of play.

The Trevor Project

www.thetrevorproject.org

Providing crisis intervention and suicide prevention services to LGBTQ+ people under twenty-five.

True Colors United

www.truecolorsunited.org

Committed to aiding the global crisis of LGBTQ+ homelessness.

Victory Fund

www.victoryfund.org

American political action committee dedicated to increasing the number of openly LGBTQ+ public officials in the United States.

Voices 4

@voices4_

Adam Eli's (page 231) activist group working to create positive change for the LGBTQ+ community around the world in a nonviolent way.

Selected Reading

Beyond the Gender Binary by Alok Vaid-Menon

Diversity in the Power Elite: How it Happened, Why It Matters by G. William Domhoff and Richard L. Zweigenhaft

Gay Like Me: A Father Writes to His Son by Richie Jackson

Going the Other Way: An Intimate Memoir of Life In and Out of Major League Baseball by Billy Bean

I'm Special: And Other Lies We Tell Ourselves by Ryan O'Connell

I'm the One That I Want by Margaret Cho

It Gets Better: Coming Out, Overcoming Bullying, and Creating a Life Worth Living by Dan Savage and Terry Miller

It's About Damn Time: How to Turn Being Underestimated into Your Greatest Advantage by Arlan Hamilton

Making Gay History: The Half-Century Fight for Lesbian and Gay Equal Rights by Eric Marcus

Mama's Boy: A Story from Our Americas by Dustin Lance Black

Pressure Is a Privilege: Lessons I've Learned from Life and the Battle of the Sexes by Billie Jean King

Queer in America: Sex, the Media, and the Closets of Power by Michelangelo Signorile

She's Not There: A Life in Two Genders by Jennifer Finney Boylan

She Wants It: Desire, Power, and Toppling the Patriarchy by Joey Soloway

343

Sissy: A Coming-of-Gender Story by Jacob Tobia

The Best Little Boy in the World by Andrew Tobias

The Gilded Razor by Sam Lansky

The Glass Closet: Why Coming Out Is Good Business by John Browne

The G Quotient: Why Gay Executives Are Excelling as Leaders ... and What Every Manager Needs to Know by Kirk Snyder

The New Queer Conscience by Adam Eli

The Transsexual from Tobago by Dominique Jackson

Why Marriage Matters: America, Equality, and Gay People's Right to Marry by Evan Wolfson

Acknowledgments

THIS BOOK WOULD NOT exist if it were not for the fifty-one inspiring leaders featured within these pages. Thank you for being so generous with your time and giving so freely of your hurdles and triumphs. I consider myself one of the luckiest people to have had the opportunity to speak with and learn from you all.

Thank you to my agent, Ian Bonaparte, who took a leap of faith with me and helped bring my idea to life. You have been a constant reassurance and guidepost, patiently leading me through this journey. You have changed my life.

Thank you to David Lamb for acquiring *The Queer Advantage* and bringing this project to Hachette Go. Thank you to my talented editor, Mollie Weisenfeld, who skillfully brought the book to the finish line, and to the rest of the Hachette Go team, who put so much work into making this book the best it could be. This list includes Cisca Schreefel, Anna Hall, Michael Barrs, Rick Willett, Ashley Kiedrowski, Lauren Rosenthal, Mandy Kain, and many more.

A big thank-you to: the publicists, managers, agents, and assistants for your help in scheduling these interviews; Lindsey Pipia for listening to countless hours of recordings and diligently transcribing every world; Tracy Shaffer and Jill Demling, my Hollywood gurus, for lending your expertise; Andrew Goldberg and Elisa Rivlin for your legal savvy; Rooney for your delightful illustrations; Marla

Farrell and Lauren Gold for lending your brilliant publicity minds; and Daniel Salas for encouraging me to pursue this, and bearing with me throughout the process.

And lastly, to my family, who nurtured their queer son and brother with the fiercest compassion and love, and championed me as I found my way.